Consuming Government

Flywheels, Ideas, and Individual Actions to Better Manage the Government Services You Buy

Steven Borne

ISBN: 978-1-7331500-0-2

Library of Congress Control No.

Published by Consuming Government Publications
An imprint of Peter E. Randall Publisher
Portsmouth, NH 03801

Illustrations by John Klossner, www.jklossner.com

Book design: Grace Peirce

To my father, "JB," Jerry Borne

A son learns many things from a father, in that department
I was blessed.

Contents

Introduction

Collectively as Americans, the biggest thing we buy every year is government. Think about all of those taxes you pay (income, property, sales, rooms and meals, etc.), and then picture walking into a store and spending all that money and not getting great value for your single biggest annual purchase. You then come back and spend even more the next year.

We are irresponsible consumers for all of the government services we buy, and we feel powerless to fix our predicament. I hear it's too big, the system is too entrenched, you can't fight City Hall, as we drown in a deluge of pessimism.

To change how things work today, none of us has to do a lot, but we all need to be doing a little. Shifting our national behavior is the goal of this book. Flywheel mechanics is used to create a common vernacular so we can discuss options for challenges such as fixing the broken business of medicine, addressing crime, the opioid crises, national debt, and how we manage our elected officials and governmental groups. There will be the Way Things Are Today (WTAT) flywheel and then we will relate our economy to a flywheel, so our economic flywheel. The secret sauce is starting actions locally, where we have a more tangible impact. As we build skills, tools, habits, processes, and expectations, we can work our way up to managing larger portions of our government and national challenges. This approach can lead to a large cultural shift in how we view and act upon our civic responsibility.

I don't golf, I don't fish, but for almost two decades I have been working towards getting our democracy to work better. I am not driven by any ideology, but by a desire to fix what is not working effectively and efficiently for those consuming services from our government. The current modus operandi is effective for those with the money, who advantageously tip the playing field. The energy in the current "system" (Way Things Are Today, or WTAT) is considerable, and there is little or no incentive for it to fix itself. It is futile to hope for change under the existing system, so we, the citizens, need another approach.

Sidetracked by the Symptoms

As a mechanical engineer, I learned how to analyze and solve problems. Working for multinational corporations and earning my MBA at night, I gained insights into technology and business. In 1998, I decided I should be more active in the New Hampshire primaries. That was my first great insight into how inefficient the political process was. I had never experienced such poor use of resources and technology as I witnessed on political campaigns.

I stumbled through many other endeavors—supporting more candidates, campaign finance reform, independent candidates, non-partisan organizations, and more—only to realize I was being sidetracked by the symptoms. You can get by with quick fixes, band-aids, software patches, and duct tape for only so long; at some point, you have to stop and fix the root cause.

It's the individual people who are failing in our representative democracy. The root cause of our democracy's failure to address national problems is that we the people are not putting in the time and effort to manage all of the government services we buy.

The root cause of our democracy's failure to address national problems is that we the people are not putting in the time and effort to manage all of the government services we buy.

It has taken our collective democratic health a long time to get to this point and for our national challenges to reach their current state of disrepair, so the correction will be no small effort. Just as there was no singular action that brought us to this point, getting out will require collective and concerted efforts by the people of the United States. The summation of those efforts can return our nation to a shining light of democracy and strengthen our global economic leadership.

Hope for our nation may be at a low point, and many may not see a path that will lead to change. Similar to Dorothy's slippers in

The Wizard of Oz, the solution has always been right at our feet; the trick is knowing it and choosing to use it. Monstrous and seemingly insurmountable obstacles lie in front of us, but American will, determination, ingenuity, spirit, and commitment are what makes anything possible for our nation. The challenge is to get "We the people" to take responsibility and put our tremendous potential into action.

We have been irresponsible consumers who have been spending generously yet ignoring the return on our investment. We can't take our money to another provider of governmental services. There are no laws of physics, nature, or economics that say government operations must be inefficient, bureaucratic, corrupt, and not improving (this is different than the democratic process, which is designed to require lots of effort). Our current government inefficiency is what it is because we tolerate it. We can choose to be much more demanding consumers, reestablishing our expectations for quality, value, and effectiveness of government. In equal proportions we must be willing to assume responsibility and invest the required time to be engaged.

You and I are the consumers who purchase governmental services, and collectively we serve on the board of directors, responsible for hiring, funding and directing the elected people who appropriate our money to deliver governmental services and make long-term investments.

Part 1: Boundary Conditions

For those who have yet to experience the joys of differential equations, you may not see the similarities. To solve differential equations, you need to make assumptions or create boundary conditions; these must remain true for the differential equation to be solved. If the boundary conditions change (no longer hold true), then the previously developed solution is no longer valid. The math or what the founding fathers developed is not at fault, but the boundary conditions changed. This helps explain how a well-designed democracy strayed off course.

Chapter 1. How Did We Get Here?

A problem cannot be solved before you understand what the problem is, and understanding what changed can be incredibly helpful. The pre-Socratic Greek philosopher Heraclitus said, "The only thing that is constant is change." Our Founding Fathers clearly understood that point, so the democratic framework they constructed was designed to adapt and change as the world evolved. Over the years, I pondered what had gone wrong with this well-designed system, and I realized that some of their core assumptions were no longer holding true. The boundary conditions were no longer valid.

A problem cannot be solved before you understand what the problem is and understanding what changed can be incredibly helpful.

The world has changed over the past 230-plus years. Some of the initial concerns and trepidations of the Founding Fathers have come to fruition. The challenge is, how can we re-establish those boundary conditions so the democratic equation can function as designed? We need to look at those original boundary conditions before we begin taking actions for establishing boundaries that will work now and hopefully for many future generations.

1.1. Boundary Condition: Discussion and Debate

For us to cooperate and effectively maintain and propagate our shared economy, we need to work together. If we choose not to live in a hierarchical, aristocratic, or dictatorial form of government, we will need to communicate with each other. Unfortunately, the boundary conditions of discussion and debate with people who have different views are now a minuscule fraction of how we form our opinions.

Think of the contrast between the amount of time in the late 1700s people spent in taverns, community-based activities, family discussions, and with colleagues, compared with how we engage with people today. Many people work from home and do not have daily in-person exchange with colleagues. I regularly see groups of people with their faces glued to small screens, not even verbally talking to each other.

To clearly explain something to someone, you must first truly understand the topic or perspective.

The process of actively discussing something is also crucial to understanding. To clearly explain something to someone, you must first truly understand the topic or perspective. To present your case or to help someone understand something, you must first organize your ideas and thoughts before you explain them. Without this essential step, what we hear, think, and believe does not get organized. If you are not actively discussing and trying to persuade people, you may not fully understand a subject. Today, too many people think they are discussing, but are much closer to regurgitating a stream of sound bites. Repeating without thinking things through first is not a rational discussion.

In the days before radio, TV, smartphones, and the internet, when the sun set, you could sit in your house, go see your neighbors, or visit the local tavern. You did not watch *Monday Night Football*, but instead talked. The subjects could be gossip, weather, business, or, believe it or not, politics. Yes, there was a time when friends, neighbors, and others were perfectly comfortable talking politics, local, state, and national. Before print, there were storytellers, songs, and other community activities that shaped political thought, answered questions, established values, and reinforced societal norms. For the most part, that has disappeared from our society.

Citizens formed their positions not based on paid talking heads, but from having discussions and friendly debates. Most communities had more than one newspaper, so it was convenient to educate yourself on opposing opinions. We learned from each other and our opinions evolved through these discussions. While people did not have to agree with all they heard, many of these discussions occurred between people with an established relationship. There was a certain level of trust or skepticism based on one's experience with another individual.

Discussion and friendly debate on a regular basis were part of what people did in the late 1700s[1]. The act of discussion teaches the individual what they truly comprehend and what is less supportable. To debate, you must listen, hear and think about what was said, in order to have an interactive discussion. You don't have to agree, but at least you were exposed to other ways of seeing things. Hence, your brain is much more active in the process of forming opinions than the more passive mode of hearing people talk at you, such as on TV or radio.

Issues, problems, and alternatives were discussed on a much more regular basis by individuals. How many in-depth political discussions do you have about local or state issues each day, each week? If you are spending a good portion of your money each year on these services, are you even talking about what is happening with your money? Personally, I like having these discussions, but with our go, go, go and home-based lifestyles, we are hard pressed to have these discussions.

1.2. Boundary Condition: The Press

Opinions, like religions, are neither right nor wrong, only different. Opinions are formed based on the perception each of us has, and each of our vantage points is uniquely different. We consider a fact to be an absolute truth, but those truths may appear differently to each of us based on our perceptions. If half of your view is blocked and you don't see something, does it exist? While people only receive information coming from one side or source, they are blind to other perspectives. How much do they really understand of that other perspective? In the days of our Founding Fathers, that visibility came from newspapers, flyers, and pamphlets.

For much of our past, newspapers were the primary source for information. There were many different and competing newspapers that would take stances or positions on topics. Similar to how today's TV and radio programs have a bias, so did newspapers. However, many people would get information from multiple sources, exposing them to multiple perspectives. I am old enough to remember a time when we had morning, afternoon, and evening editions of the big-city papers. There was plenty to read and journalists had the time to go deep into issues covering many different national and local topics. The first step for having an educated electorate is information, and the newspapers were the primary means of information.

Yes, the internet, TV, and radio provide more information, but that information tends to be narrowly focused. The scope is limited in alternative views, perspective, and focus. Is more information better if all that is consumed by an individual is one-sided? Streams of disconnected, sometimes unfounded information and opinion do not provide the visibility and information we need to efficiently manage our government.

I don't fault the media for any of this change. They are not a public service, but a business entity attempting to make a profit. In a crowded and fragmented market, survival is a function of succeeding in defined niches where loyalty can be established. If people are not willing to pay for the value of investigative journalism, then why should businesses invest resources in helping to keep our government open and honest?

The First Amendment includes the right of freedom of the press. So, what is our government's responsibility to protect this right? The press or media is a business, not an arm of government. All our government should do is help assure a level playing field. What the press is will change over time. Fewer people rely on TV and news networks, but it can be argued that the monopolization of any media source (e.g., Fox or Sinclair in TV) has slanted the playing field. Anti-trust laws are not to create competing businesses but to prevent massive clumping in an area that significantly tips the playing field.

I have found the following thought experiment helpful for showing how this single-perspective situation prevents us from productive dialogue. I hope you and your kids have had the fun of playing with Play-Doh at some point. Play-Doh is just a blob of stuff that has to be formed. When Play-Doh is taken out of the can and dumped on a table, what is it? Well, it's Play-Doh. Now let's assume the clump of Play-Doh represents a problem, issue, question, or anything else our society needs to address. In our democratic society, we use our political process to take action on the problem. The Play-Doh represents the problem or challenge and not just a toy to occupy our time.

If we are sitting around the table with Play-Doh (i.e., an issue) in front of us, we can have a rational discussion about it, share ideas and develop a course of action. However, something happens to that Play-Doh. Take the room of people, separate that same color Play-Doh, and put an equal number of people around three tables. Some of the Play-Doh kits come with plastic molds that help you form the Play-Doh. One table had the Play-Doh first go through a square, another a circle, and the last a star mold before it hit the table. Each table looks at a different shape.

If you ask the people at each table what they are looking at, the majority are going to tell you they are looking at a square, circle, or star. Some may say "shaped Play-Doh," but the emphasis will most likely be on the shape, not the Play-Doh. Our media are the molds that shape the issues and strongly influence what we perceive. All three are looking at the same Play-Doh or issue, but their perspective is based on which filter or mold they are looking through. If you bring the groups together, one will be talking about a circle, one about a square, and one about a star, so the shape—their ideology—becomes dominant, not the common problem.

If we are going to work together and find solutions to our problems, we have to take what the media gives us, squish it back into a blob of the original Play-Doh, then start to figure out what to do. Informed discussion and debate is the process that helps us forget about the shape and focus on what the problem is—Play-Doh—rather than a shape.

1.3. Boundary Condition: New Ideas and Opinions

The Founding Fathers assumed that if you had new ideas or wanted to get your point across, you could post a few flyers on the oak tree at the town common and print some pamphlets, and your ideas would get disseminated and discussed at local taverns. Back then, people actually read "public notices." When was the last time you went to a town/city Hall or your local library and read a public notice? There are new tools today, but they are far from effective in getting new ideas or opinions across to many locally, statewide, or regionally. The tools that are available tend to only be utilized by a small fraction of the population. Even social media is broken into niche markets and virtually tribal access paths. A poster in the Colonial-era town common got a higher percentage of the eyeballs than today's high-tech solutions.

Information people get today tends to be one-sided and biased. If they read a newspaper, it is just one newspaper; the same for TV news. Each of these will tend to offer only one perspective on issues. The internet makes it much easier for an individual to post something, but unlike the oak tree in the town square, only those who tend to already agree or lean in that direction are going to see it. Additionally, the messages are shorter, whether they arrive as sound bites or tweets, lacking the depth that inspires individual analysis. These shorter messages tend to be accepted and not questioned.

1.4. Boundary Condition: Civic Responsibility

We have all heard the phrase from the Revolutionary War: "No taxation without representation." Now do you think the colonists wanted the ability to have a say in whether Britain built a new London Bridge or more Navy ships? More likely, they just did not like seeing economic energy (their money) being sucked out of their economy. Britain was slowing down the colonial economic flywheel, so pulling money (energy) out was hitting the colonists where it hurt the most—their economy's ability to build energy.

Howard Zinn's book *The People's History of the United States* made it clear that one of the key goals of the Founding Fathers was to create an environment that would take care of their economy. The Declaration of Independence contains the phrase "endowed by their Creator with certain unalienable rights." Those rights did not include the right to vote for those who did not own property. Why was that?

People who enjoy paying taxes are few and far between, but a stable currency, infrastructure, a legal system, secure borders, and other common systems are essential elements for commerce. If you were poor and had no assets, you were not contributing to these common systems. If you are not vested, how much do you care about how effectively and efficiently other people's money is being utilized? So, if you don't personally have skin in the game or an interest in how your money (taxes paid) was being used, how much time and effort would you invest in managing other people's money? If those government services cost more, were inefficient or did not meet expectations, how engaged would you be about other people's spending. Observation and history had shown the Founding Fathers that people who paid for the government cared much more than those who did not contribute. Many at that time feared the power of the not-vested masses of people.

While all humans are created equal and have the same inalienable rights, not all would put in the same effort to manage the government. Voting initially required citizens to have skin in the game. If you owned property, then you cared about the value of that asset, and it was assumed you would pay attention to activities that increased or decreased the value of your asset. Those who would pay attention and take care of the economic flywheel had the right to vote. Unfortunately, the Founding Fathers did not include women or non-white men as eligible to vote, regardless of property ownership.

The courageous and dedicated activities of many reversed this injustice to women and non-whites, giving them the responsibility of managing our government. But the abolishment of those prejudicial practices did not weaken the original boundary condition that directly tied your economic interest with the people you hired to manage your investments in government (taxes paid). That correlation between direct self-interest and the effort of monitoring who you hired (elected or appointed) to manage the money you were forking over for governmental services eroded over time.

Today, all citizens have a say in the care and maintenance of our economy (mostly through voting). There no longer is the requirement that all people be vested or directly impacted by how their money is being utilized. The much wider responsibility base (voter base) is more disconnected as some don't have skin in the game, and for those that do, their vested interest carries the same weight as the non-vested interest. The assumption that those who voted would put the time and effort in to make sure their money was being utilized effectively has been highly diluted by those who are less economically vested.

While the number of voters has been expanded, the motivation and responsibility for staying informed, educated and participating in managing our government did not go away. Too many people have abandoned their civic responsibility. Now a large portion of voters don't understand what is happening with our government. Some feel it has grown too big or too complex, or that it intentionally hides what is going on. We have become irresponsible purchasers of our government, and as a nation we are failing in our fiduciary responsibilities to take care of our economy. Many who are engaged have been sucked up in the whirlwind of the two-party competition and associated polarization.

1.5. The Way Things Are Today (WTAT)

How would you feel if every time you did something, someone else came along and gave an equal push in the opposite direction? The polarization being created by the opposing political parties and their alternating directional activities is not helping us build our economy or address our challenges.

Can you feel the stress of the seesaw ready to snap from all of the polarization? If you think it is about to snap, welcome to our democratic reality.

Abraham Lincoln said, "A house divided against itself cannot stand." It is hard to deny what is happening in our nation. Our nation needs to acknowledge our current predicament driven from our "mediatainment" (partisan media that is more entertainment than trustable news) and the billions spent on campaigns and lobbyists. While there is nothing wrong with the seesaw gently rocking back and forth, it is either going to tip completely left or right, or it will break. None of the three options will work out well for our nation, but that is what we are facing.

An element of the divide is also becoming economic as well as ideological. When we hear about the 1% of the nation who continues to own an ever-growing percentage of our national wealth, what does that mean? Well the seesaw is tipping one way, and those that don't climb into the 1% are continually sliding to the other end of the seesaw. The steeper it gets, the fewer that can stick with the 1%. The middle class is getting stretched with a few popping up towards the 1% end, but most falling behind where their parents used to be. For many, staring up at the incline is getting more daunting.

Now take a step back and make some observations from how things are looking from each side of the seesaw. If you're falling to the low side or unable to fight your way up the slope of today's economic challenges, you wonder: what ever happened to the level playing field? It never was level, so don't kid yourself, but it never seemed so insurmountable, and it is getting worse. How did it get so super-duper slanted? It's pretty straightforward, for those who put the politicians in place. While everyone who pays taxes is buying government, it's not your tax dollars that tip the playing field, it is the two-party, money-driven system that keeps politicians in power. Who has the discretionary wealth to feed political marketing machines that influence the other 99% on how to vote? It's the 1%, and thanks to the Citizens United ruling, corporations, businesses, and unions.

These wealthy people and entities are not stupid; they would not be spending if they were not getting value for everything they give to political campaigns. There needs to be visible return on investments. If some are buying political influence, so laws or lack of laws create situations where their companies or businesses can make more money, shouldn't they do it too? This is creating two sections of the economic flywheel. The 1% is living off the outer ring or edge of the flywheel, where there's more kinetic energy; they are getting wealthier, receiving more benefits, and building on top of the rest of the nation. There is a theoretical gap between the high-energy outer ring and the inside portion. While we spin as one national economic flywheel, there are two distinct sections: money on the outside and everyone else on the inside.

These wealthy people and entities are not stupid; they would not be spending if they were not getting value for everything they give to political campaigns.

From the other perspective, the wealthy who believe their efforts have pulled more of the mass to the outer rim of the flywheel are concerned that what they have earned will be pulled down so that all can share the economic energy. Benjamin Franklin said, "When the people find that they can vote themselves money, that will herald the end of the republic." The number of people whose economic fortune keeps them regulated to the inner rings of the flywheel outnumber those in the outer rings, and they will vote to shift the wealth (mass) back down to the lower rings. The money can be benefits or other economic advantages, so more of what others have earned is redistributed to those who are not being self-supportive.

The perspective of those who don't have skin in the game feel that since the playing field is so slanted, why shouldn't more of the money from the 1% and others be going to those who are suffering or not as well off? They have legitimate needs, they are citizens of this nation, and a just society should be addressing them. At the time of the original publication, the opposite is happening: the few with the money are assuring that more of the economic growth (mass) goes mostly to the outer ring and is not equally distributed.

Of course, it just isn't that simple. Those who have created value from ingenuity and hard work should not have to give up what they earned. There are views from both sides, and like discussion and debate, if we aren't exposed and don't discuss these, it is hard to see both perspectives.

Growing up and learning from sports, my dad, his friends, and other role models, I just assumed everybody gave 110% all the time, since that is what I was taught to do. The other perspective was opened up to me early in my career when a boss had to explain that there are two types of employees: those who earn paychecks and those who collect paychecks. The ones who collect paychecks are getting paid for doing their job; they do their job and no more, hopefully not less.

Additionally I learned from my sister, who was working as a social worker in NYC and explained to me her view of the mentality of welfare generations. Some people living on welfare as they grow up see that our government is responsible for taking care of them. Their view is that because they are citizens (part of the flywheel), they get their due in the form of healthcare, food stamps, housing help, and other assistance. Gaming the system to get the most out of it is how you climb to higher-energy portions of the flywheel.

These different vantage points are neither right nor wrong, they are just different views. Perception is reality and what you see from where you stand is how the world looks. From my perspective it is not blue or red, it's purple, but our two-party system needs to keep voters in the blue and red camps.

Fractional Logic

Many a time, I have wondered why intelligent people with similar backgrounds, education, and circumstances would have opinions so radically different from me. I could not understand why they were not questioning the views and perspectives they were regurgitating. It may have been from an e-mail that was forwarded, tuning to a radio station I don't normally listen to, or multiple instances that exposed me to what was happening. Opinionated groups have become adept at leveraging something I refer to as "fractional logic": only a small piece of the total argument or statements is based on the initial true fact.

The starting point is true or rationally believable. Since the person already leans in that direction, it is easy to take them further in that direction. Picture someone or something about to fall: it does not take much effort to complete the fall, nor is there much natural resistance to falling at that point. There is momentum that takes less energy, or in this case, unquestioning acceptance, to keep going in that direction. The individual is still rooted in that original truth, so that acceptance carries forward to the rest of what they are being told. The driver of the fractional logic now takes that person down a path that is far less connected to the original fact. By the time the ride ends, the original fact is now just a small portion or fraction of what they have accepted, but the conviction of its truth applies to all the ideas and opinions they have absorbed.

A fraction of logic is the original lever that gets people accepting and believing an argument or perspective that was started with a fact, but has crossed the line to opinion or simply to conjecture. There is a difference between a fact and everything that could be built from it. We can lean on the fact, but not all of the opinion that follows. Skilled entertainers are adroit at this craft, and you will find many of them on talk radio and TV programs that contain news. While I am not encouraging anyone to listen to political talk radio (remember, these shows are entertainment), if you pay attention you will clearly see the pattern of fact and then a journey to somewhere else.

If you go outside and shoot some baskets, maybe play a little two-on-two basketball, you are playing a sport. When you are watching an NBA game, you are being entertained. Those athletes are not running up and down the court for their recreation; they are highly paid entertainers. The same is true of all of the political talking heads, whether they are on TV, the radio, or online. There is nothing wrong with what they are doing, and it's our responsibility to remember that. We can't expect them to start with a disclosure reminding us of that fact. In a fragmented competitive market, success hinges on building and maintaining a niche following.

Who Represents Us?

By the time you finish this book, you will hopefully have a different view on how we take care of our economic flywheel. Today, too many of us think we just hire the maintenance crew (elected officials) and then sit in the stands and watch until the next election. In our representative democracy model, what does it take to do a good job representing the people's responsibility for managing the delivery and quality of government we are buying? Originally, it was not the responsibility of career politicians.[2] Originally, political office was a temporary activity earned by some of the most outstanding leaders in a community or state. In fact, term limits were a topic of discussion during the Continental Congress, as some felt it important to have fresh individuals serving in these roles. New Hampshire included this voter responsibility provision in the 1798 Bill of Rights portion of the state constitution. When I first read this, I had to look up what "emolument" meant (a salary, fee, or profit from employment or office). Unfortunately, it is a term little used these days, but it was warning of the danger of employing career politicians. Today, many states have a minimum age requirement for representing residents in our federal government, so that candidates must theoretically attain some level of maturity and experience prior to taking a public service role.

[Art.] 10. [Right of Revolution.]

Government being instituted for the common benefit, protection, and security, of the whole community, and not for the private interest or emolument of any one man, family, or class of men; therefore, whenever the ends of government are perverted, and public liberty manifestly endangered, and all other means of redress are ineffectual, the people may, and of right ought to reform the old, or establish a new government. The doctrine of nonresistance against arbitrary power, and oppression, is absurd, slavish, and destructive of the good and happiness of mankind.

Part 2: The Flywheel Model

In his book *Good to Great*, Jim Collins uses a flywheel analogy to describe how a new idea can take hold at a corporation. At the time I read the book, I was working for a multinational corporation, and that concept resonated and has always stayed with me. In this book, we are going to use a flywheel to give us hope and to develop a common way to understand and discuss how we go about managing the government we buy. I also tag, or label, my ideas and suggested actions "flywheel ideas."

Chapter 2. The Flywheel Concept

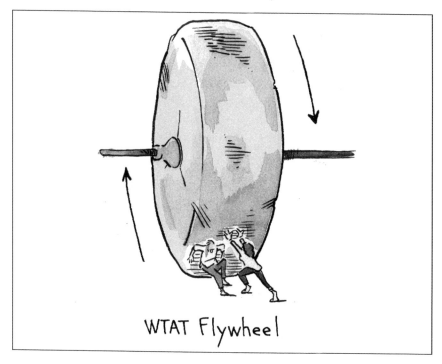

WTAT Flywheel

How our democracy is currently working is a massive flywheel, spinning with a tremendous amount of energy: we'll call it the Way Things Are Today (WTAT) flywheel. It is unfathomable that a single individual is going to be able to make an impact. Some refer to this flywheel as the "system" or "how things work."

Currently our money-driven and party-focused political process offers few solutions to our collective problems, since government services for the most part are anything but efficiently delivered or value driven. Until we the people demand change, we will be unable to vote our way out of our current situation. Albert Einstein has been frequently quoted as saying, "Repeating the same actions and expecting different results is a sure sign of insanity." It is time to start to do things differently. He also said, "Problems cannot be solved with the same mindset that created them."

A catastrophe or massive crises could also stop and change this WTAT flywheel, but I would prefer to avoid that. If the financial meltdown of 2007 and 2008 did not bring about substantial change, the next catastrophe is going to have to be much, much bigger to make an impact. The other way to change would be a little bit at a time. At first our actions will not have any visible impact, but if sustained, these local actions and cultural changes will begin to sap the energy from the WTAT flywheel. As that flywheel slows, our efforts are going to have more and more of an impact on that flywheel until we bring it to a stop and get it moving in a new direction.

Most of this book will focus on a second flywheel: our economic flywheel, which provides a framework for discussion and debate. For all of those who live in our nation, our economy is a great common bond. If the economy is not humming along, just about everyone is in trouble. When our economic flywheel is moving and growing, all can benefit and prosper, and it makes national investments affordable. All of our decisions and actions can be discussed in respect to how they affect our economic flywheel. A common vernacular will set the framework as we respectfully debate our choices. The most cost-effective and efficient government will translate to more economic flywheel energy, creating a competitive advantage that will be hard for other nations to ever catch.

Think about Wikipedia. No one would have ever paid to build and maintain Wikipedia, nor would money motivate the multitude of people who provide the content. Something massive has been accomplished from many small individual actions. When you get done with this book, you will have started thinking about what you are going to do to bring about this change in American culture. It's not a radical change, just a shift towards actions that make our democracy and economy as healthy as possible.

One of the chief roles of government is to maintain an environment where commerce can flourish. This includes our currency, legal framework, part of our infrastructure, national security, and other areas. We hire the people who are responsible for assuring that our economic flywheel keeps on spinning and adds mass. As our economic flywheel spins on its axle, we need to make sure we keep the axle well lubricated and maintained. The economic flywheel ideas and actions will enable us to control the "system" and not be driven by the "system."

The "system" is how the management of our government works today. What the Founding Fathers developed at the federal level, states and local communities also deployed at their level. It is a well-designed system, but in many aspects it is not operating as designed. Maintenance and repairs are needed and those are replacing the functions of the original boundary questions.

The heart of this book is focused on the repairs to be made. A problem is discussed and I introduce flywheel ideas for corrective action. For some ideas, I include what can be done at the local level to begin the implementation of the repairs. The ideas and suggested local actions are catalysts to get citizens engaged and working on repairs. These initial actions start to slow down the WTAT and should draw in more individual investment of time and skills. Some of these ideas may be fully implemented; others will evolve; and still others will introduce additional ideas and actions.

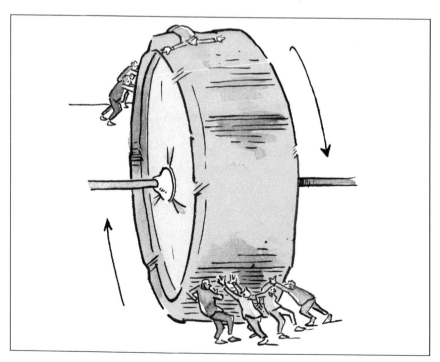

To put many different topics and ideas in context, this book looks at what impacts our economic flywheel. There will be forces that act as brakes, sucking out energy on every revolution; the broken business of medicine is one. There will be other forces we created that are weights connected to our economic flywheel that we have to fight through on every revolution, such as the size of our national debt and annual interest payments, both of which are illustrated later on. Think of the salary and other operational costs of the United States Congress when they are a "do-nothing Congress" that acts as sand on the flywheel axle. When we do take actions to better manage our government, that helps the flywheel and acts as grease on the axle; I use many examples of that from what we have been doing locally with the Rye Civic League.

The net result of these actions will be the rebuilding of the boundary conditions. The world has changed, so they won't look like the boundary conditions of almost two hundred and fifty years ago, but they will serve the same function in today's day and age.

Chapter 3. Applying the Flywheel Concept to Government

Sitting on the deck with friends recently, we got into a political discussion. One friend started defending the Bush-era tax cuts, while another said that the fiscal stimulus after the 2008 financial meltdown worked to stimulate the economy. They were both right and vastly wrong. Tax cuts and government money pour energy into the economy, but they no longer have the impact they used to. How could these two friends both be right and wrong at the same time? Enter the economic flywheel model.

Picture a large stone flywheel: a heavy, large wheel that takes a fair amount of energy to get moving, but once going requires less energy to maintain its angular momentum. Inertia is the energy that a mass holds as it is moving. Imagine pushing a boulder; it takes a lot of energy to get rolling, but once it is moving, it takes less effort to keep it going. If it smashes into something, the damage is from its mass and velocity, not the little bit of energy you just put in. The flywheel inertia is our economic energy. Keeping this flywheel inertia growing and not shrinking is how we achieve increasing gross domestic product (GDP). Assuming we always have some inflation, we need GDP to be going up if we want to earn more money and have job opportunities for a growing working population.

Assume the Democrats control 100% of Congress and ramp up federal, state, and local spending to drive the economy. The push comes from the top of the flywheel and it does add energy to the economic flywheel. The same is true of Republican approaches: cutting taxes and mitigating government burdens on businesses will also push the flywheel in the same direction. Picture that energy coming from the bottom (you can swap them, top or bottom, it is irrelevant). Either approach unfettered will add energy and help our economy; the problem is the impact just doesn't work like it used to. Like it or not, the world has changed and will continue to do so.

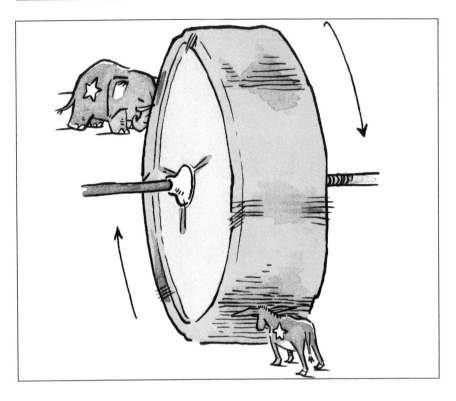

Ever since there has been trade, economies have been connected. Currently, the US is the biggest flywheel; the economies we trade with are smaller and stack up adjacent to ours, all spinning on parallel independent axes. All of those other flywheels add up to something greater than the US economy, but the connection is more important. Now take some ropes, elastics, or chains and connect the flywheels to each other. When our flywheel starts to spin, it has an effect on the other economies. If we slow down or speed up, we can impact other economies. This is a model and not a detailed simulation of what happens, but it shows basic relationships.

As the world gets smaller, the connections between these flywheels become more rigid, that is, stiff. So, tighten those chains, shorten those elastics, take the slack out of those ropes, so energy from our spinning flywheel gets transferred to other flywheels much more effectively. Some economic models from the 2007-2008 financial stimulus talked about jobs that would be created; while some jobs were created, there were not as many jobs as predicted. So where did the jobs go? Look at the other flywheels. Jobs were created, but some showed up in other economies. While those workers may go to US chains abroad or buy products/services that come from US companies, for the most part, their spending and support from those jobs went to the non-US economy.

Our ability to directly impact the US economy from cutting taxes or more government spending has lost its punch. If either the Republicans or Democrats dominated government, their actions would have some impact, but there is no way that either can pour enough energy into our flywheel to allow our economy to build sustainable economic energy to permanently fight off our fiscal (flywheel) inhibitors (brakes, weights, and sand on the axle).

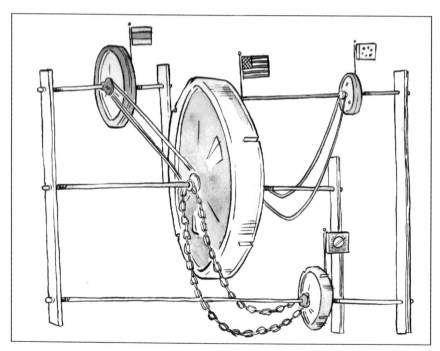

It's not just this dissipation of energy to other economies. Our economic flywheel has two other big problems. We will treat one of them as a brake. Take a big, solid piece of wood or a huge beam, fix one end into the ground in front of our flywheel, and stick the other end against the flywheel at 2 o'clock or 10 o'clock, opposing the direction of the spin. This brake pushing against the flywheel is sucking energy out of our economy. On every flywheel turn, the brake is pulling energy out of our economy. For example, the business of medicine in this country is severely broken and it is sucking resources out of our economy, so our inefficient healthcare system acts as a huge brake on our economic flywheel.

Healthcare is only part of the battle. On the other side of our flywheel, we have buckets of weight attached to our flywheel: our national debt. While some debt is OK, for our economy to spin, we have to fight through the weight of that debt on every revolution. Why? Well, for starters, the interest on that debt was $268B in 2017, 7% of the total federal budget.[3] What do you think would happen to our economy if businesses and/or individuals had an additional $200B each year to spend, save, or invest? Having those $200B payments pulls money out of our economy. Debt is not all evil; it can be prudent to use other people's money to get things done, and many Americans invest in US savings bonds. Like your house mortgage, what can you afford to pay in interest and principal payments given all of the other personal expenses? The annual interest payments are painful, but the $22,000,000,000,000 ($22 trillion) that we owe is a massive burden[4] on our economic flywheel.

The less debt we have, the less we have to pay in taxes. The challenge is that the debt will only go down through a combination of higher tax revenue and government reduction. While some may argue that it's theoretically possible to spend or cut our way out of our national debt problem, the chances of that happening are mighty, mighty slim. The current policies of either political party are inadequate for the challenge and the current global economics.

When you hear of other countries collapsing economically, many times it is because they have piled up so much debt that their economy can't power through the next revolution, and their flywheel stops spinning. That could happen to the United States; our debt is so large that a strong recession, along with the flywheel brakes, could create enough drag that our economy slows to a crawl.

Here comes the sand. If you were wondering how our do-nothing Congress fits into the equation, picture the flywheel axle, nice and lubricated so that it spins freely. Now what happens if we dump sand on the axle? How well do you think our economic flywheel will spin, lubricated with sand? Well, like our economy, a flywheel has lots of momentum and can power through interference. So, the do-nothing Congress takes energy out of the economy since the flywheel has to turn on sand, not the smooth lubricant. If you were not feeling bad enough, remember we are paying Congress, and for the most part, when they do nothing or take completely partisan action, our money is being used to take energy out of our economic flywheel.

My generation grew up knowing our parents worked hard and their lives were better than my grandparents' lives. From stories I've heard, my grandparents were much better off than their grandparents. While it is not true for all Americans, it held true for the millions of us whose families migrated to the United States from the late 1800s to the 1980s. If we worked hard, developed a skilled trade, or went to college, the odds of being better off were in our favor. Unless something changes, that will not be the United States our children or grandchildren will compete in. As our economic flywheel loses momentum from our inability to fix the forces we allowed to evolve, the flywheel energy future generations need for better lives, opportunities, and welfare just won't be there.

Part 3: Flywheel Brakes

As I introduced earlier, there are manmade forces that impact the rotation of our flywheel. If you've ever worked on bikes or cars, you are familiar with brakes. My first homemade go-cart had a brake. It was a wooden 2x4 nailed to the side of the frame. When I wanted to slow down or stop, I just pulled back on the piece of wood and it scraped along the pavement, slowing me down. Brakes on the economic flywheel are similar to that go-cart brake, like a lever that pushes against the spinning flywheel. The more force pushing down on that brake, the more energy is going to be sucked out of our spinning flywheel. It takes a lot to bring a flywheel to a complete stop, but the brake can drain lots of energy.

Smaller brakes can be removed cleanly, but larger brakes may not be completely removed. However, if we take actions to mitigate how hard the brakes are pressing against our flywheel, even small changes can add up to more economic energy.

As we step through these sections, picture a big beam being pushed against the economic flywheel. Some brakes will be bigger than others, but they all are taking energy from our flywheel.

Chapter 4. The Big Brake: Healthcare

Do you see the elephant in the room? We seem to skirt around the fundamental fact that the business of medicine is broken and is sucking energy out of our economy. This is everything from the 17%+ of our GDP that goes to healthcare, our overall poor health (obesity, diabetes, opioid epidemic, and other issues) to the countless hours fighting with health insurance providers. The brake is the massive volume of capital, poor health, and our time that pulls energy out of our economic flywheel. While there are lots of healthcare jobs, the net effect of the broken business of medicine is a big old brake on our economic flywheel.

The first time I heard "The business of medicine is broken," I was at dinner with a group of first-year doctors. They had gone from residency to varying types of medicine, from research and specialties to primary care. They were shocked at how broken the business of medicine was. They lamented how little this aspect was covered during their medical education. One doctor was fighting to get basic care to keep patients alive, while a friend had just spent a week in Hawaii thanks to a pharmaceutical company. Those pharmaceutical boondoggles have come to an end, but just count the drug advertisements you see these days. For all we spend on healthcare, the money is not being efficiently allocated to give the most return to our society. Having a few hugely profitable people at the top of the healthcare chain does not drive our economy. We are at the point where even the middle class is making economic choices between, for example, home repair and healthcare.

4.1. Government and Healthcare

It's not all of healthcare that is the brake, only the inefficiencies and misuse of what we spend. Healthcare, like the automotive industry was, is a big part of our economy. In the 70s, about one quarter of our total economy was related to the automotive business (cars, gas, parts, steel, electronics, repair, insurance, advertising, etc.). Healthcare is now a similar proportion of today's flywheel energy.

We invest much more of our GDP on healthcare than needs to be spent. There is plenty of money going into the system, but it can't be going to the right places. If it were, we would see higher levels of health, more people being covered, and the total cost invested in healthcare begin to decrease year over year. We will discuss some suggestions, but whatever we agree to do, not having a more efficient system or business for medicine is a detriment to our economy. The World Bank shows that the US spent 16.84% of our 2015 GDP on healthcare, which is up from 12.51% in 2000, so we are moving in the wrong direction.[5] Compare to countries with socialized medicine: the same table shows the UK spent 9.88% and Canada spent 10.44% on healthcare in 2015. Yes, this is a smaller percentage, but the numbers can only be viewed in parallel to the quality of care, results, and treatment options.

This disproportional amount of GDP going to our healthcare slows down our economy. There is no need to argue about best care, slow care, or the faults and merits of different approaches. We are paying a GDP premium and are not getting premium results. The disparity in spending versus results is the brake on our flywheel.

From my perspective, the Affordable Care Act of 2010 addressed the unacceptable practice of denying people healthcare insurance for pre-existing conditions. It did not address the fundamental mechanics of the inefficient healthcare system. Besides unhealthy lifestyles, two of the big drivers of healthcare spending are what gets spent on those who are near the end of life and emergency room visits.

Think of the 80/20 rule (80% of the costs go to 20% of the population). A vast majority of our healthcare spend goes to those at the end of their lives. Overall, the almost 17% of GDP spent on healthcare is over $3.2 trillion. We have the baby boomers cascading towards the last phase of their lives, and that volume of people will drive increased spending on healthcare.

Today, everyone who pays for healthcare is sharing emergency room visit costs for the uninsured. People without insurance wait until it's an emergency and then get treated. Not everyone needs to go to emergency rooms, but it is the place required by law to admit and care for people. The primary way to keep people out of emergency rooms is to make sure everyone has access to medical care. Notice I did not say insurance.

4.2. Reducing the Healthcare Brakes

Some will argue healthcare is a basic right in our society and not a business. Currently, the only right or privilege in our country is that you will not die on the emergency room doorstep. As long as we say that, there is going to be some sort of shared-cost model. Those who can afford to contribute will need to do so.

Now, what if we change our minds and say that if someone does not have a means to pay for the care they are about to receive, then tough luck? If we go that way, the healthcare equation gets much simpler. Why? Well, there is no dead weight the system has to carry, and a big cost variable is removed from the healthcare system. But I just don't see us doing that, nor do I want to promote that as a viable option.

If we continue to not let people die at the hospital doorstep when we have the ability to help, the healthcare equation stays complicated by the shared cost to treat people who cannot pay for their emergency care. There is no market for paying that cost and if we are going to be funding this care, we certainly don't want to be paying for a failing system. So, nationally, there is a role for a centralized entity to step in, we just need to figure out what we want our government or this new entity (a non-governmental organization) to be doing.

There are three choices. We can have fully socialized healthcare where everyone gets a minimum degree of health care from our government, and there is no fee for basic services. The second is to require everyone to participate in a base level of insurance. For those who can't afford insurance, taxes will pay their insurance. The third is to create a tax-fed fund that goes directly to hospitals and pays them directly for costs incurred preventing people from dying at the hospital doorstep. This last approach says, no dying at the hospital doorstep, but you have to have insurance for everything else. Yes, I know people will do nothing until it's too late, then go to the emergency room. Well, guess what? With today's high deductibles, people are procrastinating with preventive care, and doctors are seeing insured patients wait until they are desperate before seeking care[6].

How healthcare money flows and who makes cost, care, and value decisions must change. It's not an easy pill to swallow, but we need to do it sooner rather than later. Our government in its current dysfunctional state is incapable of tackling this challenge. This change will be hard on everyone, but we need to admit there is an elephant in the room, roll up our sleeves, and work together to get it out of the way.

4.3. National Healthcare Discussion

Lobbyists, insurers, hospital chains, and others submitting proposals to Congress are not a national discussion. The Affordable Care Act and Obamacare are two equally poor names for the legislation that got shoved through with minimal nonpartisan discussion. As the legislation had to be marketed for or against, those were the names the opposing views assigned. If we were in the practice of calling a spade a spade, we would have called it "Healthcare Insurance Reform." It was the unequitable practices of denying health insurance for pre-existing conditions of the Affordable Care Act that had national support.

Huge amounts of our money went into getting this legislation through Congress, and it would be horrifying if we could calculate the accumulated costs. Additionally, the people we pay to manage our government spent countless dollars and congressional time attempting to repeal the legislation, while not addressing the many other challenges facing our nation.

Politics has kept us distracted from having the national dialog we desperately need. That is, what is the best way to keep people from dying at the hospital doorstep and to modify our healthcare system so overall health is improved at a much smaller percentage of our GDP? Those are the questions we need to be discussing.

While we are having the discussion, we need to remind ourselves that we live in a complex world. No matter what we end up doing, there may not be a perfect solution. No matter how good our new technology (artificial intelligence software, pills that send a signal when ingested, etc.) can be, there are going to be lots of gray areas. Since our decisions will not all be binary (1 or 0), we are going to need the human element to make choices.

4.4. Single-Payer System?

My two cents on this option is that we are not ready for it. Feel free to disagree, but I for one do not think we have the skills, tools, habits, process, and a host of other attributes required to manage this increased volume of shared investment. One day, we may decide that a single-payer insurance system is the right decision for our nation. Feel free to pile up all of the cost efficiency arguments for a single-payer system, and I will agree that in isolation there is a valid logical argument. However, if we are unable to execute on the implementation and management, then this value is only theoretical given our current set of management capabilities for the centralized services we buy (government). More simply put, until we can efficiently manage government services, more government just makes a bad problem worse.

Someday in the future, when we are much, much better at managing our government and have a much higher degree of confidence, where we can effectively manage our government providing a single-payer system, then we could discuss this option. By then we'll have developed the skills, systems, and process to guarantee government-provided healthcare will be cost effective and efficient and will provide incremental value year over year at lower costs.

4.5. We Have Single-Payer Systems Already

We have four forms of government single-payer systems now: Medicare and Medicaid, the Veterans Health Administration, and the healthcare/insurance program for federal employees. Those are all sizable programs. While these programs should keep people from dying on the hospital doorstep, they too are a combination of health/wellness and insurance, and those aspects need to be separated.

We can ignore the federal program for now, since this should be no different than any large employer contributing to prevent dying at the doors of the hospital, as well as promoting wellness/health and providing insurance for when bad things happen.

4.6. Flywheel Idea: Separating Healthcare into Components

Note: This is the first of many sections that are going to be prefaced with "flywheel idea." This denotes that this section is an idea. Flywheel ideas are introduced to be a catalyst for discussion. I am serving these ideas up to get this discussion, debate, and actions started. In some sections, the flywheel ideas will be followed by sections labeled "Taking Local Action." These are suggestions for what you could begin to do now in your community.

To fix the business of medicine in this country, we need to tackle three different and intertwined components of healthcare. Those components are: people dying on the hospital doorstep, wellness (or health), and insurance. The combination of all three is what makes up the healthcare delivery system.

Without an individual mandate for insurance coverage (payment), and with a culture that says we are not going to refuse care when a person's life is on the line, we have the problem of people gambling they will not require costly medical care. Worst case, they become destitute and get caught in the Medicaid safety net. If we go look to Maslow's Hierarchy of Needs (physiological, safety, love and belonging, esteem, and self-actualization), we can see he did not include healthcare or healthcare insurance. Why not? Well, healthcare insurance is not a need, but a planning or risk management tool. We no longer have the luxury of knowing that if I get sick and need a doctor, I will always be able to compensate her with a cow from my farm or product from my store, or to exchange some non-cash asset for compensation.

Additionally, many Americans have a fundamental problem with our government telling them how they have to spend their money, i.e., paying for health insurance. This steps over a line when government starts to tell people what they have to do with the money they keep after taxes. The insurance requirement was part of the math for the Affordable Care Act, since it is about insurance and insurance is a math game. The math requires people to put in more money than gets drawn out so that the insurance companies can make a profit. If people are not contributing, why should they get insurance? We need to step back and get out of this insurance trap.

Definition of When Government Should Provide a Service

There will never be a one-size-fits-all, black-and-white answer to this question, but some guidelines can help. The two key components are: there is no competitive market to provide the service, *and* we can't afford a failure of that service. The military is an example. There are many military equipment providers, but there can never be a provider of complete military protection with the power to enlist residents (meaning that there is no market). Additionally, we can't afford to have our military service be a failure. The judicial system would be another example; there is no market, as we can't have multiple sets of overlapping laws. It's the same with having centralized currency supply control (I am not saying there can only be one currency, but there can only be one backbone currency). There is a market of firms who would be more than willing to garner fees from managing our Social Security funds, but for those who depend on Social Security, they can't afford for the money managers to fail. Remember that a past administration was lobbying for privatizing Social Security around the same time this same group of taxpayers were being abused with subprime mortgages and CDOs that lined the pockets of Wall Street.

4.7. Flywheel Healthcare System Component: Emergency Rooms

The first problem we have to discuss is people coming into emergency rooms. We have emergency rooms because emergencies are inevitable. I think emergency rooms are something that fall under the definitions of a government service we need (see the side note). We can argue the market question, but we should agree that this is a level of service we can't afford to fail. If you have a heart attack, your local municipality ambulance service (which could be outsourced) can pick you up, but when you get to the hospital, do you really want a failed emergency room? No, I am not saying that our government should be running emergency rooms, but we do need to make sure they are not failing.

We need to come up with a formula that provides fixed funding to emergency rooms. This process may also address the oversaturation and underserved portions of our country for hospitals. I live in a hospital-saturated area, but there are others who are underserved (rural, suburban, or metropolitan). Part of the cost for someone who chooses to live in a rural area is that they do not have the right to a minimum amount of time to get transported to an emergency room.

Whatever the formula works out to be, the funders are going to be wellness programs with the balance from taxes. Why the wellness programs? No matter how healthy you are, you could break your leg skiing, go over your bike handlebars, get hit by a car, etc. It is reasonable to say the average person will have some use of the emergency room, so something we plan for and hence not an unpredictable cost we should be using insurance for. The funder of that visit is going to have to be us, not Medicaid/Medicare or another mechanism that covers the gap for all those not in a wellness program. Insurance companies need to be left out of this entire program of funding emergency rooms. Once the person is discharged from the emergency room (either home or into the hospital), then insurance can kick in to cover the non-wellness costs of treating the now non-emergency situation.

Emergency rooms become a business within the hospital. They will no longer be a leading profit generator for a hospital. However, they will be the gateway for additional hospital business. If the broken leg requires an overnight visit or if the orthopedic doctor uses a hospital x-ray facility for follow ups, that is when the hospital will generate revenue. Now the patient is not obligated to give their business to that hospital, but can and must make choices as to where and how they will manage the next treatment/recovery steps.

Will this be simple? No. One of my favorite lines when people offer up excuses for why we can't do something is: "If we have a Jeep driving around on Mars, we can figure this one out." The program could be based around a system of credits, where each payer gets a fixed amount of credits for their contribution to the emergency room. After those credits have been used up, that funder will need to begin to pay the additional costs. So, it's not a flat fee, and you can consume all of the emergency services you need. Each funder is going to have to manage who goes to the emergency room, so they don't burn through emergency room credits. All of the wellness funders will have an incentive to keep people out of the emergency room.

The Veterans Affairs (VA) hospitals should not have emergency rooms, unless that hospital emergency room is the only option for a community. A veteran should go to the nearest emergency room at no cost and then the VA would have the option of having them admitted or moving them to the VA hospital on a case-by-case basis. That leaves the VA to focus on health and wellness. It's our debt to veterans to be the wellness and insurance provider for their health needs.

Here is the tough part. What about people who are not in a wellness program and have no overriding insurance? They are the ones who use the emergency room as primary care. If anyone (those with no wellness or insurance program) does get to this point, there is a probability they also have a mental health injury.[7] How we support those who are not getting mental health care will be discussed later, but those actions and solutions are going to take money. The best way to make sure we can afford to take those mental healthcare actions is to make sure our economic flywheel is constantly generating more energy. If our economic flywheel energy is increasing, then our economy will have the energy to assure our definitions of wellness and health are inclusive of mental health injuries.

The transition time between now and the beginning of adequate mental health capabilities and support will be the hardest. Once we are on top of our mental health challenges, anyone using the emergency room for primary care will get the assistance required and would be able to stay clear of the emergency rooms for avoidable emergencies. Others who do not have mental health injuries and perpetually visit emergency rooms are going to have to be held accountable for excessive usage. This may not be monetary; they may provide gifts in kind or exchange labor hours to offset their accumulated costs. They are going to have to work off the cost, potentially with community service hours. If not, why should we continue to keep providing expensive care if they are not going to help with the cost?

If it is a mental health injury, that is one thing, but rational, conscious decisions to continually leverage emergency rooms without attempts to offset the costs should not be allowed. This last point will be a complex (costly) sticky wicket. Remember we're not talking about people who are destitute, but only those mentally stable people who refuse to be in a wellness program and have insurance and want to use emergency rooms for primary care. In a true emergency, we would need to absorb the cost of stabilizing someone's condition, but without a compensation path for treatment/recovery, they would be discharged.

4.8. Recap ... and Breathe!

Let's recap, since I have most likely managed to upset many people. We need emergency rooms, but we can't have them used as primary care. As a society we should develop a formula and management that provides enough funding to keep emergency rooms solvent and cost effective. Emergency rooms will be like the doughnut or sandwich shop inside a gas station. They pay rent but are a separate business inside the gas station. We the people will be the ones funding and overseeing the operations of emergency rooms that run inside the hospital or paying for the service delivered from emergency care clinics. You can think of these emergency care clinics as a franchise.

Where there is oversaturation of emergency rooms, we will not fund excess supply. When a given wellness group (where our health maintenance comes from) consumes all of their emergency room credits (from a formula), that wellness group will need to provide incremental funding. When that happens, the emergency rooms can earn profits, since all fixed costs will be covered for the year. Emergency rooms are going to be socialized medicine. It is a service that we can't afford to have fail. Even if there is a competitive market, a competitive business wouldn't provide service to those who can't pay.

The hard decisions and solutions will focus on keeping people from creating emergencies through a lack of wellness coverage, and keeping people from leveraging emergency rooms as primary care. With this in place, the business of medicine can shift to two components, wellness coverage and insurance.

4.9. Flywheel Healthcare System Component: Wellness

Many groups are currently trying a multitude of ideas to get people to not only be more responsible for their health, but also for the financial costs of maintaining their health. Wellness is not your insurance for anything that may go wrong or for accidents, but a plan for maintaining your health. Ideally, for many this may be all the healthcare they ever need, or all they need most years of their lives.

Some who have employer-sponsored health insurance are familiar with wellness programs that insurance providers push. The wellness portion should be separated from the insurance program. We can provide standalone wellness programs for an individual. It would include all of the basic health maintenance we should be doing each and every year: our annual checkups, biannual dentist appointments, eye exams, age-based precautionary exams, etc. It should also include mental healthcare, physical therapy, occupational therapy, nutritionists, and possibly personal trainers. Who pays for these programs will be a mix of individual, employer, and subsidized. Employers originally got into the mix as a way to retain employees and not incur additional payroll taxes. Whether companies or employers choose to support wellness programs should be up to them, with no obligation to do so. There can also be wellness plans that are partially subsidized for those who do not have the economic means to pay, but the goal should be to continually decrease the percentage of subsidized costs.

The cost of this basic wellness should be fixed for the year. So, none of this high-deductible plans and other insurance gizmos that can actually prevent timely actions for care. Access to information is essential for people to make rational economic choices and it's what we don't do today. Efficient markets require buyers to make informed economic decisions. maintain health. It will be a team approach, with incentives all the way around to reward wellness and cost efficiencies. So, unlike some hospital-employed primary care physicians, the primary care doctor would not be encouraged to drive up hospital utilization and maximize office throughput. Their goals will be to maximize health and minimize total costs for the group. These groups will also have specialists who work with the doctor and patient to help guide the pros and cons of next steps (quality, care, costs, and other attributes).

Say, for example, you have back pain. What are the options? What are the associated monetary costs and impact to daily routine? You may just need some muscle relaxants for the short term, then a shift to a physical therapist. Or maybe, head right to a personal trainer or occupational therapist to immediately eliminate the cause of the problem vs. focusing on alleviating the symptoms. The specialist will not just say "Go see a physical therapist," but will come armed with key decision-making information about therapists, such as customer satisfaction ratings, office wait times, cost, disposition of therapist, types of patients they work best with, and other information consumers should possess before making economic decisions. You will never walk into an appointment without knowing cost and other specific quality metrics.

These wellness plans will have a set amount of money used for the zone between basic health maintenance and when we need to do a little more. If this set amount of funds is not used in a year, some should go to your team (your primary care doctor and the wellness specialist that help you make those cost/quality/results decisions), and some should go towards your wellness budget for next year. When something unplanned or bad comes up, this is when "insurance" kicks in. You don't use your automobile insurance for gas, getting your inspection sticker, buying new tires, etc., but you do use it when you have an accident. That is what health insurance needs to be, not the omnipotent force that dictates what you can and can't do with your healthcare.

Your wellness team wouldn't just see you at your annual check-up and say, "All looks fine, we will see you next year." Given our less active lifestyles, staying healthy can't be taken for granted. Most of us need to be proactive about maintaining our health. This includes taking medications, nutrition, exercising, mental health, reducing stress, and other key wellness components. Not only is the wellness team going to focus on everything you need to be doing to improve your wellness, they are also going to score your effort, looking at factors such as whether you've been taking your meds, doing the things to lose the weight that you and your team agreed was a practical goal for this period, and cutting back on less healthy habits.

Why does your effort need to be scored? Well, if you are not putting in the effort to improve your wellness, should you be paying more or less for your wellness and insurance? If I am doing everything I am told to, reducing the amount of resources dedicated to my healthcare, should I be paying the same as someone who doesn't exercise and makes less healthy eating choices? Your effort grades should influence what you pay to maintain your wellness and for insurance. Discounts to those who work hard to maintain wellness may be minimal, but more importantly those who choose to not put in an effort should have economic consequences.

A key point is to not confuse this with initial or pre-existing conditions. When the program starts, it doesn't matter if you are a healthcare wreck or on the cover of fitness magazines; all that matters is your effort going forward. Those who are a healthcare wreck or suffer from chronic conditions or diseases may have more responsibilities moving forward than someone who is in great health, but we look at the completion percentage of those efforts. So, an overweight smoker who is doing nine out of ten actions could be paying less for insurance or wellness costs than another person, since they are doing all their medical team thinks they should to improve their health. The other person may be generally healthy, but is only completing three out of five actions, such as not showing up for screenings, taking a preventive medication, etc., so they are a bigger insurance risk based on effort to remain healthy.

Technology will play a huge part in this. Unfulfilled medical prescriptions are one example. While research studies differ, approximately 30% of prescriptions are not filled,[8] so many people are not responding to the guidance of doctors. With the opioid epidemic, some of that could be a good thing. Refill rates for medications also drop off significantly. It may feel like we are giving up some of our privacy rights, but tracking this data and getting it to your medical teams is not that difficult. If existing privacy laws add disproportional costs to this information flow, we may have to modify those laws to avoid extraneous investments.

Think of the information from Fitbits, such as location

information or options to import food information from labels or menus. There can be many methods to automatically capture information and pass it to you or your wellness team. Or it may be your responsibility to present what you have been doing. It would be your job to document your efforts. Advances in other technologies will be able to gather key information directly and pass to your wellness team or tracking system. This may include monitoring data that would provide guidance to change your instructions without having to spend time going to see your wellness team. I could go on and on, but use of technology for monitoring could remove a fair amount of the subjective components of the wellness effort scoring.

Moving forward, when we talk about healthcare, it will more closely match the term. We will all take care to ensure we are healthy. The focus will be on health: not deductibles, not complaining, not co-pays, but what we are doing to maintain health, cost effectively. This may not have immediate impact on the total dollars towards health, and that may turn out to be a good thing for our economy. The big benefit to our society could be greater upfront investments that should reduce the volume of expensive and disruptive health issues. We will be on the job more, we will be doing more active things, and we could spend less time in waiting rooms or battling insurance companies.

4.10. Flywheel Healthcare System Component: Insurance

Insurance can go back to being insurance. We need to keep the good insurance elements from the Affordable Care Act, such as preventing insurance companies from denying coverage for pre-existing conditions. Insurance companies should not be able to charge more for pre-existing conditions. However, they could offer discounts to those of us who get good wellness effort scores. This would have nothing to do with your current state of health, but instead the effort you are putting in to maintain or improve health. Many car insurance companies give safe driver points and we can do the same for health. However, they can't penalize you for pre-existing conditions or for accidents.

Insurance can also be funded the same way our wellness is funded.

The insurance can be paid for by individuals, employers' contribution (but never 100%), or subsidized for those who do not have the economic means. However, you won't get subsidized insurance unless you are in a wellness program. You can get insurance without being in a wellness program, but expect to pay more for that insurance.

Insurance goes back to being insurance. The automobile is a close analogy. If you have an out-of-warranty mechanical failure, you need to pay for that; it is not covered by your insurance. Health insurance would be for those mechanical breakdowns of our body (mental and physical). If the records show you never bothered to ever change your oil and thus you have a mechanical failure, your insurance to help cover that cost should be more compared to someone who regularly changes their engine oil.

4.11. Flywheel Healthcare System Component: Pharmaceuticals

Pharmaceuticals are another topic we need to discuss. On one hand, if someone makes a brilliant discovery or invests lots of money, they should be able to reap reasonable rewards for their ingenuity, efforts, and risks. We also have a problem of charging hundreds of thousands of dollars for a dose of medicine. To address this challenge, we are going to have to attack this from a safety, cost, and process perspective. It will behoove us all if we choose to make investments that will help pharmaceutical companies lower development costs associated with regulation. Interstate commerce laws prevent states from introducing laws that add unnecessary costs and complexities to conducting business. We must act similarly between nations and the costs of drug approvals.

If we can get our economic flywheel spinning with maximum efficiency, we can leverage that energy to fund a pharmaceutical program. Once we have paid down enough of our debt, we can allocate blocks of capital that improve the investment equation for pharmaceutical companies. This will be used to lower the net present value (NPV) calculations (a way of normalizing investments that have different timelines) for pharmaceutical companies. By providing contributions to offset costs, we are lowering the returns required for the research project (investment) to be profitable. This should not be just throwing money at an industry; we must manage this investment just like we manage all governmental services.

We (our government) should not be the ones telling industries how to spend their money. We should be helping their business case by providing funds based on results near the end of the process or once a new drug is available. These payments will reduce the payback period (time) for these companies, and in exchange we'll require them to lower prices once a certain percentage of their investment has been covered. The only influence we can assert on the industry is with the volume of funds we make available for specific diseases. Theoretically a larger pool of funds available for a specific malady should encourage more investment.

The money does not come from the theory of trickle-down benefits. Creating these funds should be a collective goal of our nation. If we work together to reduce the total money that goes toward medical treatment and care, some of these savings would go towards this fund. For example, by taking better care of ourselves, there will be excess money from our wellness programs, or we can agree to exchange lower insurance fees for more investments in cures and better treatments.

The public's role should be to help make more drugs economical to bring to market by lowering regulatory costs (nationally and then attempting the same globally) and helping the winners become profitable more quickly. A shorter road to profitability means prices could be capped. If companies do not agree and want to maximize profits from higher prices, then we'll change the patent laws and shorten the patent protection for companies who do not cap prices. The goal is not to take money away from pharmaceuticals, but to change the timing of when they get to reap profits.

Chapter 5. Reducing the Healthcare Brake

These are big changes. Guess what the impacted businesses will do? Even if they believe this is the right thing to do, they will fight. Why? They have to deliver to the bottom line. They have a great gig right now. Even if change is in our national interests, it is not in their personal or stockholders' interest. They are obligated to do what helps keep their companies as profitable as possible, ignoring what is best for us and our country.

This discussion can't be driven by the people who have a lot to lose. This is the established system, and the system funds your government representatives. That's right, the same people we are paying to represent us. If you sit back and wait for change, I don't recommend holding your breath.

If we are going to make this move, then communities need to start having this discussion. First, people need to buy into the concept. If we start with the gory details, those create edges, which opponents will use to flip and spin the discussion. *(See Fractional Logic discussion on page 14-15.)*

It makes a lot of sense for opponents to spend money to slow down or stop a change that may impact their bottom line. Beware of fractional logic, and question, question, question all that you hear that opposes this approach.

The discussions need to begin with an understanding that if we are going to fix the business of medicine in this country, improve overall health, and pull the healthcare brake off our economic flywheel, we need to divide healthcare into three segments: emergency rooms, wellness, and insurance. Will your community be one of the first to pilot such a program? Once the concept is tested and some of the kinks addressed, a larger national plan can be developed. When we sent the first men to the moon, it was the government funding a group of bright and dedicated people. For this challenge, there is room and a role for all of us to play. Our job is to not be distracted and to ignore the FUD (fear, uncertainty, and doubt) that will be launched at us.

This will be an iterative process, not something we should expect to get perfect right out of the gates.

It may take time and pilot programs to help us learn. This will flush out unforeseen complications and give us opportunities to make adjustments. There may be medical practices or groups who are already taking this wellness approach, insurance companies promoting exercise, offering education when they suspect a condition, and a host of concierge medical practices. Who knows, maybe hedge fund money will jump in and create a bonanza of investments? These new entities may need new software tools, consulting support, marketing, and educational programs to deliver the skills for people to operate in new roles. Can you feel that economic flywheel picking up energy? This chapter looks at the brakes related to messaging on health, smoking, obesity (Cost of Girth), and local actions that can affect them all. There are likely more, but for these I have suggested actions for local groups that follow each section.

5.1. Flywheel Idea: Getting the Message Across

Not all marketing is bad. One way to get people ready to act or so upset they take to marching in the streets is to show them how bad things have become. The American people need to comprehend how messed up the current business model is. One idea is to create a movie, like what was done with *Supersize Me* or *Bowling for Columbine*. Here is a storyline to educate the public about how bad our business of medicine has become.

There will be three friends who all have different jobs in today's healthcare game. For people of my generation, you may remember the Ralph Wolf and Sam Sheepdog cartoon where they start the episode as friends as they walk up to the time clock to punch in for the day. Once they punch into work, they would be working against each other, but at the end of the day, they would be back to being friends.

As it turns out, there is an army of people who work against each other in our current business of medicine model. One lead character will work at a doctor's office and spend much of their time trying to get the care a patient needs. However, the patient can only get the care insurance will cover. So, this character and the doctor invest time and effort looking for ways to code activities in such a way that the insurance will pay for the care.

Once the patient is at the hospital, the second character is focused on having the hospital conduct tests and treatments so they can bill the insurance company to create revenue. The hospital focus is on revenue-creating activities, so they run all the tests possible to bill insurance. No one's goal is to maximize care.

The third lead character works for the insurance company, and they spend their entire day looking for ways to deny care or refusing to pay for activities by the hospital or the doctor. The theme that emerges is that the main focus of our healthcare business is on creating revenue for the businesses in the value chain and not finding the intersection of maximum health benefit and minimal costs. While these are generalizations and extremes, it can help get the core message across. There must be thousands of ridiculous stories people could submit and then the best could be woven into the script. I always liked the way Joseph Heller in *Catch-22* exposed how ridiculous our military establishment could become.

5.2. Flywheel Idea: New Approach to Anti-smoking Campaigns

One morning, I noticed some high school students were waiting for the bus. I was horrified to see one smoking a cigarette. I can't condemn anyone who is working on quitting smoking or who is perfectly happy with internal destruction, but I don't like that first bad decision people make when they start to smoke cigarettes. Similarly to the Scared Straight! or Crying Indian campaigns[9], there could be two sets of short videos, comics, or other media. The plot would be teenagers checking out someone of their preferred gender. They would comment on this person, then when the person turned, they would see the cigarette, and the captions above their heads would change from interest to unflattering thoughts like "Stupid," "No backbone," "Insecure," etc. The idea is to emphasize the negative messages people have when they see one of their peers smoking. The fewer people who start smoking, the fewer people will suffer the health impacts or the costs of quitting.

Theory on a Contributor to Cancer

Cancer is a cell gone bad, so what turns a cell bad? Sometimes it is just a freak mutation, other times there may be a catalyst (chemical, radiation, or other) that instigates this unfavorable mutation. We refer to these as carcinogens. We have known for a long time that decaying radon gas is a catalyst for cancer. As radon gas decays, it releases or radiates an alpha particle. Our DNA is susceptible to this radiation and that effect is a carcinogen. We find the highest concentrations of radon gas when buildings are above or near ledge, which is releasing the radon gas. Most states now require testing for radon gas when property changes hands.

However, many people have been in homes for a long time and have never tested or acted on the radon gas seeping into their homes. This problem can also be exacerbated by all of the weatherproofing we have invested in. Many of us have done a great job sealing up all of the leaks in our house, from better insulation to much more energy-efficient windows, so we retain more heat or cool air for air-conditioning. For new homes and these improved homes, that is great news from the energy efficiency front. The bad news is, our homes no longer breathe.

Our homes are getting much less fresh air flowing. It also means that less air (gas) is getting out. As radon gas seeps into our homes from basements, the concentration of gas can be increasing. This would be the most intense in basements or rooms that sit above garages or basements. We don't continuously measure for radon gas. When we test for it, we assume that radon gas flow is consistent, and we measure over a three-day period that represents the volume of radon gas at any time during the year. But what if there are large peaks and valleys of when that gas flows into our house? If we measured at a peak, we most likely installed a radon remediation system. If we measured during a valley, we most likely did nothing.

The New Hampshire Seacoast community has been hit hard by a number of rare childhood cancers, so a task force was assembled to investigate. As with many government-driven efforts, they did the best they could but nothing conclusive was discovered.[10] At the same time, local residents have discovered several older landfills that are leaching PFOAs (perfluorooctanoic acids, which are carcinogens from manmade products) into our groundwater and streams. Many local residents also feel that our area has an abnormally high cancer rate, but since it is many different types of cancers, there is nothing substantial enough for our government to act on. The high N.H. cancer rate was reported by a 2018 Center for Disease Control & Prevention (CDC) study that cited New Hampshire for having some of the highest pediatric cancer rates.[11]

A neighbor who hails from Long Island commented that similar coastal communities also seem to have high rates of cancers. It is the rare exception when a smoking gun is discovered from a cancer cluster investigation. (See study below.)[12] Maybe there is no one smoking gun, but a combination of effects that are making more cells then expected turn bad. What if these PFOAs or the many other non-natural agents from foods and our environment are accumulating in our bodies? They may only be dangerous in large concentrations, but what if these non-natural things in our bodies started to be radiated (as with radiation from power lines, radio waves, medical testing (X-rays), or radon gas)? So, what if there is not one thing (a specific carcinogen) causing a single type of cancer (all that we can investigate and take action on), but a combination of things triggering a wide range of cancers?

Focusing on radon gas, is there any reason why coastal homes would be exposed to more radon gas? I believe there may be. We know that liquids and gases move away from high pressure towards low pressure, which is why things leak. So, a gas bumping into an area of high pressure would drift or flow away from the high pressure, seeking out low-pressure areas to escape.

What do we have at a coastline? We have beaches, marshes and layers of much more porous sediment. Some coastlines may be ledgy and not as attractive to escaping gas. The adjacent ocean is huge and all of that water weighs a lot, much more than the air above our coastlines. So, there is a lot more atmospheric pressure on the ocean floor than there is on the coastline. Radon gas would thus flow towards the lower-pressure coast to escape. If there are large volumes of radon gas trying to escape from beneath the ocean or lake floor, it could all be moving towards the coastline.

So, if there is a lot of radon gas trying to escape near a coastline, there could be a flow of radon gas moving towards the coasts. Homes in these areas may be more susceptible to higher concentrations of radon gas flowing up from the ground and finding it harder to escape from our well-insulated homes. We know this gas will accelerate lung cancer in smokers and, to a lesser extent, nonsmokers. In addition to all of the other types of radiation we are exposed to, there is also the radiation from the decaying radon gas added to the mix of total radiation and non-natural substances in our bodies.

My theory is that there may not be a smoking gun to explain instances of higher cancer rates, but the accumulated effects from these non-natural substances being radiated along with normal cell risk from radiation are what causes more people to be attacked by cancer. It's a theory and needs testing or a deep-dive analysis of existing data.

If this proves to be true, we will need to start to put more attention on radon remediation in homes. People can be more conscious of getting fresh air into basements and other rooms when they have a chance. That may be it for direct action. From a group perspective, we can put the focus on gathering data and getting the people with the knowledge, skills and data to focus on proving or disproving this combination is contributing to a portion of cancer cases. As with many of our challenges, there will not be one single action that solves the problem.

5.3. Cost of Girth

It is hard to not classify body weight as a "weight," but our national girth is not a weight that our economic flywheel has to work through. It is more of a brake, sucking energy out of our economic flywheel.

The total girth is a national crisis, and it is not just the health-care costs. All of that mass needs to be fed, clothed, and transported, which just sucks up resources and energy. If the average American is 23 pounds (CDC number from a 2009 study) overweight, that is about 4.8 billion pounds of extra mass; that number may be even higher today.[13] If the average person is 160 pounds, that extra mass is the equivalent of about 30 million people being fed, clothed, and moved. When I first looked at this, our fat (converted to the average weight of a person) would be the 44th largest country in the world by population (between Venezuela and Saudi Arabia).

A June 13, 2017 *USA Today* article stated there are 79.4 million obese people in the US.[14] According to Wikipedia, if all of these people where in one place, they would be the twentieth most populated country in the world, more populous than the United Kingdom, France, or Italy. If you have ever been to one of those countries, picture every single person there as overweight. Now think about what additional costs are required to maintain the health of that nation. In the US, the problem will only get worse as of those 79.4 million obese people, 13% of them are children and young adults.

There are plenty of studies, reports, and data points discussing the costs associated with diabetes and other ailments we must pay to treat and that are directly correlated to obesity in adults and children. For example, the American Diabetes Association's 2017 report states that 1 in 4 healthcare dollars go to people with diabetes.[15] That same study reports $237B in costs from those diagnosed with diabetes, and another $90B in lost productivity.

How would you feel if you lived in an impoverished nation where people are lacking food, unemployment is high, and the US is feeding more fat than people who live in your country? While a country's current economic situation may have nothing to do with any US past actions, it would be reasonable for that country to feel a level of animosity towards the US. During one of my Leadership New Hampshire classes (a yearlong program to educate civic leaders across the state: www.leadershipnh.org), one of my classmates pointed out how people in developing nations are mystified that Americans flush toilets with drinkable water.

No matter how or why someone is overweight, no one should be punished or treated unfairly for their current size. However, moving forward, individuals need to be held responsible if they are not making an effort to stop weight gain and ideally reduce girth. If not, we go back to the wellness and insurance sections, and if there is no effort to improve, then their contributions towards wellness and insurance need to be greater than those who put in the effort.

The size of our girth needs to be put front and center for Americans. We need to compare it to something tangible, like the weight of Empire State Building (365,000 tons or 700,000,000 pounds) or the

Golden Gate Bridge (887,000 tons or 1,774,000,000 pounds). So, if we use the rough math of there being 4.8B pounds of extra weight, that is almost 7 Empire State buildings or 2.7 Golden Gate bridges. Think what it would cost to feed an Empire State Building-sized person, or the energy that would be required to move the Golden Gate Bridge?

We then need to set a path that incrementally reduces the total amount of girth, so a national goal of getting down to six Empire State buildings or to reduce the Golden Gate Bridge by a certain number of spans. The goal is not to have a nation of waif-thin people, but to incrementally reduce the total girth. We need to avoid putting more of a stigma on currently overweight people and instead put the societal pressure on those who are not working towards reducing girth. You are what you are; the focus needs to be on what an individual is doing moving forward.

This would be a multipronged approach around nutrition, eliminating food deserts (urban or rural areas with few healthy food options and too many cheap carbohydrates). What is available to people in food deserts is low cost and not the best nutritional options for people who need to be losing weight. However, nationally, citizens need to be willing and able to pay more for healthier food.

Reducing our total girth needs to be a national goal, and progress should be reported as part of the State of the Union Address until we get this under control. This is a health/economic crisis. Notice that I am avoiding the BMI (body mass index) standard, since by this standard I am obese. I am not. In the summer, when I am getting ready for my 175-mile bike ride that raises funds to fight cancer (www.pmc.org), I sink in swimming pools, evidence of my low body fat at that time. It is not about how big you are or how much you weigh, but how much additional or extra weight you are carrying around. This additional weight is what stresses our body mechanics and organs.

The goal is to free up the capital excessive girth consumes in resources and healthcare spending. Picture the brake on our economic flywheel pulling back and the flywheel picking up more economic energy.

5.4. Taking Local Action: Approach to Reducing Girth

While this is a national issue, the best way to do this would be to start local efforts (non-tax dollars) to drive and motivate local efforts. Small and large companies could also get involved. Rotaries from one town or area can challenge other areas based on numbers from members or whole communities who participate in fat reduction competitions and activities.

The focus should not be the weight of any individual person, but the progress a community is making to decrease girth. While fat helps us stay warm in the winter, I do not believe it helps people stay cooler in the summer.

Communities could provide activities to communicate the difficulties of staying cool or completing additional tasks when the extra weight is included, such as requiring people to wear fleece jackets when it is warm out, or to wear backpacks with additional weight. A community can also drive helpful activities such as exercise, better nutrition information, ways to get people less sedentary, and any other ideas.

Chapter 6. The Mental Healthcare Brake

Having a better understanding and acceptance of mental health has the potential to bring huge savings from multiple areas. I will share a few stories that helped put mental health in perspective for me.

I heard a moving discussion by former NH Supreme Court Judge John T. Broderick as part of the 2017 Leadership New Hampshire program. He shared his personal story, but the key message was that our cultural problem with mental health must change. What resonated with me is that his son took a logical and effective course of action to address his mental health injury—or at least it was logical to his son. The judge's intelligent and capable son suffered from severe anxiety and learned that staying intoxicated numbed the fears and kept them at bay. Unfortunately, the side effects of being perpetually intoxicated led to his son beating Judge Broderick nearly to death. Judge Broderick ended up in intensive care and his son ended up in prison.

It was only in prison that social workers were able to diagnose the severe anxiety. With the problem diagnosed and treated, his son was able to leave prison and get back to the life Judge Broderick and his wife always envisioned for him.

Here were two highly educated people who did not understand the severe challenges their son was facing. While the signs were there, similar to a lazy eye or a learning disability, we are not conditioned to recognize and acknowledge these types of injuries. The opposite happens: we are trained or conditioned to hide and ignore mental health injuries. We don't talk about mental health, but unfortunately many of us have had friends, family, or others with mental health injuries. Our society has put a taboo on mental health as something not to be discussed, instead labeling it as something to be embarrassed by. If you have never suffered from a mental health injury or been close with someone who has, you may not understand mental health injuries.

What would happen if we addressed heart disease like we address mental health injuries? Everyone with high blood pressure or high cholesterol would be deemed in no state to take an active or leading role in our economy. We would create homes for them, pretend they did not exist, be embarrassed that they are in our family. What would be the effect on our economic flywheel if we removed all of these people from our functioning economy? Since it is not practical to remove them, people with mental health injuries stay right here and drain economic energy from our flywheel as we "deal or not deal" with them.

The more we ignore mental health injuries and continue to ostracize those with mental health injures, the harder we press that brake against our economic flywheel.

My Story

I will admit, I once was one of those people for many years who thought depression was just in your head. I assumed someone was weak if they could not shake off or fight through depression; I was extremely wrong. When I was twenty-nine and my older brother was thirty-two, he committed suicide. Years later, my sister's medical school professors described what happened to him as a psychotic break. I had never heard of it. The best analogy is that it's like having a nightmare, but you are wide awake and physically functioning. We now suspect the psychotic break could have been related to CTE, as he got many concussions during his years playing high school and collegiate football.

After he died, I had to close down his life and business and keep an eye on my parents, family, and his friends. After about three months, friends suggested I go see a therapist. I had never gone to a therapist and I took an apprehensive approach. I tried one therapist, but it did not feel right. After a few more tries, I found someone I felt comfortable with. I explained to the therapist that I did not want to go out with friends. I did not think I was worthy of dating anyone. I had lost the spring in my step; I could go through the motions, but it was a struggle to get moving. I was not happy, and I did not want to be unhappy. I don't think the therapist actually laughed at me, but when I asked what was wrong, she said something like, "You are depressed—what do you think depression is?"

I thought the therapist had to be wrong. I had way too much energy and I got too much done to be a person with depression. But once I stopped being defensive, it all sunk in. This was depression. I did not ask to be depressed. I did not want to be depressed, but I was. She offered me the option of medication, but that was not me. She said I could continue meeting with her and look for ways for me to fight back. In the end, I had to let go. I had to stop fighting. Yes, I got more depressed: I described the feeling as knowing you're falling down a deep, dark shaft. The bottom was coming up fast and I feared I would shatter when I hit it. After a while, I realized I was not getting worse, so the next step was to get better. It took time—many, many months—but time helped me climb out of it.

I walked away with a whole new appreciation for mental health and depression. When someone has mental health injuries, it's not because they chose to be injured. It's not a personality flaw, but an injury. I wear glasses for my vision; our son wears hearing aids; some people walk with a cane; you can wear braces and fix your teeth. But you can't just slap something on a mental health injury and forget about it.

6.1. Taking Local Action: Know the Five Signs

Judge Broderick is leading a regional partnership in the state of New Hampshire as part of a national effort known as the Campaign to Change Direction (changedirection.org). The campaign was started by Dr. Barbara Van Dahlen, the founder and president of Give an Hour. The goal is to change the culture of mental health. When many hear Judge Broderick speak, they are moved and understand this is a worthy cause, similar to fighting a disease or one of the many great injustices still plaguing our world. For me, I realized that changing the national perception and attitude on mental health must be a national evolutionary step.

The Campaign to Change Direction's approach is to achieve results similar to and hopefully surpassing what the American Heart Association accomplished with heart attacks. Almost all Americans know the signs of an impending heart attack; we have gone to war against cholesterol; we've invested massively in CPR training and defibrillators. All of this has contributed to huge heart attack death reductions. We all have mental health, just as we all have physical health. The Campaign asks that everyone learn the Five Signs of Emotional Suffering that mean someone is in emotional pain and might need help. The goal is twofold: first, to start a mental health conversation on a grassroots level and provide a common language, the Five Signs. If someone is suffering, the Campaign asks that people connect, reach out, inspire hope, and offer help in order to find a solution when a person may not have the will or drive to do it alone. The greater goal is to change the culture of mental health so that all those in need receive the care and support they deserve. This common language will help change the conversation and therefore our culture.

Take the case of Judge Broderick's son. He is an incredibly bright and talented person, but he had an injury he did not talk about, and no one around him knew how to recognize what was going on. His injury was uncontrollable anxiety. Yes, we all have anxiety, but what would you do if in every situation the anxiety was not a little feeling, but 200 times louder—too loud to ignore or to fight through? Remember, perception is reality. To you, it could be just one of life's challenges that people need to learn to deal with. However, there is something physically broken (not by choice) with some people. When an anxiety-causing situation occurs, their body does not just deliver 5 units of anxiety, it delivers 500 units. We all know 500 units of anxiety is way out of proportion (the norm) for the situation. But for the same situation, you have to cope with 5 units of anxiety and they have to cope with 500 units of anxiety. It doesn't matter how you would handle the situation with your level of anxiety, the volume (500 units) of anxiety is very, very real to them.

It's not fair. I don't want to have bad eyes, but I do. People with mental health injuries need more help. It can start with removing society-imposed mental health stigma and then making mental health care as commonplace as brushing our teeth, nutrition, and exercise.

Step one is education. While we can donate to the Campaign to Change Direction, we can also make a pledge or commit to become an individual or group partner to share the Five Signs of Emotional Suffering at changedirection.org. We should empower our school systems to order the educational tools directly and include this support as part of our publicly funded education. We have physical education as a class, but not mental health education. I don't think mental health has to be an everyday class, but once or twice a week would be helpful. We need to ensure school budgets include the educational materials, the discussions, and additional staff to support improving our mental health (avoiding and early intervention of mental health injuries).

In New Hampshire, the state has implemented a 211 calling service that helps people in need get information on available supportive services. (Go to www.211.org for the services in your state.) Yes, there are many suicide prevention phone numbers, but if a person has progressed that far without our help and attention, we have already failed as a society.

For some injuries, medication is the right thing, or in combination with therapy. Unfortunately, many from my generation thought therapy was like the *Bob Newhart Show*. Therapy is not a sitcom; it can be effective, or it can be a waste of time and money. Personally, I have experienced both. The only way to address the potential dichotomy is for those who are paying to be responsible to find the right fit. Sometimes it's hard to know. Our daycare administrator told us to go to a therapist for one of our children, suggesting a "play therapist." At the end of the time-consuming sessions, the conclusion was off by a country mile. We found someone else, and during the preparation discussion my wife and I had with her, she correctly diagnosed the root cause. All she had to do was listen and she had an accurate assessment.

The bottom line is that our wellness programs need to include therapy for mental health injuries.

We all have to decide to change the way we think about people. No more saying things like "Stay clear of that person, they are crazy." It has to shift to, "That person has an injury." While it is easy to make an association with injury when we see a cast or crutches, we need to have the same view when we observe someone with a mental health injury. We need to view the days when families secluded relatives with mental health injuries or avoided discussion as misconceived views of the past. Similar to when we read about doctors using leeches or bleeding people, future generations will have the same dismay at how our society ignored the proper way to work with those with mental health injuries.

Each of us can start now, agreeing to change our perceptions. Make a commitment to make sure your family and friends all learn the Five Signs. Correct your vernacular when you are discussing anyone with a mental health injury. This is not a problem you should be waiting for your government to address. This is a societal issue and the responsibility lies with us as individuals.

6.2. Mass Murder is Mass Murder

While this may not impact the flywheel much, it is something that is important to me and potentially all of the other people who have lost a friend or relative to suicide.

The American Foundation for Suicide Prevention showed in the fall of 2018 that suicide is the 10th leading cause of death in the US (over 44,000 deaths per year). For every successful suicide, 25 attempt suicide, with the total impact of suicide and self-injury to the US economy costing $69 billion a year (suicide and self-injury).[16] While the 2018 World Population Review shows the US with only the 27th highest suicide rate (15.3 suicides per 100K people), the loss of those 44,000 people a year is a cost we should reduce.[17]

6.3. Flywheel Idea: Do Not Glorify Suicide

There are many things we can be doing to reduce suicides; one that grates on me is how we use the term when it is associated with mass murders.

Unfortunately, many of us have had to endure tragedies or the pain of losing someone, so you know how sensitive you can be to anything associated with that painful event. For example, when the date my brother died pops up on a digital clock, I look away if I haven't already had the shivers. Those first few years, whenever I heard or read the word "suicide," a wave of sadness would wash over me. However, when someone goes out of their way to kill random people, regardless of their motivation or intent, they are randomly murdering people. They are first and foremost mass murderers. They are bombers, they are terrorists, they are villains—much different from my brother and the countless others whose mental health injuries led them to suicide.

If someone is going to put in the effort to randomly kill people they don't know, how relevant is it that they were also willing to die? By using the word suicide alongside the way they mass-murdered people, we are putting the emphasis on their life and not on the victims. By emphasizing suicide, we are glorifying killing a bunch of random people, since it implies the murders are making a sacrifice. We need to remove the word "suicide" from the news coverage of these mass murders.

If people insist the distinction is necessary, then come up with a different term, such as a mass murderer who was considerate enough to save us the costs of incarcerating them for life. Come up with anything else, just stop using the word "suicide" for mass murderers.

Like most things, nothing is going to change unless you and others take action. The initial step is getting our feedback to the media. Thank you, social media. It is now much easier to post a comment on a media outlet's site, or post anywhere else and include a hashtag so they may see it. Put it on your own social media sites every time this happens. If people can create a game, a challenge to motivate people to remember and make the point to the media, the more the merrier.

Groups of volunteers who come together can also provide awards or recognition to newspapers, radio, internet news sites, etc. This is an example of how a multitude of skills and interests can be applied to make things happen. For the entities who do this the least, they could be recognized. I would encourage more of a carrot approach for media groups. The stick approach is using social media, writing letters to the editor, picketing, and other actions to cajole media to choose to actively change how they describe and report on mass murders where the assailant also perishes.

Suicide prevention and education groups could also use this campaign to gain awareness by pointing out the difference every time the media uses the word "suicide" associated with murder. This gives them an opportunity to draw out the differences, as most suicides are the results of mental health injuries.

The media is more likely to pay more attention to the murder of a large group of people than to a single individual. So, the suicide prevention and education groups can ride this wave of attention and focus to call out the big differences, how the media has got it wrong (the definition of suicide would be updated to refer strictly to taking one's own life in isolation), and to create more awareness of the available help for those who have mental health injuries. There will no longer be any glorified or sympathetic component (the sacrifice of the murderer also choosing to die) to killing people, and people who must deal with the tragedy of suicide will no longer have to cringe when a horrible act is associated with the loss of a friend of loved one.

Chapter 7. The Opioid Brake: We Are Losing the Opioid War

In March 2018, *Time* magazine produced a picture documentary issue dedicated to our opioid crisis.[18] The *Time* story emphasized the staggering death tolls, greater than the total number of deaths in all wars after World War II, but we seem oblivious, hence the pictorial approach.

We can't call on our military, as our armed forces are not to be deployed on American soil (the Posse Comitatus Act of 1878 and the Insurrection Act of 1807). So how should we respond to this attack? Wait for our government to act effectively and efficiently to repel the danger?

There is no panacea. Like many of our challenges, we will need a multipronged approach and it will be painful—literally. Much of the problem started from prescribed painkillers. No one wants to be in pain, but we are going to have to deal with pain ideally using opioid-less approaches. Every time you take an addictive medicine, you are on the front line and could be another war casualty. There is no basic training, so you are responsible for your own survival. Not your doctor, but you. If you are in need of managing any kind of physical pain, it's your job to either stay away from these drugs, or do all you can to minimize what you take and to get off and away from them as soon as possible.

7.1. Flywheel Idea: Hold Your Doctor Accountable on Opioids

If you feel your doctor or medical team is being too liberal with offering opioid-based pain medication, you need to speak up. Whether you are on the front lines or not, our job is to change the culture so we are hypersensitive when anyone starts taking these pain medications. Pharmaceutical companies have no incentive to not be pushing these medications, but we are the market and we must pull the plug on the demand side. For instance, we could only buy single doses of these painkillers, or we could hand our medications to someone who controls how much and how frequently we can have these. Yes, there will be more suffering, but there is a huge downside risk with every single dose.

Think of this as attacking the enemy supply lines. Opioids are how some start to get addicted, but we still have to deal with enemy troops (the addictions, not the people) on our soil. These are the countless addictions in almost every state. If we had real enemy troops on our soil, how many of us would turn a blind eye, waiting for others to take care of the problem? Don't you think you would do something to help out? If we want to win this war, we need to be in wartime mode.

For starters, I would like to know what our society's attack strategy is. Do you know what our plan is to win this war? I certainly don't. I hear about calling attention to the need to spend more money, but is that for someone else to fight, or for us to rally around some concrete actions that leverages the might of our nation's will?

Pulling the plug on the demand is the best way to fight drug dealers. If there are no customers, there is no market for pushing addictive drugs. If we mitigate new people getting addicted and we drive hard to get as many people as possible in recovery, we will turn the tide.

Does every community have a militia (armed with the appropriate tools) for this? We need to develop local militias that can do the heavy lifting of getting people off these drugs and then getting them in positions that keep them from going back.

7.2. Taking Local Action: T Teams and Box Scores

It will be great if we can slow down and theoretically stop more people from becoming addicts, but we have a huge challenge of assuring that as many people as possible can turn around their lives.

T stands for turnarounds. Each and every community needs to focus on driving up the number of people we have helped turn their lives around. The first steps will be to develop standards for measuring the volume of people at different stages of "turning around." It will start with estimates of the number of addicts in a given population.

Communities can leverage data points, such as police incidents, volume of Narcan used or sold in an area (think the Internet of Things and how we can leverage technology to provide information), number of months off drugs, turn-around people who have new jobs, turn-around people in a new job for one year, or turn-around people who have been promoted. While there may be some privacy concerns that will inflate costs, we have to be realistic about the balance of costs and paralysis until the crisis diminishes.

We can develop some standard box scores for all communities. If you are not a sports fan, go to a sports section and look at the statistics that are kept for players or teams. These box scores allow you to track how someone or a team is doing against peers. Communities are not competing for a trophy, but to drive awareness, focus, and actions to help people turn around their lives.

We need something similar to the World War II stories of how communities came together and everyone pitched in to support the war effort. If not, how do you think we are going to win? The box scores measure the results of our actions. What is missing or needs drastic improvements are our actions. The box scores help establish a framework to focus our actions. Can you help direct or find employment opportunities for people joining the T-Teams? Can you help or initiate activities that help T-Team people move to new social circles to help them stay clear of forces that could drag them back down? This is our responsibility, and if we don't take responsibility, the alternative is to turn over our money in the form of more taxes.

Maybe you're not cut out for the front lines, but you have creative communications skills. Your contribution could be researching and communicating the best-in-class solutions, and helping spread the word on what works and what doesn't. This just one example of pitching in based on skills and experience. It's working directly towards activities that will help our shared economic flywheel.

Unfortunately, there are many more parts of the healthcare equation that could be drastically improved to provide improved care at a total lower cost. There are also additional brakes to our economic flywheel, so we need to move on to those.

Chapter 8. The Crime Brake: Crime and the Drain on Economy and Society

Crime sucks up money and causes suffering. Anything we can do that minimizes crime helps our economy. A 2017 US Government Accountability Office report showed that depending on the accounting method, the cost of crime could be between $690 billion and $3.41 trillion annually. It stated that "the Department of Justice reported that federal, state, and local governments spent more than $280 billion in 2012 on criminal justice, including police protection, the court system, and prisons."[19]

Putting that in perspective, the group National Priorities Project reported that in 2015, global defense spending was $1.6 trillion. So, our annual spend on crime (using the inclusive category definition) is almost three times what the world spends on defense.[20] In a 2018 press release, the US Comptroller reported that the proposed 2018 Department of the Defense budget would be $574.5 billion, so the conservative estimate of the cost of crime is more than we spend on defense annually.[21]

Growing up, my farther refused to lock our home. His rationale was that the replacement cost of anything someone would steal would be less than the cost and hassle of replacing a door or window. Even for simple vandalism, the replacement cost may be minor, but it is a cost of distraction (time and resources not invested in economic or leisure activities). We replace a broken window, but it is lost opportunity cost of our time.

Of all of the people who die in a crime-related death, who knows the lost value to society or to a local economy? We'll never know what the person could have contributed, what destinies will go unfulfilled. So, whether it's theft, physical harm, scams, or malicious activity, they all suck energy out of our economic flywheel. The impact of crime on victims drains away economic energy from our flywheel. From that alone, any decrease in crime provides an overall benefit to our economy and society.

8.1. Non-value-added Costs of Crime

Courts, prisons, and police are not going to go away. Our society is always going to fund some level of fixed cost each year to assure we have police, a civil court system, and prisons. Beyond the cost of making sure we have these institutions, what are variable costs? If we could bring down crime rates, how much could police forces shrink, how many prisons could we eliminate, how fewer less public defenders would we need to employ, how much smaller could the court system be? The size of these cost components are the variables we must control.

For all we invest in police forces, how much of the cost is associated with crime prevention, crime investigation, crime prosecution, and other activities? For small communities, there will not be much of a savings, since they may not be able to reduce the number of officers, but they could focus on other savings. Larger communities could see a more significant change. I could have said savings, and there just may be, but the focus should be on incremental value for the community? On the old TV show *Adam-12*, the police cruisers were emblazoned with the words "to protect and to serve." With less resources going to crime prevention, investigation, and prosecution, protection could go up and there may be new and better ways to serve the community.

Prisons and the court system also have a fixed cost and variable costs that will be reduced with less crime. Those two systems will be discussed shortly, but first we should focus on crime reduction.

8.2. Flywheel Idea: Reducing Crime

Some violent crime can be impulsive, but premeditated crime can't happen without people choosing to take actions. In the same amount of time it takes to act, there is more than enough time to ask yourself questions before the action. To help people make the time to make noncriminal choices, we need to create a culture where we all view crime as really, really bad because it sucks up so much economic energy. Right now, we use the loss of freedoms as the primary deterrent for crime. To reduce the total volume of crime, we need everyone in our nation to understand how much crime costs all of us. The idea is not to turn into a nation of snitches and tattletales, but a community that prevents crime from happening in the first place. The goal is to not have annual costs that are as big as our national defense budget.

Let's make the assumption that every single criminal has a family and a friend or two. Those people make up the front lines of criminal defense. They are in the best position to prevent a crime from occurring. So, the challenge becomes how to motivate people to want to reduce and eliminate crime. You are not responsible for the stranger on the street, but for your close circle of people. More than a dozen States have implemented "Red Flag Laws" that allow a judge to step in and order firearms to be removed from a family member or friend whom the judge rules a potential threat to themselves and others.

How do we mold a sociodynamic force that helps people choose to not commit crimes? In this context, I am referring to creating a norm that committing crimes, or engaging in any types of activities that require our police or court costs, is completely unacceptable. So, it's not cool and is actually incredibly embarrassing to have a friend or family member to be found guilty of a crime. The Puritans put people in stocks in the common square as a punishment. The character Hester Prynne had to wear the large letter A on her clothing in Nathaniel Hawthorne's *The Scarlet Letter*. These acts "branded" people and their families, so it was not just you who was in jail, but also the immediate family of the criminal.

For example, for a white-collar crime, the immediate family of the criminal could get a sticker that goes on a license plate or on personal identification or credit cards. The concept is that a criminal's circle of family, friends, and neighbors have something to lose or would need to carry a burden if someone from their inner circle was found guilty of a crime. A judge could only put a requirement on the defendant, but if we can find ways to put more negative association with friends, family, and neighbors, they become the first line of crime prevention.

We need to get to a point where the opinions and perceptions from the people that matter the most to us will influence the choices we make.

The simplest motivation needs to be protecting our economic energy. Every single one of us needs to be personally insulted by every single crime. When a robbery happens, the storeowner is not the sole victim, so every one of us should feel the burden of being victimized. Each crime is taking energy from our economic flywheel. Note, we can't prevent cyberattacks and cybercrime launched from overseas, but we can be working to eliminate burglary, vandalism, assaults, and all forms of violence against humans in our own country.

Initially steps would be marketing and communications of what we spend on crime. Start locally by looking at police and breaking out what percentage of costs is related to the local criminal court system. (Federal courts are harder to investigate the local impact and locally controllable costs.) These are opportunities for individuals to step up to produce the cost data and come up with marketing communication plans around current costs and promoting local actions.

Every community needs to take responsibility for their crime rate and steps to continually reduce the local crime rates. All communities should be focused on driving crime rates down. While we should not use public money, sponsorship money (for advertising) could be raised to provide recognition and awards to communities who lower crime rates. So entire communities could benefit, and financial awards could go to school systems or other local activities or places. Fast forward and you will start hearing announcers at high school events report how we are doing on lowering crime rates.

8.3. Flywheel Idea: Creative Sentencing

Another approach many creative judges have taken is to sentence those with minor crimes to tasks or labor with a factor of embarrassment to ideally discourage repetitive behavior. The next step is to connect family and others in this responsibility as part of a sentence. The general idea is if there are family or friends who were in a position to engage or influence this person and didn't, they should be called out in some way.

8.4. The Prison Brake (not "break"!): A Big Part of the Crime Brake

Of the many massive costs driven by crime, prisons are a huge percentage. In 2018, the US prison population was reported to be around 2.3 million people, which means that in the US, only New York, Los Angeles, Chicago, and Houston have a greater population than our prison system. Houston is close to that number, so drive around Houston and picture it as one big prison, as that is about how many people we have incarcerated in the US. A 2010 study by the Vera Institute calculated the 2010 U.S. cost of the prison system as $34 billion.[22] Every year we are paying for the equivalent of the fourth largest city in the US for housing, food, heating or cooling, medical costs, guards, and management. That is a lot of energy getting drained out of our economic flywheel. Some communities do benefit from prison jobs and government spending, but it's a change communities will need to adapt to. Our efforts in reducing crime will not be instantaneous; unfortunately, we are still going to need prisons for all the current criminals and new ones. The question around prisons needs to be focused on reducing net costs (not slashing budgets) and reducing the recidivism rate. These two goals can be approached together.

8.5. Flywheel Idea: Reducing Recidivism Rates

Prisons are to protect society from those who prove they cannot choose to act in ways acceptable to and within the laws of our society. Prisons should be organized so when it is time for someone to return to society, they should never end up back in prison (this is called "recidivism"). For inmates who will leave prison at some point, their time in prison should be focused on developing skills or training to enable them to take a different path and avoid situations that led to choosing to commit a crime. Prisons can't be an alternative to schools, so the time in prison must be unpleasant enough so that the fear of returning alters the behaviors that lead to criminal decisions.

Prisoner tasks and activities will need to be grueling but effective in developing employable skills. The goal is not to drive people to abhor the activity from unneeded repetition; the time in prison needs to be difficult, but not inhumane. It may be a fine line between being cruel and unpleasant enough to make people want to avoid prisons.

This will be challenging, but when we start to look at the $40 billion or more annual cost of prisons and the high recidivism rates, we need to take action. States and possibly counties can start to develop goals, with the communities keeping close tabs on what is being done and how things are working. Once again, the monitoring and reporting create a host of small tasks for people to step up and do their small part. The community engagement could be key to help local prisons identify local employment opportunities and help assure that the people who are released are prepared to succeed in roles they have been trained in.

The last area for change needs to be in having prisons drive down operating costs. Most of us have seen the movies of prisoners being abused when they are forced to work. There is also the challenge of free labor upsetting and disrupting local businesses. The focus should be around keeping the net cost of prisons as low as possible. For example, the services that prisons outsource should be minimized as much as possible. So, beyond the simple tasks of laundry, food services, etc., the in-house labor should be developed to minimize costs at the facilities.

What about prisoners with lifetime sentences? From a fiscal equation, it does not make much sense to pay all that money to just to keep someone alive for tens of years. But it is also expensive to pursue the death penalty. It was hard to find studies or data points from clearly neutral sources, but a considerable volume of publications imply that the costs of pursuing a death penalty and cost of execution outweigh lifetime imprisonment costs.

Some people feel strongly that some crimes are so horrible, those convicted should forfeit their lives. I will not argue with people who feel that way, but I do struggle with the notion we can play the role of a divine being and choose who lives and who dies. The challenge is those people who we will be paying to keep alive; what can be done to get some return on all of that cost? For those permanently incarcerated, the trick may be finding or developing a skill that provides long-term value to the prison system. It could be becoming a teacher for other inmates or training for a level of operational expertise and service that outstrips the cost of incarceration. What if a lifetime prisoner decides to become a nurse or maybe even a doctor? If so, it is easy to see how they could eventually provide more value to the prison system than the cost of incarceration.

There is no one solution to the costs of incarceration. It will need to be a multipronged approach that minimizes the incoming flow of prisoners, pushes recidivism rates towards zero, and helps minimize total costs of prisons. One of the key components of reducing recidivism is housing. Where affordable housing is difficult to find, communities will need to be more active to develop local solutions as part of the complex equation and help lower the drivers of criminal choices. There are several published studies that show how housing correlates to lowering recidivism, so it is intuitive that a lack of housing would have the opposite impact.[23]

8.6. Flywheel Idea: End the Slaughter

Every time you grimace at the news of random people being murdered, what is the impact to our economic flywheel? Do you think having schools implement and practice lockdown drills helps the return on our education value? How about when business or nonprofits invest time to implement and maintain safety procedures and protocols? How much are we paying for police details at mosques and temples? These activities are brakes on our economic flywheel.

Let me say this: Americans will always own handguns and hunting rifles. I just said Americans will always own handguns and hunting rifles. If this statement is not clear, let me restate it, Americans will always own handguns and hunting rifles. Theoretically, now that you have heard me say this three times, there is a high probability that you'll believe what I said. However, some will read the following argument three times and feel I am launching an attack on the Second Amendment. Most likely, fragments will be pulled, put out of context, and twisted to support opposing views or paranoia. They will ignore the supportive reality when I clearly stated handguns and hunting rifles are part of our culture and this is not going to change.

What must change is the senseless slaughter. It is unacceptable when children are being killed in schools and Americans are killing random Americans (terrorism is a different discussion). It needs to end.

Does a person have the right to own a military-style arsenal?

Assume the answer is yes under the Second Amendment. If it is true, we need to add a caveat from the Second Amendment—you know, the first part that people tend not to mention: "*A well-regulated militia, being necessary to the security of a free State, the right of the people to bear Arms, shall not be infringed.*" If people feel compelled to possess an arsenal of weapons, then the government will not infringe on those groups if and only if they are part of a well-regulated militia. States no longer have militias; instead they have a National Guard or state police force. The government militia these days is mostly with the federal armed services. So, let's apply the part of the Second Amendment to all things beyond simple handguns and rifles for hunting native animals.

If you are going to own an arsenal, it can only be in conjunction with a well-regulated militia. From the people's standpoint, this group is only well regulated as long as no one in this group uses these weapons in any sort of crime. If that does happen, all of those people in this supposedly well-regulated militia group should lose their right to be in the possession of anything more than handguns and basic hunting rifles for a period of, say, five or more years. They would also be prohibited from joining any other militia groups for the same period of time.

Some will say this means our government will know who has these arsenals, and a driver for having the arsenals is that they don't trust our government. It's a good point. However, until these multiple firing weapons are no longer being used to slaughter people, this level of government oversight has become a necessity. Now, say twenty-five or thirty years from now, there has not been a single occurrence of any of these types of mass murders, then we can enter into a discussion about scaling back government oversight.

Each of these groups can determine how they regulate themselves, who they allow to join the group, etc., but they are 100% responsible for the actions of anyone in this group who has access to any weapons, body armor, ammunition, etc. Any training, self-monitoring, psychiatric checking, inventory control, and other steps will be their responsibility to implement and enforce. They will need to self-regulate all members to assure they do not commit any crimes with these weapons. Yes, it will cost money, but the National Rifle Association (NRA) operating budget was $475 million in 2016,[24] so there is a good starting point for funds.

Programs can be established to build community awareness of who has these weapons and where they are. So, while arsenals may not be banned, the ownership of arsenals could be reported and tracked in communities.

Any crime using these weapons by anyone in the well-regulated militia group will cause all of this group's access rights to these weapons to be suspended. This means confiscating what they own already and returning at the end of the penalty period. There will be a large effort to get an inventory of what is already owned. We must be willing to invest in the costs of getting these arsenals inventoried. Once the line is crossed when all such weapons can only be in the possession of someone in a well-regulated militia, the gun sales laws would keep the tracking up to date.

New laws would make it unlawful to be in possession of any of these weapons without being part of a well-regulated militia. So, if there is a drug bust, the crime may not have a severe consequence, but the possession of any weapons outside of nonrepeating handguns and hunting rifles will be severe. Think of it as a "Go directly to jail" card. We'll save on the court and lawyer fees, and it's off to jail they go.

The other approach is to have as many communities as possible enact local control (districts, towns, cities or states) through laws to move us in this direction. Possibilities could include putting limits on the number of weapons that can be in a community and are not associated with a well-regulated militia. The goal is not to purge communities of handguns, but to know when a community is oversaturated with weapons. If this is the case, what is the cause of the fear: violence, crime, predators, hate, or bigotry? Get to the root cause and address what could be causing an abnormally high need to be armed.

8.7. Better Decisions with Weapons

Mandatory minimum sentencing ideas have been around for a long time. However, if someone has made the decision to commit a crime, getting slapped really hard compared to being slapped hard doesn't significantly alter the decision equation. However, mandatory minimums may help reduce the use of a gun when not absolutely necessary. Say two people get in an altercation (an assault). If one of them has a gun in their possession, the possible severity of the physical damage can be much more severe. The weapon may not have been involved in the incident, but if someone is carrying a weapon, they need to make sure they stay well clear of any trouble, since they risk much more severe consequences. Unfortunately, even with more stringent mandatory sentencing for excessive violence with a handgun, way too many people will still have their lives prematurely ended. So, murders and assaults with handguns are a problem that will need other solutions.

Children or others who gain access to a weapon that does not belong to them will cause harsh consequences for the owner and the owner's immediate circle who have the responsibility for assuring there are no accidents with a weapon. This will ensure no more accidents from children getting their hands on weapons. Say, your spouse keeps a handgun in the house, but you know that there are not proper safety precautions, training, and other measures in place. You, as a member of the immediate circle, would then also be motivated to police proper gun safety.

8.8. Taking Local Action: "A Well-Regulated Militia"

When you think about the steps required to bring about these changes, the conversation immediately shifts towards the NRA. What would happen if this didn't have to be a battle against the NRA, but the game could be changed so local groups found themselves working with the NRA? It can happen, but not automatically.

For over a quarter of a century, I have been annually investing a large volume of my personal time and energy raising money to fight cancer. That commitment is continuously fueled each and every time someone in my wider circle is thrust into a battle with cancer. I convert the mad and sad into action. Similarly, every sad news story of innocent victims of gun violence creates a mass cadre of people who are outraged and want the slaughter to stop. This rage can be channeled to action through current and new groups who create a large volume of awareness each and every time one of these murders is committed by a member of the NRA.

These groups will draw as much attention to the association and crimes as possible. The goal is not to eliminate or oppose the NRA, but to get them focusing on eliminating assaults and crimes committed with weapons. If it starts to impact the NRA's financials and membership, the NRA will need to either adjust or become a different kind of organization.

Also, every time you hear someone mention the Second Amendment, it should trigger an automatic response of "A well-regulated militia." Good habits start with practice. You could be at home listening to the news, in your car, at the water cooler; it doesn't matter. Whenever you hear Second Amendment, practice saying, "A well-regulated militia." Then when a politician or anyone else is speaking and only says the phrase "Second Amendment," it will require an automatic response of "A well-regulated militia." For example, if a candidate makes the statement at a political speech that they support "the Second Amendment", they should immediately be met with a chorus of "A well-regulated militia." This will continually make the point that the Second Amendment needs to be stated in its full context. Even the stand-alone statement of "our right to bear arms" would also be met with "A well-regulated militia."

Chapter 9. The Cost of Energy Brake

While economic activity creates flywheel energy, much of our economic activity consumes energy (power production, distribution, and consumption). The more of that power that comes from within our flywheel, the less we are susceptible to the pull of other economic flywheels. A 2017 *Forbes* magazine article reported that Earth Overshoot Day, the day in the year when we have consumed more power than our earth can produce in a year, was as early as August 1st that year.[25] Data points from 2005 and 2006 reported that with around 5% of the global population, our country consumes more than 20% of the world's energy.

The capital and focus required to adjust to rising tides along the coasts is also a braking action. We can pull in other weather-driven events that could be attributed to climate change, but rising tides is a substantial enough to require actions.

We only seem to discuss energy and energy independence when there is a crisis or a political discussion to open up federal lands. Fracking, the Permian Basin (western Texas/southeastern New Mexico), and natural gas have taken some of the pressure off foreign oil, but we still have energy challenges and undetermined long-term environmental impacts of fracking.

We waste a lot of energy. If we are ever going to become permanently energy independent or to improve the percentage of renewable energy, we need to waste less energy. If we reduce energy consumption, this helps lower the bar for renewable energy goals. We can increase the percentage of green energy by reducing the amount of energy we consume (the denominator). So, even if we don't add any additional green energy sources, the percentage not coming from burning carbon can go up just by reducing our energy consumption.

The lowest-hanging fruit is powering devices we are not actively using. This is the power wasted on LED and other equipment not being currently used. A 2015 story in *Inside Energy* talks about energy vampires; this California study showed 23% of our electricity going to vampire devices.[26] See the chart below from that report. Additionally, https://standby.lbl.gov/ is a site dedicated to helping you identify what devices are consuming power when you are not using them.[27] One dark night, shut off all of the lights in your house and take a stroll through your house and see how many things are glowing. Yes, clocks are on, but does your TV need to be on standby? Is your printer or internet powered on while you are asleep? Every single LED in your house is using some power. When one of our children got a clock radio, we realized it created more light than his night-light. How many light bulbs are in your bathroom vanity? Try unscrewing a few and you will notice that just a few bulbs create more than adequate brightness.

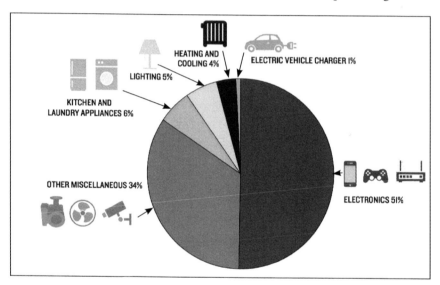

SOURCE: http://insideenergy.org/2015/05/08/ie-questions-how-much-do-energy-vampires-cost-us/

9.1. Taking Local Action: Change Your Bulbs

It took a few years, but just about every lightbulb in our house has been exchanged with energy-efficient bulbs or LED lights, so we are using less electricity. For those of us who live up north, properly winterizing our homes can also save a lot of energy. Replacing windows and proper insulation are the big ones. We left all of the child safety plugs on the outside walls when I realized how much cold air blows through outlets.

We are not fanatical, but we do what we can to use less energy. Everyone needs to work to minimize wasted energy. What one single household does is not significant, but when we all do this, we can start to move the needle. Some New Hampshire groups have gotten towns or neighborhoods to compete over the biggest reductions in energy consumption. Municipal buildings can be big culprits. Our town has a group who conducts municipal building energy audits. Poor energy efficiency is just throwing money out the window. Who is going to step up and help your town or city?

We need neighborhood, local, county, state, then national goals for reducing total energy consumption with incentives and competitions. We can have a lot of fun with goals and perks for winners. Maybe the winning neighborhood gets extra services from the local government, such as a trash pickup, paved roads, or other services. City wards or districts could have the losing groups (those with less energy reduction) complete projects for the winning group. Businesses could donate recognition signs for counties; competing cities or states could make wagers that would provide local products (maybe even build new markets for them). We could create benefits for our lawmakers, who could get preferential seating, parking, speaking order, or other awards when their constituents make the most energy-saving progress.

9.2. Taking Local Action: Energy Buying Groups

Around the time we needed to replace our windows and install a woodstove, I thought, wouldn't it make sense if a contractor could come and replace windows in some of my neighbors' homes? We could get lower prices if the contractor (or business) had lower cost of sales and economies of scale during installation. Great idea, but it was like herding cats. After going door to door and handing out flyers, my neighbors hosted a discussion. It was a nice get-together, but people said they would be interested in saving money for home heating oil. I learned that some people put a lot of energy to get the lowest possible oil price. Then there are others like me who don't have the time to chase the best deals, so if I can save a nickel, it's worth it.

For home heating oil, when there is not a lot of new home construction, the population of customers is a relatively fixed market. What is important is net new customers (how many of those customers they are taking from competition). I gathered the key information such as current vendor, estimated usage, and size of the tank, and then got local oil companies to bid. Of course, they don't make it easy for you. They all tried to have different names and positioning for how they construct pricing plans. Another key component turned out to be service and maintenance for boilers. It took a while, but we were able to normalize the bids, and I got three other people to evaluate the bids. This was important, as I had developed relationships with the vendors and we needed the selection to be free from any relationship bias. We were able to get a price that was better than others could get on their own and that included service.

9.3. Flywheel Idea: Mindset Helping Larger Energy Investments

Once everyone is more focused on reducing the energy we consume, this will help the dialog with bigger investments that will deliver energy savings in big chunks. I like the notion of getting rid of small-hop air flights. For us in the Northeast, it would mean an end to the daily shuttles from Boston to New York, or New York to Washington DC. Moving people between these shorter distances can be much more energy-efficient if we have high-speed trains. We just don't have them yet, and do you ever wonder why?

Recently a client was telling me about a California high-speed train proposal. The idea could be good, but the California government managing this is the problem. Going into a 2017 election, Californians liked the idea, but were having trouble with the mind-boggling cost. The total estimated cost divided by the number of miles worked out to $89 million per mile. (It is $164 million per mile if we include the cost of capital.[28]) While this is just an average cost, theoretically it means that for each mile of track, we would need to figure out how to spend $89 million for each mile of track. How do you come up with new ways to spend $89 million for each and every mile of track?

California will only be able to have energy-efficient high-speed trains if residents drive down the costs so that the investment can make economic sense. This is not committing to huge costs, but to working together to get the costs to be manageable. Communities would need to figure out how to take regulatory cost out of the process, providing lands and rights to make this happen. Another option is to come up with ways to use space around existing highways, providing food, lodging, or other services for workers, volunteer flaggers, and community service projects that help the construction process. It is a great challenge for American ingenuity.

9.4. Brake Component: Electrical Grid Limitations

Not everyone comprehends the problems with our electricity grid. So here is a New Hampshire example. New Hampshire businesses pay some of the highest rates for electricity in the New England region. The area known as the North Country (north of the Notch: look on a map and plan on visiting there), has unused electric generation capacity. This area is prevented from producing energy at capacity because the electric distribution system has no incentive to expand the lines to carry more power. The operator of the grid does not get enough incremental revenue to cover the additional costs of expanding the network capacity (allowing more electricity to be transported from where it is produced to where it is consumed).

Confused? The electrical lines where the energy is being produced are big enough to meet all of the electricity demands of the area. To move electricity out of the area, bigger lines in greater numbers are needed to move the additional electricity through the areas of low demand to the more populated areas. However, the people responsible for the grid (electrical transportation system) don't want to install and maintain bigger equipment in greater numbers than they need to service the local area. Why divert resources to building and maintaining something that will not deliver good returns? Those resources are better allocated to more profitable investments.

We have an electrical transportation problem where we can't move the new electricity generated from dams, windmills, and biofuel stations to where the power is needed, when it is needed.

9.5. Flywheel Idea: Overcoming Grid Limitations

Here are a few options for removing the grid limitations. One, invest in more physical transportation lines to bring electricity from where it is produced to where it is consumed. This allows locations where windmills, solar farms, or biomass generators can be built to have a cost-effective way of transporting power to where it is needed. This may qualify for a situation where government (us) would step in. The economics for non–fossil fuel power generation can make sense if the transportation costs don't crush the project. If we choose to make the transportation investment, then the financial decision to build more non-carbon energy sources makes more sense. What can local communities do to help to lower the cost component of the business equation to improve power distribution?

The second is to develop effective ways to store and transport electricity or other methods (e.g., lasers) from where it is generated to where and when it is needed. For example, assume we had energy-efficient trains (not high-speed) that could transport railcars of large rechargeable batteries. We would store power in batteries and then physically move the stored power from where it is generated to where it will be consumed (cities).

The third is to start producing more energy closer to where it is consumed. This is putting solar panels, geothermal, and waste-burning facilities much closer to the high-energy consumption zones. This is distributed energy generation compared to building large power stations and transporting over power lines. Picture rooftops with solar panels, more windmills, and biomass plants (downwind). Similar to enhancing the grid, the citizen's role is to help reduce the cost component of the installation.

Chapter 10. The Big Brake: Government Regulations

The solution to regulation is to not just repeal it. Most regulations came into place for legitimate reasons. So, I need to make some points clear about regulations to help us have more productive discussions.

Think of regulation as medicine: some is preventive, and others treat a condition once it appears. Medicine can keep you healthy, but too much of it could make you sick. Every time you make a rule, you have to have some way of making sure it is followed, and if it is not being followed, a process for punishing offenders. Those activities are flywheel economic braking costs. If you ever wondered why some beat the anti-regulation drum so loudly, it's because the monitoring and punishment, time and effort to report compliance, and other regulatory tasks suck energy out of the economy. As a rule of thumb, we should work hard to develop ways to avoid regulations (enforceable laws) as much as possible. The challenge is figuring out: what is the optimal balance of regulations and not having regulations?

It would be a beautiful thing if we could eliminate regulations. Unfortunately, excessive greed is a dark side of human nature and mandates regulations. Greed run amuck is the cancer of capitalism. Just like cancer may never go away, neither will unethical actions and greed. Similar to fighting cancer, we have to invest in ways that help us prevent it and in ways of coping with it when it metastasizes. The financial meltdown of the late 2000s is a great case in point. Looking at what lenders and investors were doing, this problem is much easier to understand. We are too quick to forget that it can happen all over again, as those who buy political influence move to mitigate how far the pendulum swings towards more regulations.

10.1. The Financial Meltdown: An Example of Why Regulation is Needed

This short explanation is from Michael Lewis's book and the movie, *The Big Short*. The takeaway from this book is not the people who profited from betting that our financial markets would crash, but how all of the greed driven banks, rating houses, mortgage companies, insurers and others made billions of dollars and walked away unscathed.

Leading up to the financial meltdown, many smart people knew something was not right, but they ignored it, because they were making money and so was everyone else. There may have been a code of conduct, but it was clearly not up to fighting greed, especially on Wall Street. Most of us can understand the cause and effects of a simple equation of A + B = C. However if we have an equation like this:

$$i h \frac{a}{at} \Psi = -\frac{h^2}{2m} \nabla^2 \Psi + V \Psi$$

(Non-relativistic time-dependent Schrodinger equation – one particle), most of us are not going to have a natural feel for the relationship between the variables.[29]

While this is a quantum mechanics equation, the point is that the intricacies of our financial system have become more like quantum mechanics than basic algebra. Those creating the complexities benefit from the fog the complexities create. If it is hard for others (monitors) to see through the fog, it's a lot easier to do what you want since your actions are obscured from others.

Let's look at the single component of home mortgages, acknowledging this is just one of many spots where our ability to prevent disasters failed. Some home loans have little risk, while others could have more; the lender just doesn't know. Financial entities (mortgage brokers) started coming to mortgage lenders and saying they would buy a block of these home loans. Mortgage lenders were willing to take less in the long term and get paid in full now. The mortgage brokers would take these packages of loans and sell them to other groups looking for ways that money could generate cash. The new set of buyers could borrow at low interest rates, much lower than the homeowners were paying for the money they borrowed, so this created a flow where many were profiting.

The credit bureaus like Moody's were supposed to be doing the due diligence when they would grade how good or bad these block of home mortgages were (bond ratings), so the buyers could gauge the risk of what they bought. There was a code of conduct for these grades, but it didn't work. Two things happened: the first was that higher grades for the mortgage blocks meant more money when you sell them. The other was that the definition of a "good" home loan from your local mortgage lender went from being one where they felt good about getting all of the payments to a loan that could quickly be packaged and sold. Mortgage lending went from making solid loans to making as many loans as possible, then flipping the risk. Do you want to buy a house you can't afford? No problem, we will lend you the money and you will be someone else's problem.

Just like we have C students getting As with grade inflation, we got "A-grade" loan packages that weren't the solid home loans of earlier years, but just a pile of much more risky home loans. One or two of these bad loan packages would have been OK. But there were many of these, and the mortgage brokers and those banks and investment houses lending money to the brokers had no idea that so many of the home mortgages were from people living in homes they couldn't afford. We had banks, insurance companies, and investment firms fail. Many people were saddled with homes that were underwater, i.e., if they sold the house, they would get less money for the home than what they borrowed to buy the home.

Others have written books on the details of this and the other situations that drove the financial meltdown. The key point is how contagious the greed was, as the blame goes all the way from the insurance companies down to the individuals who bought homes they could not afford. The collateral damage rippled through the economy as mortgage lenders and banks clamped down on lending, crushing many innocent business people and adding costs (time and money) to all of those who needed to borrow money.

10.2. Another Case of Why Regulations Are Needed

While this story is not from the United States, for some reason it always stuck with me. There was an earthquake in Greece and many of the fatalities occurred when buildings crumbled like a house of cards. During the investigation, it was discovered that builders did not build to code, and if there was a building inspection system, it failed (through corruption, incompetence, or other causes). Many people were crushed as a result of greed, incompetence, or both. See the below study for more information.[30]

Later in the book we will talk about Common Denominator Government; there needs to be some minimal level of regulation we can all agree we must have. It costs money to make some things safe, but what is a reasonable amount to be spent? Regulation discussions should help us to evaluate what we are willing to pay for safety versus the total cost of abiding by the regulation, monitoring, and enforcement.

Land Use Boards and Regulation

Planning Boards and Zoning Boards of Adjustment are referred to as land use boards. These public meetings are not the most riveting or entertaining. Since the board members have a judicial responsibility, English is converted to legalese, so it can be difficult to understand by someone not steeped in the jargon. Much happens in these meetings that shouldn't. Multiple times I have heard lawyers or builders advocate putting septic systems in wetland buffers, since these solutions are better, more high-tech systems than what are currently being used. However, this completely negates the rationale of why we have wetland buffers.

Wetland buffers (land or space between manmade things and water) are sponges and have big value for us (property) and the ecosystem when water moves in either direction. All of our modern building materials, yard toys, and other outside objects leach chemicals when it rains. This water washes towards watersheds or aquifers, but if we have enough of a sponge (land) to absorb and filter out these chemicals, their march into our ecosystem can be mitigated. When water comes up from the wetlands to encroach on our property (with all of those chemicals), the sponge (land) deters the encroachment of the water and filters when that water recedes. So, it doesn't matter how high-tech a system is, if it is in the buffer, it is taking the place of the active sponge (land).

How much buffer land do we need? It's not an exact science and there are many variables that impact one specific area—hence these ranges. We need to make compromises and monitor what is happening when we do need to make compromises. We may hire or elect people to be on these boards or committees, but we don't abdicate all of our responsibility when we put individuals in specific roles.

10.3. Taking Local Action: Regulation

It is our job to make sure monitoring groups or land use boards (see side note) are not trending one way or the other. We need to monitor them against our expectations for what we want to be happening. We need to know if they are doing a great job, are mediocre, or are highly dysfunctional. If no one is going to the meetings, if there are not short, concise, and digestible insights and analysis, then the vast majority of people do not know what is happening.

Starting with local regulations, we need to look at the value the regulations provide, the costs to the economy, and the government bodies, so we can drive them to a least-cost equilibrium point. While we push for continuous effectiveness from the regulations, existing regulations will need to remain in place. Note that the best regulations are the ones that never need to be put in place because groups are self-monitoring.

10.4. Common-sense Approaches to Regulation

Here is another good example of the challenge we have to make things better, but that does not involve inserting costly government. A May 8, 2017 *Bloomberg Businessweek* article talked about the huge volume of natural gas (mostly methane) that is leaked from the massive gas distribution system.[31] Current regulation and utilities are focused on larger leaks that can cause explosions. All of the little leaks shouldn't cause an explosion, but these leaks add up fast. The article states that "by plugging just 20 percent of the leaks, utilities can cut their methane emissions in half." Sounds simple. So why aren't they doing this?

It's a cost with no revenue incentive and only the material cost savings, so why should they? If the gas loss is a cost to the business, the gas monopoly passes this along to customers as an operational cost. Utilities don't get paid for minimizing methane gas leaks to the atmosphere. Now, regulations could set a goal and force them to do this. If so, it will cost us a lot of money to make and enforce these regulations. Here is a good opportunity for us to get creative. How can we make this happen?

10.5. Taking Local Action: Addressing Small Gas Leaks

One way would be for the current governing bodies to come up with a trade for the utilities. Can those bodies come up with ways to reduce offsetting costs (current regulations) that would offset the investments in going after these non-explosive leaks? Maybe when they find them, our government can do things that decrease the costs of fixing them, such as eliminating police at construction (flaggers), minimizing time and effort required to get construction permission from local governments, etc. These actions lower the bar, making it easier for the utilities to act. Conceptually, if the costs of fixing the leaks will be below the cost of the lost gas, they will make the repairs, because it makes good business sense. What can we do to help get the cost portion of the equation down so that the financial benefits are greater than the financial costs?

10.6. Self-Regulation

Self-regulating and self-monitoring by an industry is a much better alternative to creating regulations (which require defining, monitoring, correcting, and punishing). Groups focused on a subject should be in the best position to deploy cost-effective measures. If groups are self-regulating, then the monetary costs of failure should be high. That is, we will trust them to define standards and assure that they are maintained, but if they mess up (have an accident or get exposed for not being sufficiently monitored), the consequences must be severe, such as a large motivational financial penalty.

Companies will need to operate by a code of conduct, and breaches should be costly. Say, to get "self-regulation," this industry would need to put funds into a trust, and if there is a breach, the public gets the funds, with a doubling if a breach is not disclosed. Using insurance as a way to offset these risks should not be allowed. If these groups are operating without an insurance safety net, they will operate more prudently. If they are good, then there is no risk; they just have to put their money on the table to reap the benefits the public offers.

10.7. Flywheel Idea: Get Off the Backs of Small Businesses

Do you ever leverage the float on your credit cards (buying things at the beginning of the month, with the bill not due until the end of the following month)? If you pay in full without incurring any interest changes, you are using whatever you bought for free for a month or two. Credit card companies are fine with this since most people don't pay in full. Now, when a large corporation does business with a small one and tells the small business their payment terms are ninety days, the big company is using the product or service for ninety days for free. Who do you think is more sensitive to cash flow, the big corporation or the small company? In the aggregate, this is important to the big corporation, since by doing this to many vendors, the volume of float can be sizable.

Typically, the large corporation is in the driver's seat since they dictate the payment terms, unless the small company is the only one who can provide a specific service or product. If the small business was bidding competitively, they couldn't afford to increase price to cover the delayed payment cost. While this is perfectly legal, what do you think the impact is to the economy? Is it more important that large corporations are as profitable as possible, or that more of our nation's smaller businesses stay in operation? What is good for big companies is not necessarily good for our national flywheel. This delayed cash flow is a brake on all small businesses that sell to large companies.

Some larger corporations give improved payment terms to small businesses. There may be regulations about specific type of businesses ownerships (small, women, minority), but corporations should agree to a code of conduct for helping keep small suppliers fiscally healthy. When one large corporation is buying from another large corporation, let them battle it out on the payment terms. The large buying corporation leverages the float (using the money or product before having to pay for it), and the selling corporation may view the long payment terms as a cost of keeping customers content. For a small business these long payment terms, or having to accept less for faster payments, are a brake on the small business.

10.8. Taking Local Action: Relief for Small Businesses

This large corporation code of conduct should be scaled towards the size of the supplier. So, a small business would have payment terms of ten to fifteen days, and these terms could slowly increase until we get to large corporations. While the corporations may be forfeiting a business benefit through drawn-out payments to suppliers, they are contributing to the health of the overall economy by moving the fuel (cash) to the small business engine that drives a high percentage of jobs. One could argue that the longer payment terms may require small businesses to borrow funding, and that money lending is also fuel for the economy. While this is true, it strikes me as a less efficient way to power the economy. Pull the brake off small business and get the money to them so they can invest in people, technology, and growth.

How can you start to make this happen? Do you have large companies headquartered in your town or state, or do they have offices where you also pay taxes? If so, the first question is what can the local government be doing to help this company? It may be different in every situation. Don't just assume it is paying less local taxes. It could be some type of infrastructure improvement that helps employees, or changes in regulation that removes costs that the corporation sees as having no net value. It may just be improving the local schools. Don't assume; go and ask the large corporations what the local government can do to help them.

Once you are able to determine what your community can do that has value, you can now begin to barter. You can now do things that help the corporation and that are affordable and reasonable for the group you represent. You may have to start with only local small businesses, but I am a big fan of quid pro quo. I would also think that from a public-relations standpoint, once a community put this offer favorable to small businesses on the table, a refusal from corporations would be detrimental to their goodwill. Goodwill is important to stockholders.

A simpler approach could be to flag the largest corporations who do not have preferable payment terms for small and or local businesses, and publicize which corporations are riding on the coattails of local small businesses. While this is a little bit sneaky, I have no problem using public shame to dissuade large corporations from taking unfair advantage of smaller entities. Below is a short article on how the changes in media is making this corporate shaming more effective.[32] Think of all the fun you can have with this: ads in newspapers, billboards, letters to the editor, YouTube videos, posters where employees live, etc. Just keep on coming up with creative ways to get the word out. You could argue we should make this a law, and we could—but do we have to? This is something we should be able to get done without districting legislators. And don't forget that laws aren't free; every one of them comes with lots of incremental costs.

There may be other brakes on our economic flywheel that I have not covered here. For all other brakes, we need to apply the same process of starting locally with the discussions, and/or actions that help pull back on this brake.

Part 4: The Weights

While brakes are pushing against our economic flywheel, there are also weights attached to the flywheel. On each revolution, our flywheel needs to fight against that weight to make the next revolution. In a worst-case scenario, the weights could become such a burden that a country's flywheel could stop spinning. Our work is to reduce the weight so that our economic flywheel retains as much energy as possible. This illustration shows how our national debt is a weight on our economic flywheel.

Chapter 11. The Weight of the National Debt

The biggest weight is our national debt: more precisely, the annual interest payments on all of that money we have borrowed to pay for budgets where the spending was greater than the money coming in. We consider revenue to be money coming in, but a business earns money; our government is not earning money, but collecting it.

The $523,017,301,446.12 we needed to pay in 2018 for the interest on the money we still must pay back ($21,682,446,587,870.73, the 2018 number) is not going away.[33] It is not a brake that is leaning against our economic flywheel, but a weight that is hanging onto the flywheel. For 2018, our nation owes over $21 trillion that we have spent in past years. For that money we spent, we must pay over $523 billion of interest in 2018. If we don't pay off or down that principal ($21 trillion), we need to pay the interest every year.[34]

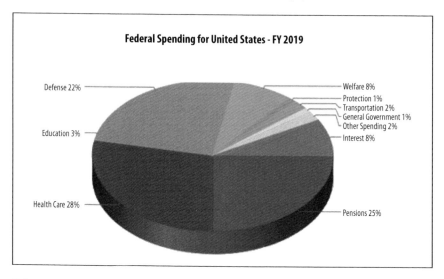

SOURCE: https://www.usgovernmentspending.com/us_fed_spending_pie_chart

This pie chart tells us that 8% of our 2019 federal spending is for the interest on our spent money.

For 2019, we are paying as much for interest as we are for federal welfare, so if we got rid of the interest payments, it would reduce the budget as much as eliminating welfare. Our general federal government (the cost of running the executive part of our government) is only 1% of the budget, so with all of that interest money, we could have eight duplicate federal executive government operations for what we are paying in interest payments every year. We are not getting anything for those interest payments; we're just paying off the interest and not the principal.

There are a number of other situations we have created that are weights fixed to our economic flywheel. Looking at the pie chart, pension payments are similar. These are massive payments for something we already used, so they are not adding energy to our flywheel, just sucking up energy on every revolution. There is a lot of money that can be doing other things for our economic flywheel.

If you have ever borrowed money to purchase a home, you know that the first payments you make are about 98% interest payment and the other 2% actually paying down what you owe. If you have a large interest payment, it makes it hard to put away money to make improvements to your house. With our huge national interest payments, it's hard to make investments to help fuel our growth.

Chapter 12. Weight: Broken Math of Pensions

Many years ago I was sending money to my sister in New York City. She was getting her master's in social work (MSW) and could not make ends meet. Here was someone with two degrees and was going to Rikers Island prison to help female inmates. Something was systematically wrong, if the people who were willing to be social workers needed a master's degree but could not even make a living. We should be grateful for all of those who choose to take these key roles in our society, like social workers, police, firefighters, and teachers. We want good people in these positions, and good people should be justly compensated for the value they bring society.

That may be why we created the pension plans for these roles, but whatever the rationale for the math, those initial assumptions about the future costs were wrong. If you have plowed through any local municipal budgets or read up about the health of centralized state pension systems, you know Social Security funding is not our only problem. Just like rising debt payments, pension costs (salaries and benefits) mitigate the future value of how current tax payments are utilized. Just as the private sector has moved away from the toxic pension equations, we must do the same in our public systems. The pension liabilities are all weights we have to fight through on all of our flywheel revolutions.

Pensions started out in many nations as a way of rewarding solders who put their lives on the line. Over time these began to change. In 1920, the Civil Service Retirement System began to pay what are referred to as "defined-benefit plans." In 1987, the Federal Employee Retirement System provided some tiers and actions and began to move federal employees off the older Civil Services Retirement System.

There was no single conference to figure out if the public would be better off in the long run, but you would hope someone did some math to test the original assumptions every time pensions were offered.

What were those initial assumptions that we would be better off paying people less while they worked and then paid them for the rest of their life with benefits? When I was in high school and college, my generation assumed people would work until they were 55 or 65 and die at around 75. These numbers were way low on life expectancy and how fast health insurance costs would escalate. If what we know now was plugged into original long-term cost equations, we would never have signed up for providing these guaranteed benefits. The accumulation of these choices has created a massive flywheel weight.

12.1. Flywheel Idea: Addressing the Pension Problem

The problem grew over time, so the remedy will take time before we fully address the situation. We need to begin to eliminate the pension systems, but that means paying more now for these civic roles. For the non-administrative jobs, such as social workers, police, fire, and other positions where we all benefit from quality people, we can use the tax system to offer relief and assistance.

For essential civic services (police, fire, teachers, social workers), new employees should not be offered pensions, but should be paid more and have a 401(k) plan. While longer-term employees will be financially better off to stay with the current pension commitments, we could create an incentive program to move as many off the current pension program as possible. For those identified roles, where we have city, state, and federal income taxes, we can choose to lower these tax rates. This way local or state taxpayers would not have to increase taxes to raise salaries. These key civic servants would have the same salary but experience a higher net income from paying lower state and/or federal income taxes. If there are no other efficiencies found, there could be some tax increases, but we have to eliminate the problem caused by an unsustainable pension system. If we all know the current math is not sustainable, we need to move to a new system, sooner rather than later.

Some of our large cities impose income taxes, so this may be a good place to start, since the city could begin to work with local unions. If a few of these cities are successful, it may turn the tide for states with income taxes to step in and add a city income tax discount. Other municipalities may not have the ability to incentivize current employees with the income tax swap, but they do need to work with unions to begin the new employee program.

This is not an effort to hammer down the compensation to drive taxes down, but to be realistic about what we need to be paying when we want quality people for specific roles. When your house is on fire, you don't want a bad firefighter. If you need an ambulance, you want a paramedic who knows what they are doing. We need to be making sure we are paying for quality services that meet our expectations. However, if the firefighter is not becoming better at their job year over year, should they be paid more than a cost of living adjustment? If they are managing people, taking on more responsibilities, and have experience that translates to better results from tasks, than we should be willing to pay for increased value. If not, the cost of living increase can be better than what the private sector gets in raises.

Our regional paper (the *Portsmouth Herald*) has been doing a good job the past few years of publishing the highest Portsmouth public salaries. This puts the salaries in perspective to private workforce salaries. (They only show base pay; it would stand out even more if the benefit packages could also be normalized so people could develop an apple-to-apples comparison to their pay and benefit programs.) There is value to experience, but it may not be linear. When does the accumulated experience demonstrate incremental value to the community?

The classic story is with teachers. If someone has been teaching for twenty-five years, they clearly have experience and wisdom they are using to be more effective in educating each and every child in a classroom. However, how does this experience stack up to a new teacher who grew up using all of the new technology and approaches to getting work done and is much closer to the skills the current workforce needs? One study by the National Center for Analysis of Longitudinal Data in Education Research shows that the experience advantage flattens out after several years.[35] Are new teachers being hired to replace more tenured teachers because they are less expensive, or are some teachers too far removed from current technologies to learn and adapt quick enough? Some may be adjusting and increasing yearly value, but others may not be. School administrators need to be able to see this match of skills and rate of adoption to determine if higher salaries justify the increased value delivered.

In schools, we may need to look at different approaches to training and evaluating teacher effectiveness. Paying lump sums for early retirement may not feel like the most fiscally prudent decision, but when the focus is on the mission of the school, these other parameters are what can help the equations make sense.

Chapter 13. Weight: Investment in Education

Walk into an area with a lot of "help wanted" signs. Visit a tech company who is getting outpaced by competitors since they just can't get workers with the skills they need. When our economy has people to feed, house, and clothe that don't have the skills employers need, that's a weight on our economic flywheel.

It's all about the economy, and a growing and changing economy needs the labor force to keep up. The subsistence economy (just keeping us alive and moving) and the added-value economy both require an educated work force. Our ability to compete globally is being hampered by the capital our subsistence economy sucks up (healthcare, national debt, etc.), leaving fewer fiscal resources for the value-add services economy that establishes our place amongst the economically healthy nations. So, our wellbeing from value-add creation (where free capital comes from) and subsistence economy can both be tied to the efficiency levels and an educated workforce.

For the common good of the total economy, we as a society benefit through investing in public education. Unfortunately, our public education approach needs to be tied to return on investment. The first step is to get all the stakeholders in primary (K-8) and secondary (high school) education, i.e., the students, parents, teachers, administrators, taxpayers, primary and secondary educators, and employers (public and private) working together. Once together, this diverse group needs a simple metric to gauge that return. No matter where a product of our primary and secondary education system (i.e., a student) ends up, the metrics need to confirm each student is sufficiently prepared to succeed when they move on from public education.

13.1. Flywheel Idea: Prepared to Succeed

We should institute a program I call "Prepared to Succeed." Each fall, we should survey employers, colleges, trade schools, the military, and other postgraduation destinations to determine if the graduates have been adequately prepared to succeed in their next endeavor. The same holds true for each grade. We should implement a one-to-seven scoring metric (similar to what businesses use, the Net Promoter Score created by Fred Reicheld, Bain & Company, and Satmetrix to ask customers if they would recommend the product or service, with seven being the high score). It will not say why or where the products of our education are not prepared, but if the scores are not sevens or improving, the why questions need to be answered. As the world continues to change and evolve, this should improve the connection between the product of our public education investments and the jobs that drive our economy. This would be an annual, dynamic process that ties the changing needs of our economy into the education system.

My first exposure to this problem was when I started in an engineering and science program (think of all our STEM talk) in the early 1980s. My university long ago established a math lab because too many incoming freshmen had insufficient math skills to enable engineering and science classes to cover the semester's workload. To stop the domino effect caused by the bottom of the class dragging down the pace of the class, students were required to spend as much time as required in math lab. While I was relatively proud that I only had to take a few modules, shockingly only 5% or 10% of freshmen in the engineering and science school passed all of the basic math requirements. The math lab is still functioning at the University of New Hampshire, so for over 30 years, public and private high schools have been delivering students to colleges and universities with insufficient skills and knowledge to succeed.

Our high school graduates must be prepared to succeed. If not, why are we paying so much for primary and secondary education? What a community pays for a K-12 education varies, but it can be anywhere from $120,000 to over $250,000 per child.[36] Let's pick on math as an example. While I am happy that my university took proactive steps so ill-equipped students were not allowed to diminish the education I was paying for, that action left the root cause of the problem in place. If high school graduates are not prepared to succeed, those end customers (schools, employers, the military, etc.) need to push back and get the problem fixed.

When implementing annual "Prepared to Succeed" surveys, high schools will get feedback from colleges, universities, trade schools, the military, local companies—wherever their products end up. From there, we push it back down the grade levels, so every set of grades has a chance to get a set of students who are prepared to succeed. Schools will be told where they are failing in their responsibility to deliver to the economy products (students) that meet the current requirements.

Now specific schools know that the seniors are not prepared to succeed, so they're going to tell us they did the best they could based on what they received in the fall. We won't argue with fact. To address this, the teachers who are responsible for the senior classes need to clearly communicate to the teachers of the junior class what they need to get done before they allow these students to move to senior-level classes. If students aren't prepared for the next year, why are they moving on? This will help drive the emphasis all the way back to grade schools.

Unlike the rigidness (and cost) of national standards, this would be a continuous system that can adapt to the needs of the job and higher education market. We would also allow the control to be with local teachers, administrators, and taxpayers.

When I have discussed this, others have brought up privacy concerns. To this excuse for not investing in fixing the problem, I respond with, "We have a Jeep-sized vehicle driving around on Mars." This is a lot less complex. Privacy concerns are a complication, not a showstopper. I shared this in vain with the principal at our regional high school, which receives students from five or more schools. I suggested that the teachers score the students, then the guidance departments match students to schools and provide the aggregated results.

13.2. Taking Local Action: Act Locally on "Prepared to Succeed"

School boards have no excuse for not taking steps to make these changes now. These activities may not be exactly the same, and that is fine. The most important part is a strong level of communication and feedback between grade levels. We should hear support from educators as this puts each of them in a much better position to deliver a solid year of educational improvements for all students.

While implementing this type of change falls on school boards and administrators to implement, it does not mean the taxpayers (not just the parents with children in the system) get a free pass. It is the responsibility of all those who pay taxes to work with, push, and monitor the school boards to implement these types of changes. Just because state or federal law does not say we must do this, a lack of a mandate is no excuse for not taking action. If we act locally, then state and federal education can be focused on other concerns.

We are also much better off letting school systems coming up with the approach that best works for their school system. School systems can learn from others and develop the most cost-effective system for them. While states and federal governments will also have a responsibility for the funds they provide to school systems, their focus should be on working with the customers (workforce, military, tech schools, colleges and universities) to assure that the outputs from school systems are prepared to succeed. Local taxes for schools are much larger than state or federal school dollars, so local responsibility is much greater.

School Board and Other Public Meetings

I am going to go out on a limb and say that many public meetings are ripe for improvements. I hear constantly from boards that they are open and receptive to public input and involvement, but we need more actions to back up those words. Conversely, we can't lose sight of the fact that these roles are voluntary or with minimal stipends, and that those who serve sacrifice countless hours towards this community service. At meetings, they need to get the work done and don't want every single meeting to be a marathon.

We need to work to a compromise that helps the public be engaged but is not overly obtrusive to the work that needs to get done. Public comments and discussions can't digress into endless complaints.

Structure is needed, and we should be able to develop methods that provide efficiency and public engagement.

For example, our town boards review and approve past meeting minutes towards the beginning of meetings. Yes, this needs to get done, but this can be moved to the end of the meeting, since little or no public interaction is required. Technology could also be utilized to improve the process for everyone. Instead of verbally walking through the documents, features such as tracked changes, projectors, or screens can be utilized with colors assigned to different members; these inputs could be reviewed before the meeting with a simple vote to approve a set of comments. The document with those changes could also be displayed on a screen, so they could be quickly reviewed and approved.

The public also has a responsibility to improve. Time limits on comments need to be in place, since some members of the public have a tendency to ramble. We also tend to hear people get off topic or repeat previous discussions. Yes, people have a right to be heard, but we need simple systems, e.g., cue cards or lights to let speakers know that they are straying off topic or that their comments are repetitive. It could be a combination of training and assigning a neutral third person to interrupt to keep the speaker focused on net new comments or information. All of this needs to be handled with respect and tact, so some training may be required. The Positive Coaching Alliance (www. positivecoach.org) advocates for a "Parent" to keep the other parents in line at youth sports, so the coach can focus on the children.

In my town, voter initiatives pushed the video streaming and recording of town meetings. The video recordings are big improvements. When I miss meetings, I can listen as I multitask. Improvements can still be made such as implementing chapters. Chapters allow meeting summaries to provide links directly to that spot in the video.

13.3. Flywheel Idea: One Level for Every Child

While "Prepared to Succeed" is a good tool to help us maximize the return on public education, it is by no means a panacea for all of the current school system challenges. States with high taxes can invest in "gifted and talented" programs, but those programs don't exist in my state and other low-tax states. These programs are good, but they highlight another change required for how we assure we are getting returns on our educational investment. While advancement to the next grade should be predicated on being prepared to succeed, teachers and administrators need to be held accountable for each and every student to advance at least one "level" each year. This is not clearing one common bar, but from where the student starts on day one of the year. Each and every child should make a minimum level of advancement each and every year.

While all students should be able to clear the "Prepared to Succeed" bar, if a student was 90% there on day one of the school year, should they only improve their knowledge or skills 10% during the year? If your school system is paying say $14,000 per year for a student that only has a 10% improvement in a year, that is not a good return for that student. All of us with children know what happens to the behavior of children who are not fully engaged in activities.

Some teachers are effective at progressing each student. After a second-grade class social event for parents, my wife and I each heard many different parents point out how the teacher was going out of her way to provide unique activities for their child. Their children were not special in this classroom; this rock star teacher was customizing the work for every single child in her class. It was just what she did.

Around that same time, I met an elementary school teacher who worked in one of the large city school districts on the other side of New Hampshire. When I discussed this concept with him, he let me know doing this with his classes that approached forty kids would be nearly impossible. He also mentioned some of the challenges of having a class of students from diverse socioeconomic backgrounds. While he did not argue with the concept, his teaching was more on survival mode with the large, diverse classes and no in-classroom support.

He may have been an incredible teacher and made sure the mean test scores cleared the mandated hurdles, but it is doubtful each child was moving up one unit of education each year. That incremental progress is what we are paying for and what we should be demanding for every student. I have no problem paying more if I know I am getting more value or return. But if I feel I am already paying a lot and the returns are not there, I am reluctant to put more money into something.

Our responsibility is to be absolutely firm on our expectations for our school systems. Overall, they must deliver to our society able-minded youths who have the skills and education to support the current requirements of our economy along each individual's chosen path. Every child deserves to advance one full educational unit each and every year. We do this by working with all of the stakeholders to assure we get on the same page and develop plans. Only a certain percentage of the tax base has students in the public schools. The rest of the taxpayers are stakeholders for the educational services they are funding and assuring our economy is fed an applicably educated work force. School boards, administrators, and teachers are the ones who need to implement the changes inside the schools, but they need our support and involvement to make fundamental changes.

13.6. No More Tenure for Primary and Secondary Teachers

For the taxpaying stakeholders, the most important thing for us to know is if the school systems are being efficiently run. We need to know that there is not a lot of fat in the system, we are not paying large salaries to less efficient teachers, administrations are lean, and the results of the school system are continually improving.

Two of the biggest changes are going to be around teachers and the pension system (discussed earlier). I am in agreement with the tenure systems at universities and colleges to protect professors' academic freedoms. We need people challenging accepted ideas, pushing the boundaries, and being unconventional to help our views and ideas evolve. These people need a degree of protection to not be persecuted or punished for being different or outside the establishment's comfort zone. However, this level of protection for ideas and pursuit of knowledge is not paramount to delivering value for primary and secondary public education.

Tenure for public education (K-12) needs to go away. That leads directly into the discussion of salaries for teachers, since the security from tenure is part of the compensation package. The first step is to establish a new rule for the way teachers' salaries are discussed in the public domain. As long as we continue the farm-based process of dismissing students for two months over the summer, we need to present adjusted salaries. Assuming teachers get four weeks of paid vacation, the salaries presented to the public need to be in terms of a full year of work. Before you jump to spreadsheets, this can't be a straight-line adjustment.

Granted, the teachers have the summer off, but their commitment to being a teacher also makes it difficult to find a high-paying job over the summer. Teachers are making a sacrifice (not working 12 months during the year), which limits their total earnings potential. Teachers don't have the same flexibility of taking their vacations when they want. Whatever we end up agreeing to for the compensation equation, it should be in terms of an adjusted base salary for a full year. So, if the budget line item is for $65K of salary (not benefits), then the adjusted full-year salary may work out to be something like $75K for an equivalent full year (working 12 months with only 3 weeks of vacation compared to 11 weeks).

Many school systems are implementing early retirement programs as a cost-containment activity. Fiscal discipline is a good thing. Experience in education provides value, but it can't just be a measurement of time in a role. Good, bad, and great teachers all gain experience from years and years of teaching, but which ones are utilizing the experience to deliver higher value? Quantitative metrics would make it simple, but how well a teacher utilizes experience is going to be more subjective and qualitative, requiring us to rely on administrators and peer teachers. The "Prepared to Succeed" surveys and feedback discussed earlier can be a component of this.

Beginning teachers fresh out of school bring new ideas, familiarity with new technologies, and lower costs, but that needs to be balanced against utilization of experience and how well current teachers adapt and incorporate those new technologies and approaches. It will be a difficult balancing act for administrators, but our job is to make sure this is not done behind closed doors. We are the board of directors for what is happening in our schools; we need to have insights and play an active role with value-based strategy.

13.7. Flywheel Idea: Teachers Are Teachers, Not Parents

If the expectations from our schools and teachers are that every student advances one level each year and is prepared with all of the skills and knowledge to succeed the following year, how successful can teachers be if time is spent not teaching? These distractions are weighing teachers down.

A good friend is a longtime fourth-grade teacher in a city with a broad socioeconomic landscape. One of the more profound things I learned from her was the challenge she faces from kids who are incredibly disruptive in class. We are not talking about the special needs or ADHD children, but children who have not been taught how to behave. There is nothing clinically wrong with these children; they just lack discipline, respect, consideration, and other basics for this age level. Too much of her bandwidth goes to raising students and not teaching. A 2016 National Bureau of Economic Research (a private, nonprofit, nonpartisan group) study reported that these disruptive classmates can have a long-term negative impact on their futures.[37] A 2014 Ofsted report (United Kingdom's Office for Standards in Education, Children's Services and Skills) estimated that low-level disruptive behavior costs classmates 38 days of the teaching year.[38]

This is a fundamental problem if we are focused on maximizing the value for what we invest in public education. Whatever the solution, it is not going to be smooth, since parents are going to have to be held accountable for a basic level of behavior and programs funded to get children to not be overly disruptive. A hard line needs to be drawn, so parents are not dumping discipline problems on teachers. If there is a clinical problem, then there should be an Individualized Education Plan (explanation is below) to coordinate special education school resources. If it is just a child who does not know how to behave, the parents need to be put on a plan with financial consequences to assure their child is not having a detrimental impact to the education we are funding.

Whatever the ultimate solution, we need to give teachers and administrators tools so teachers can teach without parenting. We are not paying for parenting, we are paying for education. Schools have been investing in school therapists and councilors for years. As long as the community is comfortable with funding this support, a minimal level is reasonable. Some children may just have spikes of behavioral challenges; in-school resources may be the most efficient way for society to support those children. However, there needs to be limits and a process that requires the parents to assure their children have a minimal negative impact on a teacher's ability to educate a total class.

How can schools address children who require basic parenting? I would suggest a program modeled after how schools address children with handicaps. Our state calls them Individualized Educational Plans (IEP), which are used by special education departments. These plans clearly set goals and the planned actions to make sure they are achieved. The big difference is that the parents are responsible for the cost of actions, not the public school system. This would cover the cost of evaluation, development, and execution of action plans required to get disruptive behavior to a minimum level. Similar to the issue with emergency room costs, if the parents do not have the financial resources, they would need to come up with other ways to make contributions. This would either be labor for the school or community services.

Note that I am not saying all kids need to be angels, but we need to address the disruptive children. Teachers are best equipped to provide the guidelines for what can be managed in class and what can't be. If a class is constantly late or behind schedule because one or more children don't respond to the teacher's directives, this is not education, but parenting. This does feel draconian, but we can no longer fail to address this problem in our schools.

13.8. Taking Local Action: Student Behavior

All of us can help the behavioral challenge without spending any money. Each and every one of us needs to crank up the level of civility in our communications. We all have opinions. None of them are right or wrong, because they are opinions or beliefs. While people's opinions or beliefs can change or adjust, it is up to each individual. Our job is to listen and try to understand, not to persuade or condemn. Before any of us renders judgment or when we begin to feel combative, we have no right to react until we have stepped into the other person's point of view. This is not accepting or supporting a different opinion or belief, but admitting that your view is only your reality and can be no less or more real than another's. Civility is about making the effort to respectfully listen and digest before attempting to move to next steps.

Children are phenomenal mimics. They mimic what we do and what they see covered by media, online, and on TV. By raising our game, how we talk and how we behave, we can have a positive impact on our children and re-establish basic norms for civil discourse.

13.9. Head Start: A Good Investment

We can't be ignoring reading to children, full-day kindergarten, and Head Start programs. The National Head Start Association provides correlating studies supporting the incremental value.[39] If we want to maximize education value, it behooves us to launch children with as much momentum as possible. It also helps assure our children are prepared to succeed once they enter the public education system. Head Start, preschool, and funded kindergarten are all programs that create this momentum. A 2010 *New York Times* story summarizes the work by these researchers on the overall impact of kindergarten.[40]

This is not to say children can't thrive without these programs; anything is possible. However, if we can give a child a positive push that will help them fully utilize our investment in their education, we should be doing it.

While I can advocate for reading to children, it's an individual parental choice. My wife and I have chosen to make time to read to our children, and we have enjoyed lots of great stories we would have never read otherwise. If you aren't reading to your kids or grandchildren, you are missing out on some fantastic books and authors. Thanks to Rick Riordan, I know more about Greek, Roman, Egyptian, and Norse mythology than I ever dreamed I would.

Adult Abstractions

How do you listen? Is the first step to wiggle your ears, maybe turn your head? How about blinking three times? With children, we tell them to listen or to think and expect them to respond. We assume they instinctively know the sequential steps. What are those steps when it comes to thinking or when we instruct someone to listen? These are adult abstractions that go right over children's heads. When you tell a child to think, how should they approach this instruction? Do they put their hands on their heads, get in the lotus position, or mimic Rodin's Thinker statue? How do they learn to master these tasks?

If I tell you as an adult to think about something, do you have a set process or procedure you follow? No, you don't, but you certainly know what to do. We never work with children to develop a process for thinking or listening, but we expect them to grasp these adult abstractions. With our children, I focused on "asking yourself questions," since that is what thinking essentially is. So, when they needed to be corrected, I would ask them if they asked themselves any questions before they did something.

While this had some good results early, it is still not a panacea for all situations. When my child slammed a door, that was one of the first times I tried this approach. You reached out, grabbed the door, you shifted your weight, your brain gave off a series of instructions, so there was plenty of time to ask questions. As the children got older and did not make optimal choices, I would ask about the questions they asked themselves before they acted. Children act impulsively, but getting them to ask themselves questions is how they learn to get in front of impulses.

Children have the same problem when we tell them to listen. How exactly do you listen? We start with the assumption that if we say something, their ears hear the sounds. Now, what happens or doesn't happen next is based on choices they make. Once they hear the words, do they dismiss them or do they take action? So, when someone is talking to them, it is their job to hear the words and make a decision. If they continue to play a game when we said we needed to go, they made the choice to hear the words but not react to their meaning. They could have heard and decided that the game was more important, but they do need to acknowledge that is a decision they made and need to be responsible. When I say we are leaving in ten minutes, I ask them how they are going to know the ten minutes have expired, and then I leave the room.

13.10. Teenagers Need to Be Vested Also

During all of these discussions around education, we tend to leave the students out of the conversation. We can do all of the right things, but if the children are not on board and motivated, we are working uphill. Elementary school students tend to be motivated, but when the workload begins to ramp up, some students begin to check out. Many years ago, I got to witness this firsthand. Before we had children, I used to spend a night a week tutoring at a boys' home for middle and high school children. The boys were there because the state had ruled their guardians were not providing a suitable environment and/or could not keep the boys out of trouble. When it came to science and math, most of the paid tutors were ill-equipped to help, so my night became science and math night.

My expectation was that when I was there, the boys would be ready to buckle down and focus on taking advantage of the opportunity to learn. I was shocked about how indifferent these boys were about school and getting homework done. Yes, they were teenagers, but there was so little motivation, ownership, or a sense of responsibility for their education. Not all kids are cut out for rigid classroom education, but this was apathy on steroids.

On one of the drives home, I figured out what was bothering me. These kids were soon going to be launched into the adult world, and through no fault of their own, they were not dealt the best cards. Given they did not have a good hand, blowing off their homework and not focusing on school was the equivalent of taking the best card they had been dealt and just tossing it aside. The biggest gift just about any of these boys was ever going to get was their free education. It was the one winning lottery ticket they each had, and they were choosing to not cash it in. Now how dumb is that?

For you or me with the wisdom of hindsight, it's extremely

clear. From the vantage point of the teenager, it may look completely different. That winning ticket may be paying out something they just can't comprehend or appreciate. They may be able to regurgitate things adults have said, but that can be a long way away from comprehension. How can you get the importance and opportunity lost to sink in for a teenager whose perception of their world is extremely clear for all they can see, but rapidly blurs beyond the narrow band of their current perception?

13.11. Flywheel Idea: Getting Students Vested: The Eighth-Grade Project

To help get the lost opportunity cost idea across, we need to implement an eighth-grade education project. This is a way of deploying experience-based learning to help students appreciate the gift from society. Each student will be required to figure out the total cash cost invested in their K-12 education. Once they have the estimated figure, they can pick any product or service that has significance to them. They then figure out the volume/delivery of those products or services the same investment amount would provide. Say, the student picked an iPhone. How many iPhones could have been purchased with what was invested in their K-12 education? Given that number of iPhones, how many fit in a shipping box, and how much volume do all of the shipping boxes take up?

We are having them convert the investment their community will be making in their individual education into something they can relate to. The dollar value cost of their education may have no relative meaning until they can associate it with something they can comprehend. Ideally each eighth-grade class could turn one of the projects into a concrete example, which could be delivered to the school, such as a tractor trailer stopping by the school.

How the math is done can be adjusted for ability, so more advanced students would have to research the real costs for each year, no rounding, adjusted for current dollars, etc. Other students could use more estimates and the presentation requirements would be adjusted. Students could also do the math for how many hours would need to be worked to save or earn that much money by different types of jobs.

If we are going to spend money on education, the recipient should at least go through this exercise to hopefully appreciate what their community has invested in their potential. The future value of money may not mean much to the teenage mind, but going through the work, and using something they would spend money on today, puts that "value" in context.

Insights into the teenage mind

If your teenager tells you they know everything, I am going to agree with them. Why would I do that? For example, since you can't tell me what the far reaches of outer space are expanding into, I am not going to hold that against you. While most adults can't clearly perceive what is beyond the edge of space, a teenager can't really understand what they can't see. A teenager clearly sees all they can perceive, and they are honest when they tell you they understand everything. It's just not everything we can see. Beyond their view it gets unclear quickly. Those items in the forefront of their vision are disproportionately clear (what their friends think, the next video game, etc.) and much more relevant than conceptual things adults talk about.

It's perception. Take going to the Friday night movies with their friends. Since all of their important peers will be there, it is a hugely important event in the evolution of their social sphere. When your teenager starts to describe the importance of this event, picture a huge plastic beach ball on top of their nose. This is what they see from their perspective. How can they be expected to focus on anything else when this beach ball is sitting on their nose? You are thinking it's just one movie. You don't even see the beach ball on their nose. When they accuse you of not understanding, they are talking about the world they see from their position; the world you see is from a point twenty or thirty years down the timeline. From your perspective, those beach balls are smaller than an atom.

Our chaotic world does not fit into nice little boxes with perfect edges allowing us to neatly stack and organize the world. As teen-agers grow into adults, their growth does not always happen in perfect proportions. Take a good look at a teenager's feet (which are bigger than the rest of their body)! This same type of sporadic or topsy-turvy growth (e.g., in brain development[41]) happens with their worldview, and this causes problems for us adults. In some areas, such as sports, music, reading, or playing video games, some children can perform at levels years ahead of their average peer. When this happens, we assume they have grown in all areas and are capable of seeing more of the world from this advanced vantage point. So, in some areas the teenager can operate at this higher level. Here they can see the world from an almost adult-like perception. In other areas, they are way down below. They can have conversations about these other areas, they know they are out there, but in reality, these areas are just a vague notion they know is out there.

I like to picture it as concentric spheres. As we mature, we can clearly see more of those spheres. When we look back, we can clearly see the paths and obstacles life presents as we journey outward from one sphere to the next outer sphere. For most, these are not smooth spherical layers; the surface of each layer for different individuals has its own contours. For some areas, such as math, sports, or music, the child may be gifted and operating at a level several spheres out (picture a mountain jutting up to new levels). While they have greater clarity about this one area (more adultlike), it does not mean their entire perceptional sphere is out at that level (think height away from the center). Conversely, that same child could struggle in some areas, so there could be valleys that prevent them from comprehending at levels most of their peers operate at.

As we get older and pile on the years of experience, the huge deltas between the valleys and mountains that create our vantage point tend to smooth out. We can still be exceptional in some areas and struggle in others, but for the most part, even our valleys have picked up years of experience, which creates better understanding from hindsight. When we look back, we can see the connection points and how one can easily travel from one sphere level to the next, and we also see where the wrong turns are. A teenager cannot look back and see the paths they could have traveled, since they are not there yet. Teenagers can't see around the corners we have already traversed.

Teenagers are living on this plane of perception, covered with peaks and valleys. There is little consistency, and at times they are not sure if they are in a valley or on a big hill. They just can't tell. When you think of it this way, it puts their challenge in perspective. It's up to us to recognize when they are on a peak and enjoy their adultlike view, but when the subject changes, they are back in a valley. They don't know they moved, but we have to adjust and shift to a new mode.

Imagine playing checkers with a young child. They could have you lined up perfectly for a multiple jump, but they can't see the path. It may not stand out to them, and it looks different from the other end of the board. They are not great at checkers, so you don't take advantage of them. However, you may switch over to chess, and since they've played a video game version of chess, they crush you. Just because they are good at chess does not mean they can see all the connections and paths in checkers.

The next time you start to get frustrated with your teenager because they just can't see what you are talking about, remember that it's you, not them, who is being unreasonable. Their focus is on what they can see. They make rational choices based on the relative importance of what they do comprehend. It is not fair to expect them to factor in variables or consequences for what is foggy and way out in the distance. As they are exposed to these adult-level concepts and points, they can talk or regurgitate what they have heard; just remember talking and true comprehension are not the same.

13.12. Weight: University and College Debt

When I was young, I heard of doctors who had staggering levels of medical school debt, but I knew that doctors would be able to work their way out of that huge debt. We now have a situation where almost any degree can pile up volumes of debt, but not all degrees get paid like doctors. The cost of pursuing an advanced degree is becoming prohibitive. How do you think that helps our economic flywheel, when it's too expensive to be trained to be a knowledge worker? Other nations highly subsidize advanced degrees, making it easier to pursue demanding degrees.

The individual weight of our personal education debt impacts our own flywheels. For us to do the things we want or to stay economically afloat, we have to have enough energy to fight through that debt.

Scholarships are great things, since they make a big difference helping many conquer the financial mountain of attending college. Currently scholarships are rewarded on potential. For some, these incremental funds are what make or break the possibility of continuing on to secondary education. Scholarships should continue making the possibility for further education a reality.

These scholarships are struggling to keep up with the cost increases of college education. Yes, we now have online institutes, but this technology is not driving down the costs of on-campus education. While the college education business model is not as broken as the business of medicine, it needs to change. The salaries businesses can pay graduates no longer come close to a timely return on investment. When the school is delivering a high-value knowledge transfer, the knowledge should have value in the workplace to compensate the educational costs. When the college or university is "training" individuals for specific roles in the workplace, the costs need to be in line with the incremental value employers receive and hence compensate new employees. Colleges and universities are key cogs in how we solve tomorrow's problems, but if the college education system costs continue to rise, the system becomes a great leak of our nation's valuable capital. Inefficient deployment of where our money goes can be an economic damper or weight on our economic flywheel.

13.13. Flywheel Idea: Different Approach for Scholarships

A potential way of motivating colleges and universities to slow down the rate of cost increase and hopefully lower the cost of college education could be to implement scholarships as debt relief. That is, a certain percentage of the students each year could receive scholarships to pay off debt (or next year's tuition) based on merit. The money or scholarships available to any schools would be directly tied to cost control to help bring down the huge total costs for college education. This money available at a college or university should help a school compete for students.

The focus will not be on those with the potential to perform in college, but for those who deliver on that potential with good grades and other assessments. Here is how these debt-relief scholarships could work. Every year, the names of, say, the top one hundred students in each program would be placed in a hat. This large pool of possibilities is to give most students a reasonable chance of getting assistance and not limiting this to the brightest students. The increased chances should help motivate more students to excel and have realistic hopes. Of the people that make the cut, the volume of available money would determine how many scholarships are awarded and their value. The higher number of scholarships increases the possibilities for each student, while the dollar value helps with the significance of the scholarships.

The funding can come from taxpayers for state schools or from alumni. Private schools would need to utilize endowments. Corporations could sponsor these scholarships in exchange for first opportunities to interview and recruit graduating classes. Stadium names tend to go to those who help get them built, but colleges could become creative with allowing other naming rights to be auctioned, with the proceeds going towards these scholarships. For smaller schools, this could open up funding from local businesses that depend on those educational establishments to produce the talent required for those industries.

Chapter 14. Weight of Insurance and Lawyers

This isn't about taking the costs out of the courts, it's about inefficient uses of capital (money). Too much money and time go into insurance, frivolous lawsuits, and CYA (cover your ass) activities. For instance, the Institute for Legal Reform's website says that US small businesses spend $100B a year on litigation and one third of small businesses report being threatened by a lawsuit.[42] The National Federation of Independent Businesses estimates that each frivolous lawsuit costs a small business $100,000. Yes, those activities drive some economic transactions, but they pull resources away from potential growth or profits. If you are brave, next time you are at the doctor's office, ask what they pay for medical insurance and how it impacts the economics of their practice.

One doctor told me it was $35,000 a year, but that was back in 2008. This cost of insurance is one of the largest drivers forcing doctors out of private practice and into larger hospital groups. Another doctor said the malpractice insurance costs are significant, but he sees the hidden costs of defensive medicine as the much larger loss of time and resources. A 2018 story in *Policy & Medicine* cited a study authored through Harvard University and the University of Melbourne that defensive medicine costs the US over $45 billion a year (2008 dollars).[43]

In our culture, the threat of legal actions (the ability to sue) can motivate businesses, individuals, or governments to avoid abusive or fraudulent behavior. Some US citizens consider our right to sue as a core US freedom. However, when the right is abused, it drives large economic inefficiencies. When we see or hear those ambulance chaser commercials, we need to ask questions. Some of the cases are truly needed, but what percentage of these legal actions are instigated with the goal of a settlement, not to correct a wrong or to protect people moving forward? The Law Dictionary estimates that 95% of pre-trial lawsuits end in settlement.[44]

There are multiple cost components associated with the legal system. I would be shocked if any of our courts are able to exist 100% on fees; in fact, I could not find any data points about how much of the costs are covered by these fees. When fees don't cover cost, guess who is funding the difference? You and me. Don't expect these costs to go away, but we should be doing whatever we can to minimize our shared costs. Big savings from reducing insurance costs can either come from more people buying insurance or from reducing the insurance payments (risk premium). The best way to reduce risk is to mitigate the volume or threat of a lawsuit. Costs of settlements and jury awards can be quantified, but what is much harder to quantify is all of the time. This is the cost of distraction.

Fortunately, I have never been involved in a lawsuit, but when I took a business law class, I was horrified at the business costs. A 2010 US Chamber report said lawsuits cost small businesses $105 billion a year.[45] It's not easy to successfully run a business; it can be even harder when the people who need to monitor the business and make decisions get handicapped by litigation. Executives, managers, and directors are pulled away from their jobs to deal with pending litigation. The mission of a business is not to defend against lawsuits, so every second not focused on the business is detrimental to success. These huge business costs force many to make the hard decision to just pay the extortion rather than incur the loss of irreplaceable time.

14.1. Flywheel Idea: Tort Reform

In some countries, if the plaintiff loses a case, then they are liable for portions of the defendant's legal costs. Until the day when individuals, businesses, and institutions are all angels, we need the power of the courts to balance these tendencies.

However, the US could adopt a portion of the European policy. We could begin with a nominal amount, say 5% of the defendant's costs when the defendant wins the case. Now, if that does not curtail the volume of frivolous lawsuits (when the main goal is to get a settlement), then the percentage would increase until these lawsuits decrease.

When the rate of these lawsuits does drop, then the percentage could be lowered until we find the acceptable equilibrium percentage.

This approach begins to put some risk on the plaintiff (person who is bringing the lawsuit forward). Today, the only deterrent for the defendant is to slap a countersuit on the plaintiff, since there is no penalty if the plaintiff loses; they just need to cover their legal costs, not the court costs. When the plaintiff wins, the defendant can be made to pay the plaintiff's costs, so a lawyer is willing to gamble their time for a payoff. For these lawyers, a settlement minimizes costs and provides a much faster path to profits. This change forces people suing to have skin in the game, so it is no longer a risk-free proposition. The goal is not to thwart all suits, but to help assure solid merits before a case moves forward.

If judges do not have the power to begin testing this approach, we need to push the legislation or vote to give them the power to start. This is a battle we will need to fight for locally, possibly with different levels or approaches to develop what works and what doesn't. It will take time and patience to achieve the right balance that comes from the threat of valid lawsuits and too many suits driving up insurance and business costs.

Maybe we can have some states be more aggressive with this approach and benefit from attracting more commerce to their state. This business development incentive (deterrent to frivolous lawsuits) may help the first-mover states reap economic gains. Will your state be a leader or a laggard?

Chapter 15. Weight of not Leveraging Our Elders

New Hampshire and many other states have an aging problem and a struggle to get employees with the skills and abilities employers need. Think of it as a basketball team with five people on the court and just a few other players on the bench. Sitting behind them are several rows of others who used to play and can still play, but maybe not full time. Our starters need a break, they can't go the whole game.

Much of our economy is running like this: people stretched too thin and doing too much. We may not need another set of starters, but just some help from people coming off the bench. This way, when we are on the court, we are giving it our all. Many years ago, as he was working for a French subsidiary in the US, a French expat astutely observed that Americans tend to have three modes: at work, on vacation, or at work and on vacation. He was making the point that without good vacations, the American knowledge workers were getting burned out and worked less intensely throughout the week. So, we have people at work that may not be operating at or near peak efficiencies. A volume of workers not operating efficiently is a weight on our economic flywheel.

15.1. Flywheel Idea: Retire Corps

We have the Peace Corps, we have AmeriCorps—what about "Retire Corps?" These people would not be going to foreign countries or teaching in urban schools, but would instead get involved in government services. In New Hampshire we have the big challenge of an aging population, so the question is: how do we flip this into an asset? Many of these people are highly talented and experienced, but may be done with the pressures of corporate life or the strains of self-proprietorship. All the baby boomers who retired at 60 or 65 could have many years left to be much more active and engaged.

This would be not for police, fire, teaching, or social work, but on he administrative side and in whatever other roles our governments require. This may create an opportunity for us to lower our cost of government and create opportunities for non-elected public service. Say you have a lot of skills and have taken an early retirement package, but could use a little income and something to do two or three days a week. How many of our local, county, state, or even federal jobs could be job-shared between two people? As part-time workers, they would not need vacation, pensions, or healthcare.

There may be two people job sharing, but the total cost we (our government) need for this role may be less. For budgeting, some companies use a multiplier of 1.5 times the salary for the total employment cost (salary and benefits). The salary for these backup people performing public services may not need to be as high, and there may not need to be any benefits (maybe some wellness contribution), vacation, accumulated leave, union procedures, or incremental costs. There could be some loss of efficiency from job sharing, more roles and documentation required, training time, etc., but if they work, say, three days a week, there could be an overall savings for us.

When one person wants to go on vacation, their co-worker would work the full week, or two others who held this role in the past could work some of these days. This type of job sharing would not work for all roles and most likely not for most senior management, but maybe enough to make a significant budget impact. As we deploy technology to improve efficiencies and expand value, older workers may choose to shift to some of these job-share roles. The influx of experienced and skilled workers may accelerate change as past practices around customer satisfaction and value delivery get incorporated. Many people are accustomed to working remotely and may only need to be onsite occasionally. Eliminating commuting helps make these roles more attractive.

Rather than conscription or draft for these roles, they would be optional for Americans who would like to play a part in public service but want to stay clear of political appointments and elections. The culture could change so that many would aspire to this type of service as semi-retirement. It can be a rough transition from fifty-, sixty-, or seventy-hour executive work weeks to not working at all. After a decompression period, these types of public service roles may be the ideal transition step as people ease into retirement.

15.2. Taking Local Action: Retire Corps

No massive federal program is required to get rolling. Start with your town, ward, or the smallest level of local government you fund. Who are some of the likely people and what are some of the roles? A growing area may be stressed with how to meet demand, but reluctant to making the long-term commitment of a full-time hire. These types of workers may provide the flexibility departments need. Ask to have discussions with local leaders about goals and plans to achieve them. Budgets and a reluctance to bring on full-time staff may be a significant impediment to providing needed services. Look for where departments are struggling and develop proposals for local arrangements. Immediate actions may not be possible, but could be planned into the next budget cycle. Contract workers may be the current solution, but compare the attitude, skill sets, cost, and motivation of a temp worker with an inspired citizen looking to be utilized and give back to the community.

15.3. Flywheel Idea: Grandparent Uber

If you are a parent with children engaged in afterschool activities, you know about the transportation problem. We live and die by the carpool coordination to get our children to all of their afterschool activities while trying to minimize the amount of time we are pulled from work. What Uber has developed could work great for this problem with a few twists—the biggest one being a local volunteer group who would vet the grandparent drivers. This vetting group will be required, through the use of interviews, reviews, and other steps, to assure that parents are completely comfortable with the driving ability and disposition of the people who will be driving their children. The child does not need the phone, but the "Grandparent Uber" driver's phone and the parents' phone can be used to confirm the child is now safely at their activity.

There also needs to be significant pool of these drivers to assure parents there is a plan to last the length of the sport season or activity. Parents need to know they will not be scrambling week to week to get children to activities. The programs may need to be membership clubs to keep a sufficient number of drivers for the number of kids and activities.

Chapter 16. The Food Equation Weight

In a global economy, we have a natural competitive advantage with our climate and soil for growing food. We are blessed with some of the best farming land in the world, but we are not maximizing the food we can be providing to our economy and to the world. Our government has become a key variable in the farming equation since the first Farm Bill in 1933. Farmaid.org does a great job explaining the pros and cons of all sections (Titles) of the Farm Bill.[46] However, we are no longer a nation of farmers. A 1988 *New York Times* article reported that the number of people living on farms had dropped to the same level as 1855, and that statistic is from thirty years ago.[47] A 2015 story in the *Economist* reported that US taxpayers paid $20 billion in farm subsidies. Some of these may be perfectly rational, but we have way too much farmland we are not leveraging.

Online, there is a chart (figure 2-4) from *Persistence Pays: U.S. Agriculture Productivity Growth and the Benefits from Public R&D Spending*, a book by Jennifer S. James, Julian M. Alston, Mathew A. Andersen, and Philip G. Pardey. It shows the percentage of people farming dropping from just under 45% of the population in 1869 to single digits in 2004, while the total population increased by around 300 million people. Taking into account that technology has increased farm yield, we are applying this technology to far less land.

We are selling ourselves short when our economic flywheel energy is not leveraging our natural competitive advantage for growing food. We should be tearing out strip malls and growing more food. Yes, we have to be sensitive to the sustainability of other countries and can't be destroying local markets by dumping food. But we should be able to find ways to maximize our yield and not crush domestic markets abroad. The food could go to storage or to world relief organizations, who could be the funder, helping the US to eliminate starvation around the globe. Only in extreme situations should we be using our money to pay farmers not to produce. Think about our debt and the infrastructure investments we are not making while financial resources are going to farmers to not grow food.

16.1. Taking Local Action: Increase Local Agriculture

Once again, Americans don't have to live under the misguided notion that government can efficiently tackle this problem, so what can you be doing in your backyard? There are many "local" farm-to-table initiatives across the country where restaurants and others put an emphasis on utilizing locally grown or farmed (animals and fish). When food is local, less energy is consumed and less pollution is caused because the supply chain is direct and efficient. Yes, the price may be slightly higher than food from mega-producers, but if the economy is humming, the total value to our society could justify any increase in price.

Demand is a powerful force, and the consumer creates demand. The challenge has always been to motivate and inspire the consumer. The demand will create a market to entice more into farming on small or a large scale. So, no federal effort may be required to increase our total farm output. This is not so we are eating more, but so that more food is produced and consumed locally. There are trends for more organically grown foods, a decrease in GMO foods, etc. and this trend can be satisfied by local farmers that a community can get to know and trust. More smaller, local farms can also help alleviate the impact of water shortages, since multiple water sources will be feeding these spread-out farms. Farmland has been dropping precipitously for years; this could change that trend. The 2012 US Agriculture Census showed the continuous drop in number of farms and the domination of total land by the largest segment of farms.[48]

We will still have large farms with all of our technology that could be ramping up production as long as there are global markets for the production. Global markets are out of the control of us locals, but if there is an upsurge in converting land back to farms, this could inspire a desire to grow, with smaller farms actually contributing to the global food supply.

Reduce, Reuse, and Recycle

Have you ever been to a large-scale landfill? If not, I suggest you do. We produce a mind-boggling volume and tonnage of garbage. Let's forget about the environmental impact, such as PFOAs leaking into our water system, and just consider the cost. All that garbage is being compacted and moved to massive landfills. My town pays by the ton for what we truck to landfills. There is a cost for disposing garbage and the best approach is to reduce, reuse, and recycle.

The reduce and reuse steps are simple, from bringing your own reusable shopping bags and washing out and reusing plastic containers to countless other ways to reduce the amount of garbage we produce. It takes effort; I am not great at remembering my reusable bag, which is why you see me walking out of stores with my pockets jammed and precariously balancing my purchases. You can read someone else's book for the gazillions of other things you can be doing. At my brother's thirtieth birthday celebration, he handed everyone *50 Simple Things You Can Do to Save the Earth* by John, Sophie, and Jesse Javna.[49]

Here is a challenge for every family in the US. Do you think you can send less weight of garbage to the landfill than we do? We are a family of four and in a normal week we barely fill a kitchen-size trash bag and it is feather-light. Besides recycling, the reason we have so little landfill garbage is that we compost our food.

We use a private company called Mr. Fox (https://mrfoxcomposting.com/) that composts food waste for homes and businesses. We pay for the pickup service, and a big bonus is that they deliver a bag of soil every spring. While our trash is feather-light, our compost bin can weigh twenty-five pounds or more after two weeks.

The volume comes from the recyclables. We don't have curbside single-stream recycling, so we separate the paper, metal, and plastic. I am incredibly efficient at organizing the car so that I am in and out of the dump when I drop off my recycling. Unfortunately, our town only takes a few of the 1- and 2-type plastics. Luckily, we have found places (neighbors and companies) that take all plastics, so we drop a bag or two of the other plastics there.

If we can do it, there is no reason why everyone else can't be doing the same thing. If our town wanted to increase the weight of food composting, they could buy a bunch of bins and develop a process where people dump their bins and can pick up a rinsed bin from the dump. Towns and cities that have a pay-to-throw program have seen great results from increased recycling.

While a fee for each bag is the most straightforward approach, weighing garbage at the transfer station or at curbside pickup is a great way to collect data and drive change. Volunteers can easily set up a scale and weigh each bag of trash. While people would not be forced to provide their names, they would hopefully provide the number of people in their household so there could be averages. The weight per person and the weight per household would be good metrics. Once the baseline is established, groups could develop campaigns to drive up recycling and composting and reduce the tonnage going to landfills.

China is a growing problem on many fronts. They are not the great market for our trash that they used to be. It is now up to us to come up with ways to make the economics work, which will create a market for reusing recycled material here in the US.

We have covered many of the brakes that suck energy out of our flywheel and weights that our economic flywheel must fight through on every other revolution. The next two parts of the book focus on the interior of the flywheel, i.e., the part that sits on the axle it spins on. First, we will look at what makes the spinning more difficult (sand on the axle). We will then look at all of the favorable ways activities can promote spinning and maximizing economic energy (putting grease on the axle).

Part 5: Sand in the Axle

Our economic flywheel can't float out in space; it needs to turn on an axle. What happens at that interface of the flywheel and the axle is where individuals can have the most significant impact to the energy of our economic flywheel. There are many ways we can draw analogies about how our actions or inactions impact the way our economic flywheel spins.

Picture a stone flywheel spinning on a shaft. If there is no lubricant, there will be lots of friction. We can measure that friction by heat, which is the energy that is coming out of our economic flywheel. If it is well lubricated, the flywheel spins efficiently without much loss of energy, so things that we do to help our economic flywheel reduce friction and spin effectively are lubrication for our flywheel. However, there are many elements that have the opposite effect, as sand. Picture sand pouring into that gap between flywheel and axle. What is happening now? More and more energy is going to be pulled out or our flywheel to fight through that sand. Lots and lots of sand is getting in the way of our economic flywheel.

Chapter 17. Too Much Money for Marketing

Nothing exemplifies our lost control of the management of our government (i.e., the Way Things Are Today or WTAT flywheel) like the massive volumes of money that position the wealthy to benefit the most from our flywheel energy.

For those providing most of the money, this aspect of government is working extremely well. Those who can afford to tip the playing field so that they are going downhill and everyone else is going uphill will think the current system works well. This is most easily observed at the federal level but can also be seen through support for local initiatives. Effective marketing is the biggest determinant for winning an election, and this marketing requires money. When people spend money, lots of money, their expectations are that they will receive sufficient returns on that expenditure. While not every candidate wins, when they do the payoff can be profitable.

While the winning candidate and their supporting political party will thank the voters, it's typically the money-driven marketing that made victory possible. The money does not want thanks, it wants results, and this comes in the form of legislation, appointments, and direction that favor positive business outcomes. If it wasn't working, businesses and the wealthy would not be throwing money away. Since having politicians and political parties indebted to businesses and industries is working, the managers of these groups are obligated to propagate the system.

If you are the one spending the money, this could feel like grease on the axle, making it spin better, but is it? Should the economic energy go to those who can afford to give money to campaigns and lobbyists? Even if you agree with that, do you still feel that our representatives should be more responsive to contributors than voters? Campaign money having more influence than taxpayers is not a balanced system, so that is sand on the axle.

Public companies have an obligation to stockholders to take actions that drive profits. If others are tipping the playing field to their advantage and a company is not, that company could be found guilty of not fulfilling their fiduciary responsibilities. Thus they could be legally liable for not taking actions in the best interest of the company. This is one reason we see large corporations donating to both political parties, hedging their bets.

Even if you feel it is morally wrong for a company to be using its profits to impact the political system, you are still obliged to participate in the practice. If you do not, others whose success would negatively impact your business are doing so, leaving you to sit idle and either take it or fight back. It is the way the system works, and if you don't play the game as the rules stand, you operate at your own peril.

The money is not limited to federal and top state (e.g., gubernatorial) positions. Large political action committees (PACs), which have no limits on the volume of money they receive, are funneling dollars to market their causes at many levels. In purple New Hampshire, an undeclared voter receives attack campaign literature and phone calls from both sides for our state representative races. This is other people's money (much of it coming from out of state) that influences who will be our representatives.

To show an example, I went to the 2018 Florida Senate race (more of an impact than the smaller New Hampshire numbers) at Opensecrets.org. Note that the below numbers are from just after the election and don't include all of the money.

Source of Funds (Campaign Committee), 2013-2018		
Type	Amount	Percentage
Small Individual Contributions (<$200)	$ 6,450,853	23.12%
Large Individual Contributions	$ 17,173,654	62%
PAC Contributions	$ 3,127,942	11%
Candidate self-financing	$ 310	0%
Other	$ 1,153,297	4%

The one thing that should jump out to you is the combination of "large individual contributions" and PACs that is almost three quarters of this campaign's money. So, who do you think the candidates are working for: all the little people, or the three quarters of the funding that helped the candidate get the job?

There are limits on how much an individual can contribute. But what the Supreme Court enabled with the Citizens United ruling was for PACs to provide unlimited amounts of money. In the above examples, it was not the dominant category, but there is nothing stopping it from being the majority of funds that fuel campaign marketing.

The above example shows that one candidate had $27 million to earn the $174K a year job for six years (leadership roles have higher salaries and all Congresspersons have separate budgets for their staff and expenses). Dividing the $27 million by six years works out to around $4.5 million a year, or a 26 to 1 ratio of campaign money to salary. What is all that money buying? It's not buying free speech, so what are the expectations for all that money?

17.1. Lobbyists and Influence

This problem is most pronounced at the federal level, but can also be seen at the state level. With politicians spending so much time raising money to keep their jobs or to support the coffers of their political party, these individuals and their staff need help. An April 26, 2016 article by Stacy Selleck for the advocacy group US Term Limits discusses how half of a Congressperson's time (up to 6 to 8 hours a day) is spent fundraising.[50]

Lobbyists help with this continual need to raise money. Not all of the business donations and money from wealthy individuals go directly to marketing candidates to the public; some goes to fund lobbyist firms who help assure the financial returns donors are seeking. They are a key part in converting investments into actions from the legislature (Congress) and the executive agencies (all of the federal departments that manage, influence, and impact industries). This is where the tipping of the playing field happens. The lobbyists craft, submit, support, and influence the creation of the laws and agency rulings that impact an industry. While they can provide a depth of understanding on topics that politicians, their staff, or executive agencies may lack, the majority of these groups are not bipartisan or representing the voters. In New Hampshire, we see "canned" legislation being fed to our representatives who insert this boilerplate advocacy into our law-making process.

The American Legal Exchange Council (ALEC) is one such lobbying group whose success has earned it much attention. As far back as April 14, 2012, a Nancy Scola story in the *Atlantic* was calling out how this conservative group was propagating legislation across states.[51] This is something both sides of the political spectrum are doing. In October 2015, *Fast Company* ran a story about how big data and analytics were being used to expose this gaming of legislation.[52]

17.2. Lobbyists

Lobbyists have come up a number of times already. As some say, as long as a government spends money, there is opportunity for corruption and there are activities to influence how our money is spent. There may not be a force that can prevent all corruption, but we can certainly do a much better job at curtailing lobbyist activity, such as banning groups from providing any legislative verbiage (writing legislation and executive instructions) at any level. Some of these groups produce the language and then find representatives who will push these laws lock, stock, and barrel. ALEC may have already provided canned legislation for the basis of the law you currently live under.

Yes, some of these groups can bring a level of expertise to a topic. But this shifts our legislative process from a deliberative one, where the best ideas percolate to the top, to one that is dictated by single-source experts. We are driven to become one-dimensional, where a single group thinks they know best. While they may know a lot, this is not democracy, but is similar to other forms of government where a small set of people claim they know best and dictate what happens. Think oligarchy or communism.

Since lobbying may be impossible to eliminate, the next best option is to create a buffer zone between our government and those who do not work directly for us. Other nations have much more stringent rules to require separation (length of time) between being part of our government and working for designated interest groups. These groups include lobbying firms, corporations, and other entities that engage with our government. Our legislators should not block off information and expertise, but when they are engaged, it must be in an open environment.

Public Citizen is one of the groups focused on lobby reform; OpenSecrets tracks financial campaign contributions to candidates. We need to make much more progress on these reforms, faster. This can happen by more people getting involved to support and drive lobby reform activities. Remember, it's our government, and voting and walking away doesn't work. Since there are so many of us, we all don't have to do a lot, just a little bit. The more coordination, the better results we will get.

17.3. The Big Shift After the Citizens United Ruling

In 2002, the Bipartisan Campaign Reform Act, commonly referred to as the McCain–Feingold Act, was a major step in capping the volume of soft money (i.e., money that is not regulated; people also refer to money coming from supposed nonprofits as "dark money") that could be poured into campaigns beyond what individuals can contribute. In 2010, the US Supreme Court ruled in the Citizens United v. Federal Election Commission case that the right of free speech applies to corporations. This opened up the floodgates for groups to pour unlimited volumes of money into the election process at all levels. Since election results are driven by effective marketing, this makes it more difficult for individual citizens to hire and direct those who provide all of the government services we pay for.

Now, the table in the upcoming "Big, Big Money" section is for money that goes directly to a candidate, so that is a good thing. There are laws that limit how much money people and groups can contribute per election (a primary is one election; the general election is another). The Citizens United ruling has nothing to do with this candidate-specific table. The US Supreme Court ruling is focused on "independent expenditures" for corporations, unions, and political action committees, not 100% dedicated to one candidate election. So, if an issue-focused PAC wants to post an ad on every single webpage you open saying "This candidate stinks" or just about anything else that can be rendered an opinion (free of libel laws), they are free to do that.

I am no lawyer, but from my perspective, a business does not walk into a voting booth. Yes, businesses pay taxes, but for a business, it is a privilege and a luxury to conduct business and make a profit. A business benefits from having a stable currency, a trusted financial marketplace, a legal system, infrastructure, an educated workforce, fire departments, and other common services to which they make supporting contributions (taxes). Businesses are not citizens or living, breathing humans. They are entities playing a key role in our society, but they do not vote and should not have a role in telling individuals who should be managing and directing our governmental services. This is compounded by the lack of transparency about what they are doing as money flows to lobbying firms, PACs ,and other channels.

17.4. Campaign Finance Reform Campaign

Finance reform is the single act that will deliver the biggest bang for the buck, i.e., do the most to eliminate the drivers of what has gone so drastically wrong with our democratic process. There are countless groups making small steps forward on campaign finance reform, but they are not all working on the same solution. Some track the money while others offer solutions.[53] The League of Women Voters does a good job of organizing these approaches by legislative, regulatory, and other approaches.[54]

As I wrote this section, I wanted to make sure I got my facts straight. Several minutes later, I had become sick to my stomach trying to understand what the Federal Election Commission laws are saying.[55]

So, let's apply the common person test to this. For the sake of argument, let's assume I am of average intelligence. If I don't get it, who else is going to understand it? It is unreasonable to think that a majority of taxpayers are motivated to figure this out.

This poses the question of whose job it is to make sure we understand these rules. It's easy to say that our government needs to do a better job communicating. However, that is going to cost us more money. As for this being our government's responsibility, I think the answer is yes and no.

17.5. Taking Local Action: Following the Money

Our government can be much better at clearly communicating what we need to understand without driving up our incremental costs. Improving how our local governments communicate to us is where Americans can step up and we should start locally. How many people are really good at creating this type of presentation materials? Those individuals can step in and do a small part. Then disseminating this information and educating the public does not have to rest on the shoulders of federal or state governments, but spreads out to local communities that must educate each other.

As long as there is money going to political campaigns or referendums, the story of where and why money is going needs to be told. We have two choices: we can agree to force everyone to contribute for an independent group to tell the story through taxes, or we can do the work ourselves. According to the 2010 Census, the average Congressional district population should be 710,767 people. If one hundred people stepped up to tell the story for their Congressperson, this is only 0.014% of the population to do this work. For our US senators, 100 people for each US senator in California is 0.00052%. For Wyoming, it would be 0.034% of the population committed to telling the story.

In a great democracy, don't you think we can come up with a few hundred people per state who could work together to collect, check, write, and produce a bipartisan report every year on where money is coming from and what it tells us? The hard work is tying the money back to what each representative has been doing as far as legislation, oversight, and other activities, and correlating those actions to where that money is coming from.

Once templates and a process are developed and best-in-class examples shared, efficiencies should go up. Imagine in the future that before you start to do your background and fact-checking or attend any type of campaign event, you can first see an overview of where campaign money has been coming from and what it tells us.

I can tell you from experience that the first stories will be much harder to tell. I have gone to OpenSecrets, the FEC, and our state elections site for research to support letters to the editor. As you can guess, there is lots of room for improvement in the timing, organization, analysis tools, and detail of what is currently available. But it is getting better over time, and more emphasis and attention from you could accelerate the value we are getting from our tax dollars.

17.6. Campaign Finance: Federal Laws

Individual states have jurisdiction restrictions for state financing of state campaigns, so I will not go into all of those details, but will call out a few states that are acting differently. In a few more pages, there is a table from the National Conference of State Legislatures website (**www.ncsl.org**) that details what specific states are doing.

Poor man's signs

I started by painting signs to promote just showing up at the local town election. I graduated to four- by eight-foot plywood I had kicking around in the basement. During the Iraq invasion, our Republican US Congressman got me wound up when he responded to my suggestion (see below) with a form letter telling me Iraq had weapons of mass destructions (WMD). This was during George W. Bush's first term, when we were in the rebuilding stages in Iraq, not still looking for WMD. See the 2008 FactCheck.org item cited below,[56] as not everyone of voting age will remember how we were misled by our government.

My idea was for our government to not ship new infrastructure to Iraq, but instead to send older US equipment. I was in telecom infrastructure and we were always trying to get the phone companies to install new equipment. I suggested that we buy old equipment from US companies to use for rebuilding Iraq infrastructure. This would incentivize a US company to accelerate purchasing new equipment and technology that would help their business. This would lower the financial bar for new purchases and the older equipment would go to Iraq. The other benefit would be that the installation and service of

---

this equipment would give the manufacturer (hopefully US vendors) a competitive advantage when Iraq could afford to buy new equipment.

So, for the 2006 and 2008 elections, I got behind a grassroots candidate (who eventually became skewed by the money-driven system as well). I took my painting idea to the next level by making a four- by eight-foot stencil from tarpaper. This allowed me to mass produce four-by eight-foot hand-painted candidate campaign signs.

17.7. Big, Big Money

Our current campaign finance rules are far from being clear and comprehensible to the average voter. The following information comes from the Federal Elections Commission website in February 2019.[57]

CONTRIBUTION LIMITS FOR 2019-2020					
	RECIPIENTS				
DONORS	Candidate Committee	PAC¹ (SSF and Nonconnected)	State/District/ Local Party Committee	National Party Committee	Additional National Party Committee Accounts³
Individual	$2,800* per election	$5,000 per year	$10,000 per year (combined)	$35,500* per year	$106,500* per account, per year
Candidate Committee	$2,000 per election	$5,000 per year	Unlimited Transfers	Unlimited Transfers	
PAC Multicandidate	$5,000 per election	$5,000 per year	$5,000 per year (combined)	$15,000 per year	$45,000 per account, per year
PAC Nonmulticandidate	$2,800* per election	$5,000 per year	$10,000 per year (combined)	$35,500* per year	$106,500* per account, per year
State/District/Local Party Committee	$5,000 per election (combined)	$5,000 per year (combined)	Unlimited Transfers		
National Party Committee	$5,000 per election³	$5,000 per year			

Source: https://www.fec.gov/resources/cms-content/documents/contribution_limits_chart_2019-2020.pdf

Here are the basics for an individual giving to the top line. Each time you go to the polls counts as its own election, so the primary and other runoff elections before the final election are separate. The $2,800 can be given for each election. All of the other lines under "donor" refer to limits on money that can be shifted from these groups to others. Understanding these nuances is mostly immaterial unless someone does not follow the rules. These are little sums when compared to the millions a federal or gubernatorial candidate will raise.

There are two big variables driving the volumes of money. First, there is no limit on how many PACs can exist. So, one person can give to countless different PACs. So, you could give $2,800 to a candidate but also $280,000 across a hundred PACs. The second big variable is the super PACs. For these there are no limits to what any group, business, or individual can contribute. However, they can't spend money on actions that directly advocate for a specific candidate. They are not prevented from saying bad things about other candidates or from flooding media channels with information telling you what not to do.

So, like my really big yard sign that says who I support and what my opinion is, I can be louder than other people; corporations and those with the most money can be even louder. Those with the money can send the most messages over unlimited communication channels telling us not only who they support, but what we should not be doing, or why someone is not good. We have leaped over the boundaries of free speech from someone who can walk into a voting both to massive influence by entities who can't walk into a voting booth.

I can't put up a yard sign in someone else's yard. And if I don't vote in the next town or the neighboring state, what right do I have telling someone my opinion about someone who is not going to be representing me? Geographical limits on where and how loudly an individual can broadcast their opinion should apply to everything but the US presidential election. If we curtail what corporations and entities (unions and other groups) can do, we can get the conversations, discussions, and debates about who represents us to be local.

Under our current laws, neither the "official" candidate nor the "official" party can coordinate the use of PAC funds. However, there is nothing stopping the PAC and the candidate/party from communicating with each other.

Political campaigns are now warped from these unlimited corporate contributions and unlimited number of PACs. All of this has combined to raise the bar for spending to beat the other choice in our overwhelmingly two-choice environment. With the bar so high to be in the "game" to keep their jobs, it shifts much of the focus of elected officials from doing the work we are paying them for to the work of keeping their jobs and raising money for their political party.

17.8. Fixing the Campaign Finance Problem

There are lots of ideas and many people doing a phenomenal job of pulling for their selected approach. There is almost universal agreement across these groups that we need to reduce the volume of money and unbalanced influence, but their energy gets diluted across multiple approaches. The end result is that nothing much is changing.

Here is a sample of some of the national initiatives. Some are focused on building awareness while others are driving specific approaches.

17.9. Public Funding of Elections

The pros and cons of each option are beyond the scope of this book, but for states who have yet to take action, this would be a wonderful subject for community discussions.

I found the National Conference of State Legislatures website (www.ncsl.org) helpful; these tables and other information come from that site.

In general, these election campaign financing control programs provide public (state) money to candidates in exchange for limiting what they spend on a campaign and/or what they receive from any one donor group or individual.

As of 2016, here is what the NCSL was showing:

Governor/Lieutenant Governer	State Ligislative Offices	State Supreme Court
Ariizona	Arizona	New Mexico
Connecticut	Connecticut	West Virginia
Florida	Hawaii	
Hawaii	Maine	
Maine	Minnesota	
Maryland		
Massachusetts		
Michigan		
Minnesota		
Rhode Island		
Vermont		

SOURCE: http://www.ncsl.org/research/elections-and-campaigns/public-financing-of-campaigns-overview.aspx

Arizona, Connecticut, and Maine have programs known as "Clean Elections," in which candidates must raise small amounts from a minimum number of voters to qualify for public money. All candidates are not required to participate in the Clean Elections program so a candidate risks being outspent by an opponent who does not commit to the Clean Election requirements.

Hawaii and Florida have a slightly different program known as a "Matching Program," in which state money matches raised campaign dollars (limited to a percentage of the campaign expenditure limit) in exchange for limitations on what they receive from groups/individuals or agree to spend on the campaign.

17.10. Taking Local Action: Constitutional Amendment

There is no reason why every single community or voting district in the country can't pass resolutions for campaign finance reform. A number of states and countless groups have already done this.

In 2015, I worked with another town resident (Diedre Smyrnos) to put a "Get the big money out of politics" warrant article on the ballot; it passed by almost a 2 to 1 margin. The article, like others across New Hampshire, required our town leaders to notify our state representatives about the will of the people. Since New Hampshire state rep terms are only for two years, I will continue to request our town manager resend the letter whenever we have new representatives.

17.11. The Open Secret

I have been talking about the website OpenSecrets for years, but as I began to compose this section, I finally got the meaning of the phrase "Open Secrets." While it may not be quite the double entendre that the creators were thinking of, I view it this way: if the information is unhidden but no one really understands what is happening, it's just as safe as a well-guarded secret. Information or data is not actionable until its story is told.

We are in desperate need of storytellers. For every single politician, someone else needs to be looking at where all of the money is coming from and the story the funding tells. Why? Until things change, who do you think your representatives work for? A politician may start out with all of the best intentions, but if they want to serve more than one term, what do you think is more important: your one vote or the money that influences many votes?

Here are some interesting tidbits from Norah O'Donnell's April 24, 2016 *60 Minutes* story "Are Members of Congress becoming telemarketers?"[58]

- A new member of Congress should be raising $18,000 a day for their reelection
- Congressional work schedule is adjusted to make time for making fundraising calls from their party's phone banks (they can't be doing this from the office we pay for)
- 30 hours a week should be spent telemarketing

Huffington Post published this from an orientation for new US Congressmen; it is also included in the *60 Minutes* story.[59]

Model Daily Schedule – DC

Call Time	4 hours
Constituent Visits	1-2 hours
Committee/Floor	2 hours
Strategic Outreach	1 hour
Recharge Time	1 hour

The accuracy of these numbers is not the point; it's the directional information we take from them. A good amount of the people we are paying to manage our government are not spending all of the hours working for us. By far, the biggest block of time in a Congressperson's day is "call time."

An October 15, 2015 *New York Times* story by Nicholas Confessore, Sarah Cohen, and Karen Yourish caught a lot of people's attention.[60] Looking at the early presidential contributions, they were able to say that nearly one half (almost 50%) of those contributions came from just 158 families and the corporations they control (out of the 120 million families in our country). For those who say money is free speech, you tell me if you think that those 158 families (or 0.00013% of the population) are equal to the other 119,999,842 (or 99.99987%) families in a democracy. These 158 families have a disproportional amount of influence on what happens in our national election. These numbers are just a point in time, but they offer a fair approximation of the imbalanced influence.

While I support continued efforts to reduce the volume of money invested in installing politicians to positions that control what happens with my money, campaigns are still going to require some level of funds. So, even when we do get a much better system of minimizing the fiscal volume and magnification of inequities of one individual or group's free speech over others, there are still going to be campaign contributions.

If you are feeling overwhelmed or unmotivated, just compare yourself to Doris Haddock, known as Granny D.

17.12. Granny D: How Do You Stack Up?

We are all busy with TV, books, video games, crossword puzzles, social media, jobs, and more. However, my father always told his children, "There is time for what you choose to make the time for." Until we all choose to invest much more of our time and efforts into managing our government, we have no right to complain. We also can't quit before we start. Change is not easy; if it were easy, it would have happened already. It takes a lot of time, effort, and dedication.

How much do we each need to invest?

For starters, we should all see how we stack up against Granny D. There are several books and a short documentary already released about Doris Haddock,[61] who was concerned we were losing our democracy to corporations and those with the most money. On January 1, 1999, at 89 years of age, she started walking the 3,200 miles from Pasadena, California, to Washington DC to raise campaign finance awareness. Think about the effort to walk three miles; how about thirty-two miles (more than a marathon)? How about 320 miles (Washington DC to Columbus Ohio), or ten times that to march across the country?

It took Granny D fourteen months to make the journey at her age. What do you think you are capable of? Voting? Attending a meeting? Spend some time to get facts. Invest in hearing multiple sides of an issue or question. If an 89-year-old grandmother can walk across the country, you can surely do more than read this book?

Better management of our government and those we hire is the absolute minimum we need to be doing. There are a multitude of choices and options, so everyone should have the flexibility to contribute in appealing ways. Granny D continues to be an inspiration to many groups; I was involved with the NH Rebellion (www.nhrebellion.org) and joined several walks.

Chapter 18. Gerrymandering

Gerrymandering may not be sand in the axle, but think of two extremes pulling at that round axle so that it is now oblong. How is our economic flywheel spinning if the axle is no longer round? That polarization is warping our axle.

> ## It is a hard "G" in Gerrymandering
>
> Too many people pronounce this term incorrectly, as it should be said with a hard "G" like Gary, game, etc. Gerrymandering is named after Elbridge Gerry who also hails from Marblehead, Massachusetts and I told the Marblehead Select Board I would help people pronounce this term correctly.
>
> Gerrymandering benefits political parties, since parties pick their voters. Should Congressional districts consist of well-defined geometrical shapes or absolutely bizarre puzzle pieces? These odd puzzle pieces group opposing party supporters together, resulting in a voting district more loyal to one party. How bizarre are these districts? For some examples, Ranker provides a list of the twelve worst gerrymandered districts.[62]

18.1. A Gerrymandering Example

Prior to the Revolutionary War, New Hampshire colonists convinced the king of England that his appointed governor should have the allocation of local taxes be approved by an executive council. Thus New Hampshire is split into five executive councilor districts. Historically, New Hampshire was Republican, but many years of immigration from Massachusetts and other factors have changed the demographics considerably. New Hampshire has countless colleges and universities, two of which are the main University of New Hampshire (UNH) campus in the east and Keene State in the west. The more liberal Seacoast, anchored by Portsmouth, is tucked between Maine and Massachusetts. What gerrymandering did was to connect the pockets of Democrats in the west around Keene with the Concord area and UNH and neighboring cities of Dover and Rochester in the east. So, this thin district (District 2 in the image below) groups a large percentage of Democrats into one executive council district, but it pulls them out of the adjacent districts so that Republican candidates have a much better chance of winning.

In a gerrymandered district, the state's majority (or controlling) party is going to win that seat. So, the primary election becomes the deciding factor, and only those registered in that party can vote for who will represent that district. In most cases, whoever wins the primary is the most extreme Republican or Democratic candidate. Moderate candidates don't survive primaries.

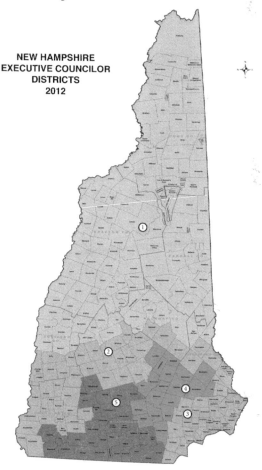

Source: New Hampshire Secretary of State.

18.2. Effect of Gerrymandering: Polarization

Gerrymandering leaves few US Congressional competitive districts, i.e., where a candidate from either party has approximately the same chance of winning the Congressional seat. This makes the party primaries the most important Congressional races, and only a small percentage of the electorate votes in a primary.

Guess what happens to moderates in the primary process? They get crushed. Who wins, well the most right or left candidate. For the most part, the US Congress is composed of people who represent the opposing ends of the spectrum. Once you understand this, it is easy to see why nothing gets done in Congress. Many go to Congress with the best of intentions but are quickly sucked into the money-raising process and party-protecting mindset. These days, the top mission of the minority party in Congress is to make the majority look as bad as possible for the next election cycle.

How does this serve you, the purchaser of all of this government? Not well, since it's no longer about you, it's about who pays to keep people in Congress. We have polar opposites amassing on opposite ends, with far too few people remaining in the middle to broker compromise. Also, these groups shun anyone from their own party who entertains making any form of concessions. If you cross the line, don't plan on coming back.

Chapter 19. Fighting Apathy

Going back to how brakes sucked energy out of our flywheel, picture apathy as a brake starting at the axle. The more apathy there is, the more sand or other objects that enter between the flywheel and the axle, keeping the axle from spinning efficiently.

Just as greed run amuck is the cancer of capitalism, apathy is the cancer of democracy. To stay healthy, the people need to be informed and engaged. Looking at voter participation, the numbers are abysmal. When I started to get involved in my town, only about 20% of eligible voters participated in the town election, which is just one in every five people. While it's certainly not an apples-to-apples comparison, a higher percentage of the town's population served in the Revolutionary War. Participation is higher for presidential primaries and elections, but how educated and informed are voters? Approximately twice as many town residents vote in a Presidential election.

A 2018 story in *Bizjournals* reported on research conducted by Woodrow Wilson National Foundation and the research firm Lincoln Park Strategies, which showed only a third of Americans would pass the naturalization exam to become a U.S. citizen.[63]

An inability to regurgitate facts may not be directly correlated to high levels of apathy, but knowledge about our country's history and government is a civic responsibility. A common business adage is to be careful what you measure, as measurements drive behavior. In the science, technology, engineering, and math (STEM) shift, many states no longer test or have standards for civics and history. Take your own poll of middle and high school students to find out the depth of education we are providing about civics in our public schools.

The bottom line is that not enough people are choosing to manage the government we are paying for. The more people abdicate these responsibilities, the more the control gets concentrated in the hands of fewer individuals. When people do want to participate, the amount of reception and inclusion they encounter can leave a lot to be desired. Unfortunately, at some local meetings you can see the

"Stay out of my sandbox, we've got this under control" attitude from officials.

At the local level, we have low participation and plenty of room for transparency and inclusion improvements. At the state and federal level, we have an entrenched system dominated by two self-preserving power brokers (the Democratic and Republican parties). It can feel daunting for an individual to believe they can impact these billion-dollar entities. In the middle, regional or county governments tend to be more of an enigma, too far from Washington to get involved and just big enough to thwart more active engagement. There is an abundance of reasons why we are not more involved, but the justifications do not negate or excuse our democratic responsibilities.

A healthy and thriving democracy is not a given. As an individual, you can feel utterly powerless to do anything about it. It is easy to fall down; gravity and momentum do all of the hard work. There is no magic force to push us back up the hill. We need to create that force through the individual choices we make. We can either choose to be responsible consumers of our government services and be educated and informed, or to be spectators to our crumbling democracy.

Downhill is faster. Easier and uphill may take more time, but the alternative is grim. Our children and our grandchildren are the most obvious rallying cries, but guilt can help. My wife and I read *Bunker Hill* (by Nathaniel Philbrick) and *1776* (by David McCullough) with our oldest child, and I was struck by the courage, fortitude, risk, and sacrifice of the colonies to win the United States its freedoms. Now slide up the timeline through all the wars that have been fought in the name of those freedoms and in serving our nation. Is paying attention to the government we buy and demanding efficiencies and better value for our taxes that hard in comparison?

Much of the nation is stuck in a rut. When many people follow the same path, they build a trail that is easier to traverse. That trail has become a ravine or a rut with steep sides. Once people are pulled onto that path, the walls of escape are steep and they are trapped in this deep rut. All they can see and hear is what the people around them are saying or what they are being shown on the cliff walls. There may be other paths (views or perspectives), but they are now shielded by the high walls and the strong pull of all the similar people traveling with them. Once in this rut, the party machines do all they can to keep people in these ruts and following the path the parties maintain. The more time spent in the rut dictated by the political party, the harder it is to see beyond or to climb out.

19.1. Flywheel Idea: Voting and Thanking Veterans

A 2018 Pew Research Study found the US has been averaging less than 60% voter turnout in a presidential election year and around 40% in the non-presidential election years.[64] Comparing the US to other member countries in the Organization for Economic Cooperation and Development (OECD), the US placed 26th (out of 32) in voter turnout.

I find it disrespectful that we have low voter turnout and then a week later we celebrate our veterans. We have one group of Americans who are willing to put their lives on the line to protect our freedom, ideals, and yes, economy, but a large percentage of us can't make the time to vote in elections. I would like us to develop a culture where voting is a core way we say thank you to our veterans. We can start simply by having veterans be at the polls and building the correlation between voting and veterans. Election coverage can have guest veterans who would be the ones to present the voter turnout numbers. The goal is to make citizens as respectful of veterans as we can be, as well as respectful of our responsibility to vote.

19.2. Flywheel Idea: Creating National Civics Day

Federal elections should be moved to the Friday after Thanksgiving and become a National Civics Day federal holiday. The holiday would be every year, but there are only federal/state elections every other year. Yes, people are traveling, others are working, but can it be any worse than a random Tuesday? Not many people go on a last-minute trip Thanksgiving weekend; we know our Thanksgiving plans well in advance. This leaves plenty of time for absentee voting. We then add a Thanksgiving Dinner ritual to toast all those who already voted to create social voting pressure. The toast can also be a catalyst for discussions with friends and family about voting the next day. We will also ban all broadcasted political advertisements starting on Tuesday, so there can only be discussion, debate, and individual research before we vote.

National Civics Day would make it easier for people to volunteer around voting, and kids would not have to miss school, since many schools close for voting. For those who want to travel for Thanksgiving and be part of the election, they should sync their alternating plans to allow them to be home during election years. Those non-election years, the focus should be on civics (a Civic Duty section is coming up).

What about shopping and Black Friday? Consumer-focused people would say shopping must take precedence over politics. While it is a huge shopping day, it pales in comparison to what we buy for state and federal government services. But why fight Black Friday? We should combine the two. We can get a lot of mileage out of those "I Voted Stickers" (include them with absentee ballots). How about store express lines, special discounts, courtesy areas, food, drinks, etc., for people who voted. In November 2018, the *New York Times* reported on groups already doing this.[65] Stores that are in close proximity to a voting place could do many things to engage customers. Really patriotic stores could have an extra hour of business and only allow people with "I voted" stickers to shop.

Elections are now on Fridays, so think what restaurants and bars could do around election results. Don't just limit it to places with alcohol: maybe also social events at the YMCA, community centers, and any other places where people gather. They could involve kids or be geared toward the elderly. Maybe there could be special events to raise money for charities. There are lots of possibilities and they would all put emphasis on participating in our democratic process. This has to be much better than the current Tuesday voting, which is just a blip on the radar in the middle of a busy week.

19.3. Getting More and Better Prepared Voters

If you go back to the seesaw image of our nation ready to break under the polarization, there are some ways to relieve the pressure caused by the two-party candidate gauntlets. In doing my homework, I found www.fairvote.org to be helpful. It does a good job of explaining the different options and tracking which states are doing what. Briefly, the ranked choice approach allows you to rank your preferences. This helps address the problem of people voting against candidates and spoilers splitting votes. Many states and other countries have already implemented these approaches. Maine is next door to us, and my local paper also covers Maine, so it has been easy for me to follow the progress there as they held their first ranked choice elections for US Congress and governor in 2018.

If you support this approach, just start pushing it for your local elections and build the support for your state. Do some research and evaluate what other areas and states did. Based on what works best for where you live, pick and choose different approaches and get started.

19.4. Local Elections and Participation

Some municipalities already have local elections on Saturdays. Those places can start experimenting now and sharing what works and doesn't work for National Civics Day.

Participation drops off precipitously for local elections. A 2014 story at Governing.com confirms that this holds true across our country.[66] Whoever shows up pretty much dominates what happens in town. There is a common thread about the mindset of the people who show up to vote, those they choose to represent everyone, and the type of management we get. If you are thinking insularity, special favors, lack of disclosure, and linear thinking, you are right on the money.

I am proud to say I no longer have to hand-paint "Come out and vote" signs. The town actually promotes the election now and we have approached or surpassed 30% participation. That 10% increase is a 50% improvement, but it is still pathetic. However, if people are arriving at the polls unprepared, it can actually be counterproductive. Showing up and not truly knowing the candidates or the pros and cons of what is on the ballot does not help.

The most valuable aspects of town meetings are the public debate and discussion. You could walk into a town meeting totally uninformed, and after hearing people ask questions and speak for and against an issue, you become fairly educated. You may have entered the meeting leaning one way, and after hearing points you did not consider, change your mind. Town meeting works great for those who are there. Unless there was a controversial measure on the ballot, many don't show up, so it tends to be the same cast of characters who dictate outcomes.

19.5. Taking Local Action: Voter Participation

Locally, there is even more flexibility to come up with innovative ways to increase participation and education. For starters, I would list on the town website or in our annual report everyone who *didn't* vote, as this information is already available in the public domain. Make it clear who did not make the time or put in the effort to vote. These people can't complain and are not even completing the rudimentary acts of managing local government services. More aggressive actions such as stickers on mailboxes could be an option. So those "I voted" stickers could be made to go on your mailbox (indoor or outdoor) to let everyone know that you participated. Anything to utilize social or community pressure should be fair game. Apps for social media would also be great. Facebook would display stars and stripes around your picture when you voted.

19.6. Flywheel Idea: Voter Preparation

This idea started around the time of the 2016 presidential primary, with all of the inaccurate information being disseminated to the electorate. If we can't get people to make the time to research the issues and the candidates, what else could inspire people to choose to make the time to educate themselves for an election? How about a contest? While individual awards are nice, I would much rather see community events. The first challenge is to get the contest award or incentive established.

The municipality could step in. In my town, we have a town dump, so awards could be either concierge service at the dump or maybe even personalized trash pickup for a short period of time. On voting day, there could be an express line for participants or winners. If there is more than one school, money could be raised for a specific school. You get the idea: coming up with an award or incentive that could apply to a neighborhood or group of people. The competitions would be quiz based. How teams are divided or established can vary. Possibilities are by neighborhoods, parents of children in a specific grade, age brackets, or birthday month or day. People would compete as teams, requiring participation by all.

19.7. Taking Local Action: Elementary and Middle Schools

Money could be put up, or the winning grade could get extra recess time or treats at lunch, to motivate the kids. For the competition, the children in the grades would need to work together to develop questions. Questions for kindergarten could be simple, such as naming different departments, asking who would you call if you had this problem? Older children could develop more complex questions around candidates, general knowledge about town services we buy, or basic facts about candidates.

Our town has an active senior group, so they could develop the questions for different competing groups. Competitions could be round-robin formats, group audience (people selected at random to represent a group), *Family Feud* style. Teams could practice and train together. The competition nights would be larger community social events with potluck dinners, music, displays of local artists, or demonstrations of what students are accomplishing. Town departments could have booths or displays focused on how they are delivering against performance metrics and demonstrating incremental value year over year at lower costs. It doesn't matter what a community chooses to do; the key ingredient is creating a channel and motivation for people to learn what is happening with the local government they buy.

Once many smaller towns, wards, or cities are having this type of voter preparation, it can be shifted to state and federal questions. Keep

Chapter 20. Moving Beyond a Two-Party System

If there is one thing that the Republican and Democratic parties can violently agree on, it's that they don't want a third party. Our two political parties are more concerned about keeping their parties in power. While the competition from a third party would mean losing funding and voters, the big risk is that no one is quite sure which party would be impacted the most, so why take the risk?

Three is no magic number of political parties, but we need to move beyond the money-infused polarization of a majority two-party system. Yes, there are tons of small independent parties, but none are significant. As the two parties shift away from the center, a moderate party may be the first place for a new party to emerge. A third party just needs to be significant enough to eliminate the drastic pendulum swings as we go from one set of polarized representatives to the other. This third leg can shift the energy from swinging us back and forth to finally moving us forward.

20.1. Taking Local Action: A New Hampshire Example

Ballot laws need to be changed to make it easier to put third-party candidates on the ballot. Many years ago, I attempted to get an official Independent Party established in my state. In New Hampshire we have an elected role called the "supervisor of the checklist." This is an elected position that maintains the voting list for the person's town or ward. They don't have an office in Town Hall, and they may not have a mailbox, an official town e-mail address, or a standardized method for contacting them. For the New Hampshire secretary of state to accept a petition signature, each individual 8½ x 11-inch sheet of paper needs to be signed by the supervisor of the checklist where that voter is registered. The number of petitioners is set at 3% of the number of voters in the last statewide election.[67]

The year I tried, that stack of petitions would be 10 feet high. For each page, you have to get someone to sign, get the supervisor of the checklist to approve it, collect it, then get all the pages to the secretary of state in the proper order. When I tried, the rule was that all "nomination papers shall be signed and dated in the year of the election," so all work needed to be done between January 1 and the middle of June. Not even six months. I tried to change the New Hampshire state law. When it got to the Republican subcommittee, this group decided they were going to make it even more difficult to get petitions signed. I had to ask my state senator to scuttle the bill.

To maintain New Hampshire political party status, a candidate from that party must get at least 4% of the statewide vote. I attempted to put a slate of "independent" write-in candidates together with the hopes of achieving this 4%. When I could not get a set of independents, I put my name out there for governor as a write-in, with a slogan of "Borne for 4," that is, 4%. I did not even crack twenty votes in my hometown and I showed up as "other" in other locations. My own wife did not vote for me, saying she did not want to move to Concord if I won.

20.2. Flywheel Idea: Best Candidate Column

I did support other independents, including organizing a press conference, but they did not get much traction. If I were to ever get a New Hampshire political party established, this would create an additional column on ballots. If there was a current legislator who was moderate and worked in the aisle, then it would be counterproductive to run a candidate against them. In that case, we could list their name in the moderate column and they would also be listed with their party-affiliated column (so the same candidate would appear twice). These moderates would be a mix of center-right and center-left people, and the management "moderate" group would be the many "in the aisle people," i.e., those who work with others to get the work done.

Part 6. Greasing the Axle

Grease on the axle helps our flywheel spin better. So, anything we can do to be better managers of all of the government services we buy is putting grease on the axle. This also covers how we manage those whom we hire to manage government service.

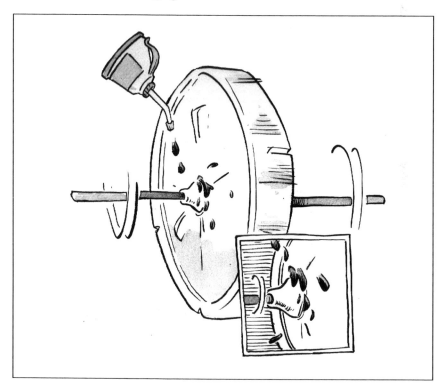

Chapter 21. Ways for Improving National Elections

As an independent in a swing or purple State I may be over sensitive to how people from outside of New Hampshire try to manipulate my opinion. As you will soon read, some of these Flywheel ideas are some of my favorites and I am hoping they are some of the first things to get implemented.

21.1 Public Speech and Volume Control

Individual expenditures are a gray area since some of us are in a better position to promote our opinion than others. Let's focus on yard signs for a moment. My family lives on what is considered a main street. So if I want to plaster our frontage with campaign signs, I can do that. This gives me an advantage in promoting our opinions over, say, a neighbor who lives in an accessory apartment across the street. Their landlord does not let this voter put up signs, so they do not have the same opportunity to promote their opinion. We own property and can display a yard sign; they don't own property and can't express their opinion. Our town has zoning laws for signs, but for some reason they don't apply to the oversized campaign signs that are popping up everywhere. What if I wanted to put up a huge billboard with lights? That is a little over the top, but if that is considered part of my free speech rights, then I can do it. Owning land on a main street enables me to be loud with my opinions.

Should we ban yard signs, since there is inequity based on where we live? Your view on this may be a function of your ability to promote your opinion. Should these signs be limited to public areas where anyone can post a sign? Maybe I worked hard, saved, and bought our house, specifically so I could post yard signs for elections. If you ban yard signs, you are preventing my ability to express my opinion. This argument goes that if yard signs are so important to someone, buy or rent a property on a main street. If I wanted more than the yard signs,

I could mail letters or postcards to everyone in town. I could take out radio ads with my opinions or have my own TV commercials if I wanted to. There are no limits on what I can do as an individual.

Now, a corporation or other entity can just as easily put up campaign signs on their property. If it is a private company, the owners have every right to express their personal opinion, regardless of the opinions of those who work there. From a consumer point of view, there are businesses in my community who will never get my business since I don't agree with their past election campaign signs. It is their choice and they are doing just fine without my business.

There is clearly an inequity here, since a corporation or union has more financial resources than I or most other citizens do. Assume we each had to pay for the signs we post on our properties. If we were all limited to putting up one two- by two-foot sign, whether that group can step into a voting booth or not, they can express their collective or singular opinion at the same volume as an individual. However, we don't have any rules that attempt to level the playing field of blasting an opinion out to others. If it were just yard signs, that would be one thing, but we are talking about millions of dollars in advertising. What does that money buy? It allows those with more resources to use many ways of getting you to vote for the candidates or referendums they favor. In most cases, these are not your neighbors but are groups from all over the country (or from other countries, e.g., Russia in 2016).

21.2. Flywheel Idea: The Following Is a Paid-For Political Message

If people have the right to free speech, we have the same right to not listen. Unfortunately, with some of our modern communication channels, the sender has an advantage. The playing field needs to be leveled so we have the option of not listening. We need a fair warning to change stations or to shut off our device. Right now, political commercials have a disclosure at the end that is too late. We need to force our representatives to change the requirements so all political commercials start with the disclosure.

All we need to know is whether the upcoming message is from the candidate or is a non-candidate political message. I want to be able to shut off or change the channel on all non-candidate messages. I will listen to a cadidate message, but if it's from any other group, I don't want to hear or see it. The same rules can be applied to printed media, where the candidate or non-candidate source must be printed clearly at the top, so the reader has the ability to discard it before its content is absorbed. No more small print on the back side. So, the lead and the largest headline should give us this information. From my perspective, this is the most important piece of information. Do I want to discard this immediately? This will also make information from the candidate stand out, since we will be looking for what we keep.

If you are an undeclared voter in a swing state, your phone rings most of the night. I will talk about those "surveys" later, but for all of those phone calls, if the call is not directly from the candidate, the phone call must start with either "Hello, this call is supported by the candidate (named)" or "Hello, this call is *not* directly supported by a candidate." While we are still not likely to pick up the phone in the first place, we need a chance to quickly hang up if we do answer. What about from the political parties? This can be murky, but if the call is not made by someone local, I don't want to hear it. I don't want people from other states telling me what to do, with their money or their voice.

We can hold our breath and dream of these practical changes coming from the top, or we can start doing something about it. We can pass local ordinances and rules that may not stand up in the courts, but it's a start. If everyone is passing local legislation saying that we need fair warning to change the station, hang up, or throw out literature, this change will get noticed. While radio ads or TV commercials may not be required to insert these words, this may not prevent the radio or TV station from preforming this service for us. So, the announcer can slip that in beforehand, the TV station can put a short message onscreen with key information, or print media can post that key text above or below the paid-for space. Influencers like out-of-state money and PACs may not like it, but if all are doing this, what choice will they have? Minimal revenue would be forfeited doing the right thing.

Why would a commercial entity help drive away listeners? Intuitively, they shouldn't, but customer satisfaction and loyalty are powerful forces and we are the masters. If a station is providing the service for me, I am more likely to just turn down the volume or hit the mute button. Maybe we will create a new social norm where we are quick to mute a station instead of changing the station. Maybe newer car radio screens could flash a "volume up" message when the non-candidate advertisement is over?

Apps or utilities could be made available that monitor on-screen information; if it is not directly from a candidate, the app will mask or hide the ad. Our armies of creative programmers can come up with other ingenious ways of pushing non-candidate information to the background.

Does this change feel less daunting? Maybe your community will be the first or the tipping point. Your local radio station could be cutting-edge enough to adopt taxpayer services. If there are competing media outlets, your demands may give one of them a first-mover advantage.

For some, this could be a fun project or activity. Having fun and improving our democracy: how is that for a novel concept? Just like Granny D did her part, this could be your time to shine! Maybe you could meet a whole bunch of new people. They may even have different political views, but who cares, you will all be working on something that you believe will help all of us in the long run.

21.3. Flywheel Idea: Return to Sender

If you are an independent or undeclared voter in a swing state, you are subjected to all of the surveys and pounds of mail from groups you have never heard of. The phone surveys are pretty easy to avoid; just don't pick up at dinnertime. Only surveys will be calling at dinner.

Third-party mailers (not directly from a candidate) tend not to be nice and are harder to stop. On top of that, our town pays by the ton to get trash hauled away. We are paying to get rid of these third-party flyers telling us what we should think and who we should not vote for. We did not ask to receive these mailers, and I want to send them back to whoever sent them. I want them to know I don't want them telling me what to think. They are not a business that needs me to go to their store or buy their product. They are certainly not a charity, as they are advocating a point of view or a candidate. However, they say they are a nonprofit and get to pay the lowest rate for bulk mail. This lower rate does not require a return address, and the post office does not return bulk mail.

Your post office barely breaks even on bulk mail. So we continue to pay more for our postage, but the political parties and third-party money can bulk-mail at rates where the post office may not even be breaking even. When I had a discussion with the US Post Office in DC, the person I spoke with implied bulk mail was close to being a money loser. Sounds like a bum deal for the average taxpayer, but don't complain since it's your government allowing this to continue.

Prior to Amazon Prime, we all knew the US Post Office was losing money and going into debt. The congressionally mandated pension obligations are a big part. Speaking with the main post office about political bulk mail, I learned there are bright people working there, but they are not allowed to do smart and innovative things because Congress controls the US Post Office. If you remember a few years back, the Post Office wanted to stop delivering mail on Saturdays, because, do we really need mail delivered on Saturdays? Businesses don't need letter delivery, since most of them are closed on weekends. What is so urgent that the US Post Office needs to deliver mail six days out of seven? But your Congress would not allow the cessation of Saturday delivery. Why? Congress works for you, so why do you let them keep the Post Office delivering mail on Saturdays?

Having post offices open on Saturday mornings makes sense, since this is the only time many of us can ever get to the post office. As with town halls and other government services, I would rather see them have a half day on Wednesdays and work Saturday mornings so people don't have to take time off from work to be served by our government. I would even be OK with them getting Mondays off and staying open later on, say, Tuesday and Thursday evenings. These changes would serve the customer.

The change we need to force through is to require all non-candidate mail associated with anything political, nonprofit or not, to pay a different rate for bulk mail. This higher rate would also require a return address on all non-candidate mail. Now, instead of your taxes or your money paying to getting rid of this mail, it could go back to the people who sent it.

It would be great feedback for some issue group to find out that 100% of the mailers they sent to your town came back. Can you come up with a better way to tell them we don't need them telling us what we should think? Also, we would no longer be requiring the local post office to perform a service for non-candidate groups at our expense. The post office could now make money on these mailers instead of losing money.

All we need is for Congress and the US Post Office's board of governors to make this change. While the Post Office would potentially see a volume decrease in bulk political mail, the higher price could lead to larger profits. If we are going to be subject to this non-candidate-funded communication, it should at least cover its own cost and be potentially profitable for the Post Office. If the US Post Office is losing money on political bulk mail, you and I are subsidizing other people's messages. To change the postage rate schedule, we need an act of Congress, since Congress controls the postage fee schedule.

Back to the fun part. Whenever you get any mail that is not directly from the candidate, you could take out your "Return to Sender" stamp and send it right back, so they can pay to get it disposed of. While this won't happen until we make the changes to bulk mail rates and rules, trust me, it's a lot of fun going stamp, stamp, stamp on these, as I had a bunch of these stamps made a few years back. If I do this again, I will have the finger pointing in the other direction as the return addresses tend to be on the left side.

Source: Stamp designed by the author.

The cost of these stamps would come way down if they were produced in volume. Groups could place large orders for these "Return to Sender" stamps and hold events to give them out. Or businesses could use them as a customer "thank you" gift, with the stamp having your local bank's logo, the name of a charity or cause, etc. A 2017 *Forbes* magazine article talks about the growing trend of "entertain or die" (to connect with their consumers, a brand must be entertaining), and these stamps are similar.[68]

21.4. Truth in Political Advertising

Advertisers are not allowed to make false claims, mislabel products, or imply unreasonable things. We have laws that protect us from misleading information. However, as consumers of government, we do not enjoy any of these protections from flat-out lying and misleading information. Considering government services are the number one product purchased in this country, it is the one place we need protection the most, so why don't we have it? Don't blame our government employees; you are the customer and you are responsible for hiring the managers of our government.

21.5. Flywheel Idea: Buyer Protection

So, how do we make sure that we are not being lied to or misled? We could have another agency, but that is more government monitoring itself. I would suggest an independent review board of people from the advertising industry who could be appointed or volunteer. In law, there is something called the "prudent man rule" (the baseline person who exercises average care, skill, and judgment). So, if the "prudent man" would not understand the difference or be able to see the truth of the matter, then it is misleading.

We could have these groups at local, state, and national levels. It's another great opportunity for people with different skill sets or interests to step up and do a small part. When there is any type of political communication around a campaign or ballot measures, these groups can monitor and be informed of potentially questionable messages. Their responsibilities would be fact-checking and applying the "prudent man" test. As the consumers and managers, we should empower (through legislation) these groups to enforce actions based on findings. They could have the ability to issue cease and desist orders and charge fines. They could also give politicians, PACs, and political parties three strikes and then they are out (not allowed to advertise for a period of time).

Political parties could be partly responsible for funding these boards through mandatory contributions. We could start with mandating that for every X dollars raised, they have to contribute Y dollars of funding. So, these boards become independent and self-funding. If the amount of work diminishes, then it will cost the political parties less each year too. Another option is to have official "paid" stickers that would have to be purchased, like stamps, to go on political signs. So, if there is no stamp on a sign, it can be removed. This may be the most cost-effective way of funding, and it would also provide a good measure of local control. If the costs of the board go down, just lower the stamp costs. I can almost feel revenue-strapped municipalities salivating over this revenue stream.

Fines should also be paid for by the political parties, so they become responsible for monitoring what the third-party groups are saying. The fines should be above and beyond the operating budget, so this surplus money would be local and state revenue, and if it is at the federal level, it would pay down the national debt. The money wouldn't go through Congressional fingers, but automatically toward paying down debt. Another option would be for local infractions to go to the United Way or other groups for a common non-political community need.

As with other great ideas, there will be a host of people who will launch FUD (fear, uncertainty, and doubt) about why this could not work. Some naysayer points may be valid, since nothing is simple. But we need to stop shutting down ideas as soon as a few complications or sticky wicket situations are pointed out. When these objections are raised, they must never be allowed to be accepted as showstoppers, but instead as challenges to be surmounted. It is folly to assume that out of the gate these types of groups will be perfect. We should assume they won't and therefore develop a process that mitigates as many concerns as possible. Remember, this is not an exact science; we are dealing with perceptions and implied concepts. Since we are protecting the voter, there is nothing wrong with starting out with strict standards, then as behavior merits, relaxing where the lines are drawn.

One of the best attributes of this approach is that it's already happening to some extent. We are seeing more fact-checking groups. It has been interesting to see in debates that most of the claims have started with an element of truth. (Remember the earlier discussion of "fractional logic.") However, they quickly slip out of the realm of reality and into the chaotic world of spin city.

Local groups can implement these ideas. No legislation or regulations are needed to get started, but the key ingredient is to assure each group maintains nonpartisan positions and is filled with community members who have earned our trust and respect (i.e., what our representative used to have to do). These would be people who have demonstrated integrity in the community and can put their own political leanings aside. As people roll out these types of groups, we will learn what works and what doesn't. Adjustments can be made, and eventually our highly efficient lawmakers may catch up to what citizens and other groups are doing.

21.6. Flywheel Idea: Survey Questions Only

Have you had a political survey call when the person or automated calling application asks something like: "If Candidate X said that we should bomb every single country, would this make you feel A) more favorable or B) less favorable about supporting them?" If you don't live in a swing state, you may think I am exaggerating, and I am, but not by much. The verbiage of these surveys can be harsh, especially when the funding is coming from an issue-focused political action committee.

The example above is not a survey question, it is issue-based FUD. If you have ever been involved in writing a real survey, it is not easy to write clean questions that are not misleading and that provide actionable data points. These phone surveys don't even try to be fair or balanced; they are purely unsolicited phone calls that trick you, the consumer of government, into listening to someone else's viewpoint (i.e., propaganda). This needs to be stopped by law or regulation.

As bad as the misleading questions are, it's just as egregious when these partisan surveys leave candidates off the list. I don't care if the list gets too long—when these surveys are cherry-picking the names they want, they are tipping the playing field unfairly. Yes, it's their money paying for the survey, but we must demand a balanced process for the information. All candidates must be listed on these unsolicited surveys or else they should list none. If the survey walks through five questions with three candidates named each time, what happens to candidates four and five? They get forgotten and the others get lifted up by name repetition.

21.7. Taking Local Action: Reducing Phone Surveys

What can we do about this? The easiest thing to do is not answer any phone-based survey. Some start off like they could be legitimate, or use a name that is similar to an established brand, but they can quickly go askew. As the consumers, we can all agree and advocate that people should not respond to any phone surveys. Those who currently profit from these activities will complain, saying that they are an essential tool for gauging public sentiment. But those people must start to self-regulate their industry. A 2017 Pew Research study reported that people not answering phones for surveys is impacting the accuracy of phone polling.[69]

If you have entered your name in the National Do Not Call Registry (https://www.donotcall.gov/) and registered your cell and landline phones, they should not be soliciting you. We can expand this to all political surveys. So, no surveys can call you, and if you do like voicing your opinions, you would lose your ability to be counted.

Local-level cable companies are major providers of fixed phone systems, with monopolistic agreements with municipalities, so there may be some ability to get them to prevent these types of surveys. These requests can be brought to your local governments to see what they can do. At the state level, this same type of push could also result in some protection, but this could be stepping on some federal toes, since much of the broadcasting industry is regulated by the Federal Communications Commission (FCC).

If these groups do not self-regulate, then we should be pushing for federal legislation to set some basic ground rules of what can and can't be asked in surveys. They obviously will need to state who they are and where the money comes from, and provide a URL address for who this group is and what will happen with the information.

21.8. Flywheel Idea: Political Signs

We talked about these quite a bit with campaign finance reform. However, here are a few changes we can make to those political signs. I would say for any sign not on private property, it would need to have a stamp that could come from the town or city hall, and the money could be used by local government. If the sign is not made out of recyclable material, perhaps it would require a more expensive stamp? While we're at it, anything over the standard size would require additional stamps. So, it would cost more the bigger the sign is.

The "bigger sign the better" faction could say that this is not fair, but really, how does a sign inform you about how this person is going to manage your money? Not much at all. You have to do that work yourself. Would this discourage anyone or make it harder for there to be as many signs, and would it reduce the number of oversized signs? Maybe. I say that's fine. For us in New Hampshire, those January presidential primary campaign signs can get snowed in until spring, and pop back up along with the spring crocuses.

This is another great thing to start up locally. Create local ordinances or laws that would institute these stamps for campaign signs. If there is debate about the money, have it go to offset taxes or go directly to schools. If the idea catches on, it could move to counties and then possibly up to the state level.

Respect for the Office

This is one of my personal peeves. I say we require a candidate's last name be displayed equally to the first name. No more first-name political campaign signs. This is not a Hollywood popularity contest. OK, maybe it has become that, but can we please make the effort to not allow first-name-only campaign signs? While we may have an issue with the person serving as president, we should all respect the office of the president of the United States. We have been a great nation and we can choose to act in great ways, so let's start with a little more respect for the office. No more first-name-only presidential campaign signs. We can start there, and hopefully this example will encourage all candidates to refrain from this marketing approach.

The rule can be fair and simple. The name on the campaign sign must match the way it appears on the ballot. If we leave all other verbiage out and just make this simple requirement, it may be hard to battle in the courts. There is nothing partisan here, just a requirement that candidates communicate clearly to the voter.

Chapter 22. Presidential Primary Process

There are a number of things we can do to improve how we elect our president.

Yes, I am spoiled, I live in New Hampshire. It's what got me roped into all of this politics and democracy stuff anyway. After looking at most of the presidential candidates during the 2000 election, I did all I could to help my preferred candidate, turning my house into a dormitory, spending most of my free time working on the campaign, and pulling an all-nighter placing the last of our campaign signs on windshields. I tried again in the 2008 campaign, this time learning that who won had less to do with candidate experience and a lot more to do with money. During that campaign I focused my activities (signs, nightly phone calls, letters to the editor) on my hometown, and while my candidate performed fifteen percent better in my town than in neighboring towns, he got crushed everywhere else. From what I learned on the ground and then closely following through the rest of the primaries, the whole process is inefficient and unfair for people in other parts of the country.

22.1. Flywheel Idea: Primary Schedule

I think what happens in New Hampshire and Iowa is a good way to start. Candidates have a long runway to get to many different places. Most years, I am able to meet many candidates in small settings. It's fun to see how candidates respond, since locals are not always a friendly audience. There are many like me checking out who these people are and wanting to see how candidates react to tough questions.

The strong tradition of paying attention and ignoring the media enables New Hampshire residents to do a fairly good job of vetting candidates. I will assume the same holds true for Iowa. That is one Northeastern state and one in the Midwest. Now, let's pick two more small states. I am fine with Nevada and South Carolina if they have primaries for all parties on the same day. I would not expand it beyond that, leaving a long runway for the four smaller states. This allows candidates to spend weeks at a time in one state and then rotate to the other states. This can greatly help campaigns minimize travel costs while forcing them into hand-to-hand campaigning versus media-focused campaigns. The four states don't have to be sequential, but can be two and two or Iowa, New Hampshire, then the other two on the same day.

Within all states, we need to do a much better job at creating efficiencies for the campaigns. Local groups, companies, and others who host candidates have to begin working together. Some groups like to have candidates in the mornings (e.g., Rotaries), others at lunch, some in the afternoons and others in the evening. We have to make it much easier for candidates to get access to groups by coordinating across groups and facilities. The same holds true for neighboring towns or cities. If a candidate will be in one place one day, we should be working to have neighboring places aligned to host that day or the next.

No more crisscrossing the state, unless they are on the back of a train. We need to get them meeting more people and traveling less (saving costs). More venues and more events should help enable more frequent and intimate interactions. Also, these smaller events do not cost huge amounts of money, taking the pressure off raising money and putting the focus on engaging voters.

Once this first round of primaries is completed, we move to the new order. We will group the remaining states into seven geographical regions. If they can be relatively balanced by total population, that would help, but keeping geographical proximity should be paramount. This allows campaign staff, media, and others to stay in a concentrated area for three weeks. This provides large cost savings. Media channels overlap state boundaries, and this improves the effectiveness of media spend. There should be additional savings and advantages, with all the debates and joint activities in the same time zone. Campaigns would have a solid three weeks to work a region, not the sporadic separations of one, two, or more weeks between primaries.

If the first group completes their primaries by the end of January, then seven regional primaries separated by three weeks would take about five months, maybe more lining up a Tuesday or Saturday. This does spread out the primaries to July. If we wanted to finish sooner, we could have the last few regional primaries only be two weeks apart. We may find that two weeks between primaries for the later regions is sufficient. Whatever method we end up with for establishing the initial order, it should rotate every four years. So, at some point each region would be first and last. The reality is that some years the races get predetermined early, and other years they're determined late. There is the possibility that some regions could never have the opportunity to be the deciding region, but no system can be completely perfect. Meaningful primaries are the best thing to help assure all voters are engaged in the process of selecting our president.

Remember, all politics are local, and the presidential primary schedules are dictated by the state political parties. We just need to tell the political parties we want this to happen. This raises a good question: how do undeclared or independent voters like myself help drive this process? If the two major parties put this to a vote, hopefully we can register for one or the other to have our voices heard. We can't threaten to boycott the primaries, since the two political parties would be perfectly happy not having us independents involved.

A good starting point is to pass local resolutions saying that the majority of residents in this voting district expect the political parties to implement this new regional primary system. Unfortunately, the political parties are not bound to implement the will of the voters. Just take a look at Congress and how they are driven more for the benefit of their parties than what is best for the whole country.

22.2. Evaluating Candidates

Would you ever hire your CEO based on a popularity contest? From the CEO to the lowest-salaried person at a firm, hiring decisions are ideally based on a person's perceived ability to succeed against a defined set of requirements and expectations.

The challenge is, who really understands what skills and experience are needed to be a successful president of the United States (POTUS)? Regardless of the winning party's agenda, our challenge is to figure out which candidate has what it takes to execute the various responsibilities of the POTUS. Yes, the strategic direction and priorities are important, but what does it take to excel in the nuances of diplomacy, lead a massive executive structure, cajole Congress to cooperate and to implement your agenda, guide and motivate a nation, and be the global spokesperson for our democratic ideals? It's a mixed bag of skills, and more emphasis needs to be put on ability to succeed.

I know I only have a fragment of an understanding of the multitude and complexity of issues, topics, and situations that face the POTUS. The ability to synthesize multiple complex issues, to delegate, and to effectively leverage those with greater intelligence and expertise are a few of the skills that separate one candidate's ability to succeed over another. Unless the candidate has held that office before, they may not have a realistic perspective of the daily burden of leading our nation. They may have run a state as governor, which is similar, but does not have the federal and national issues. They could come from Congress or have served in an executive branch that brings relevant experience. Candidates may have run major multinational corporations, which brings another set of valuable experience, but none of these roles has been as comprehensive as the role of POTUS.

22.3. Flywheel Idea: Interviewing Presidential Candidates

What would a top corporation do if they needed to find a new leader? They would start with a CEO search firm. The search firm would work with the company to understand what the board of directors' vision is and establish which skills, experience, and abilities are the most directly correlated with achieving success. Moving aside from the strategy and vision pieces, as the board of directors, how do we establish what to look for in a candidate? I think we need to go to past presidents, chiefs of staff, leaders of Congress, presidential advisors, and leaders of the executive branches, as well as possibly former leaders of other nations. Along with presidential scholars, I would say that the aforementioned group of people would have the best insights into what it takes to be a productive, efficient, and accomplished POTUS.

This group should not be picking the president, but they could conduct some structured and open-ended interviews with the candidates. We would get to watch and listen in on the deliberations of the people who do the interviewing. They would be teasing out the candidates' experience and approaches for addressing known and unknown challenges of serving in the role of POTUS. It would also serve to educate the electorate about which skills, abilities, and job experience those with firsthand experience think are the most relevant attributes.

Choosing who should lead our nation would not boil down to this job interview, but it is currently a missing component. This process should be part of the conversation with our family, friends, and neighbors when we review who we think would be the better choice for our nation. The POTUS holds a unique position, since they have the opportunity to pivot and steer our nation, so we must also vet their ideas, priorities, and direction.

These roundtable discussions with the candidates should take place at the beginning of the process, so ideally prior to the first set of primaries. While there may be too many candidates to complete all of these nationally streamed events on National Civics Day, they could be spread out over that weekend or the following week. That first week of December is a lull before the Christmas shopping is in full stride.

The burden of making these discussions happen will fall on those in the first primary states, one or more trusted and influential groups, and hopefully with full cooperation from capable past presidents. I feel that if past presidents embrace this responsibility, most others will join in. Considering the pension, benefits, and other costs we bear for our past presidents, it is not an overly taxing request we are making on them.

22.4. The Human Problem of Government Services

From the many master's and business classes I've taken, a few tidbits have struck a loud chord. I learned that if a company was not growing, it was dying. Assuming that a majority of employees would like more from their career than cost of living adjustments, where is the room to grow? People want to grow, expand skill sets, play a larger contributing role, and be compensated for the increased value they deliver to the business.

There are two aspects of this. One is that business growth creates opportunities for personal growth. This expansion creates opportunities for people to move into management functions or new business areas. The experience and skills can be compensated at greater levels when they are integral to driving growth or improving efficiencies or productivity. We spend a tremendous amount of our lives at work, and the atmosphere is much more enjoyable when the future looks bright versus impending doom. Growth helps keep people happy and engaged.

Do we want all of our government growing? If the population is not growing, do we want our police force or public works to be constantly growing? There may be exceptions, but when we don't need more people and costs to deliver services, where can that individual growth come from?

Regardless of community size, this is a problem to be addressed. A local reporter told me that our local city police department is top-heavy: there are more managerial and senior-level positions than there should be given the number of feet-on-the-street officers. A white paper by the nonprofit International City/County Management Association (ICMA) shows a huge range in staffing ratios between officers and population.

Table 1: ICMA Police Staffing Data Analysis			
Varialble Descriptives	Mean	Minimum	Maximum
Population	67,745.7	5,417.0	83,302.4
Officers per100,000 Population	201.2	35.3	465.1
Patrol Percent	**66.1**	**32.4**	**96.8**
Index Crime Rate, per 100,000	3,235.1	405.0	9,418.8

Source: https://icma.org/sites/default/files/305747_Analysis%20of%20Police%20Department%20Staffing%20_%20McCabe.pdf

Several years ago, a Veterans Affairs (VA) doctor described to me a similar problem at a VA hospital. This VA hospital had lots of managers but not enough staff to take care of the patients and to maximize utilization of key personnel, such as nurses and doctors. How do we prevent the organizations that deliver our government services from becoming top-heavy?

We have a two-part problem. We have to avoid top-heavy structures while we create opportunities for growth and advancement and incorporate the can-do culture from organizations that are crushing goals. We can no longer be the ostrich, sticking our heads in the sand and pretending we don't have this problem.

Does this situation exist in your state? It is going to be up to us to identify where our government services delivery structure is not optimal. Flagging where our money is not being optimally utilized is just the first step. The more difficult steps will be figuring out how to structure organizations so there are growth opportunities and an enthusiastic culture.

Similar to large corporations, there could be programs where people rotate or move to different functional departments. In this case it would be shifting government organizations. There will be challenges and obstacles, but Americans live for challenges.

I would like to see our institutions of higher learning step in here, especially the publicly funded ones. Professors need to shine their bright minds on developing solutions and plans. We do not need to contract consulting firms to solve this problem. Our public colleges and universities can pave the way for the future by developing approaches that provide employees challenge, career paths, and can-do cultures for our government-delivered operations.

Chapter 23. Managing Our Government

While many are frustrated with aspects of our democracy, they are also overwhelmed by the prospect of an individual doing anything against a colossal machine. My dad used to say, "You can't fight City Hall." While I had no experience fighting a city hall, it felt wrong to hear this. One individual is not going to be able to bring that huge WTAT flywheel to a stop and provide enough energy to get it spinning in the other direction.

However, that is what we need to do. It is going to take a lot of effort and time. We are left to either continue our downward spiral or to make the conscious effort to invest our time, effort, and skills and do our part. None of us have to do a lot. The key is that most of us need to do something. It does not have to be huge, just a little bit. We can be like ants that accomplish tasks much greater than their individual size and strength by all doing a little bit to contribute.

We are not going to start in Washington with our federal government. We are going to start as close to home as possible. We are doing this to build the skills to better manage the governmental services we are buying, since local issues affect us more immediately and we have more direct control at that level.

23.1. America's Strength

Doing what has never been done before or stepping up to a challenge is something our nation has been great at. American determination and spirit are a force to be reckoned with. America can rise to a challenge, we can surmount almost any obstacle, and we can do the impossible if we set our collective will to achieving the objective.

We don't need a larger-than-life charismatic figure, just most people taking more responsibility for managing our government. Believe it or not, there are more of us than there are problems. We have the power of the community. The burden of managing our government is a shared responsibility, not just for the few who currently pay attention. The first steps will be the hardest, as we move from our current modus operandi to a state where individuals know what and how to accomplish a multitude of tasks.

All problems or challenges are unique, so the approach and actions will be different for each. The common attribute to these approaches will be individual commitment to investing more of our time, effort, and skills into tackling our problems. The degree of individual effort will vary across topic. It is unreasonable to think that everyone will be doing everything. For national topics (crime, education, national debt, the broken business of medicine), all citizens should have a basic level of fact-based understanding and should be able to engage in local discussions. On other, more nuanced topics, only those whose passion, interest, experience, or skills align with these topics would be engaged.

A more proactive course of action is for each and every one of us to shift out of spectator mode and get on the field of play. No matter how daunting the goals, how steep the slope, how entrenched the current system is, we need to choose to be much more responsible for the government we are buying. Fortunately (or unfortunately), there is more than enough that needs to get done, so there are ample opportunities. Caring about the value we get for all the government we buy and being willing to commit a portion of our time, skills, and efforts every year will be a massive shift in our culture and American identity.

We should start by finding common ground; establishing parameters for the smallest level of government services we all agree we must have. This is the Common Denominator Government.

23.2. Flywheel Idea: Common Denominator Government

Take someone from the extreme left and someone from the extreme right. No matter how different they may see things, there is going to be a small set of government services they will both agree to have. That is our common denominator level of government. While nations have been trading for a few thousand years, globalization continues to tie economies tighter and tighter. This higher level of competition and lower barriers puts more pressure on nations to maximize competitive advantages. One of ours is the ability to grow food, and we can choose to make having the most cost-effective government another global economic competitive advantage.

Government is not smart enough or omnipresent enough to orchestrate an economy, but it does have the responsibility of creating a fertile environment where the natural dynamics of a capitalistic economy can thrive. Managing our government is the responsibility of all who have the ability to vote. So, we need to invest our time and efforts to force our government to be cost-effective and efficient. If we can continuously be getting increasing value from government services and paying less or stable costs year over year, that should give our national economy an advantage over all other nations who are paying more for less value.

While government spending adds energy to the economy and is needed when an economy stutters, much of it will always be a redistribution of wealth. Every dollar that does not need to go to government becomes available for other activities that can be a net benefit to our nation. This includes investment in education, business, and charity; fighting diseases; and funding consumer activities that provide value to the individual and stimulate economies. The government nirvana we should strive for is one that requires all aspects of government to be as effective and efficient as possible, so that we are constantly striving to optimize what our nation invests in government. (I am not supporting trickledown economics from tax cuts, because that is a nice theory but does not hold up to economic reality.)

In theory, capitalism (i.e., competition) creates efficiencies that help deliver better value at lower costs. While government is a monopoly, it does not have to be inefficient and does not need to have constant cost increases. Ideally, the customers and management can choose to drive it to deliver better service at lower cost year over year. In reality, what our government costs may increase faster than the inflation rate, but it is our job to manage government to minimize cost increases.

Common Denominator Government (CDG) is not a mathematical exercise, but a method for driving cultural, economic, and political change. We know that campaign finance reform is required to shift our political process away from a marketing-driven popularity contest. But with political and economic polarization and an apathetic electorate stuck in ruts, something has to change before progress can be made. Picture trying to get the massive WTAT flywheel to change direction. You can take a running start and get crumbled, or you can get low, put all of your energy into it, and push. At first nothing will happen. You have to continue to push as hard as you can. Then, after a little bit, all of that slow, hard work begins to pay off and the flywheel starts to spin. You are now exhausted, but if a few more people come along and start adding energy, they don't have to work as hard to make that flywheel build energy.

CDG will be like that. It is going to take a committed effort. This is going to be a slog, but it has to be done. It took a long time and lot of social, economic, and technological changes to get to this point, so there will be no magic panacea to rectify the situation. It must be many of us, but it will not be all of us. As the New England Patriots coach Bill Belichick preaches, just "do your job." That is what each of us needs to be doing. Don't get distracted by what others are or aren't doing, just focus on what you can do.

How each community deploys or approaches CDG will differ; there may be multiple groups working in parallel. Others may be focused on helping communities not reinvent the wheel by taking best practices and helping propagate them. Standards will help with comparisons and benchmarking, but it is more important to get going then to procrastinate waiting for the perfect solution. Americans get frustrated spending too much time creating specifications and lose patience, so it's more important to just get going. We may be veering off at 45-degree angles from our ultimate goal, but we'll take forward progress.

I picture a multitude of small vectors (different length lines pointing in a direction). When you add them all up, we begin to get progress: all those little pushes are what stops the current flywheel direction. One example is the Rye Civic League, which has come a long way in the first few years of its reincarnation (see the later sections), but we still have much more that can be done, as long as we are always working to get continually better, making adjustments and improvements.

Not all communities will move at the same pace, but some will get perpetual systems in place (like civic leagues or town administrators cut in the mold of Durham, New Hampshire's Todd Selig, who releases Friday updates that started as an e-mail and have only gotten better).[70] The next step would be to apply CDG to larger areas of our government, such as the full city, regions, counties, and states. We could develop the ability to have discussions and debates and to self-educate each other on the views and facts that surround national issues.

Through these new skills, participation, and communication norms, communities can then take actions locally that address national challenges (reducing total energy consumption, improving health and nutrition, protecting the environment, etc.). Communities will develop the ability to get different facts, have discussions, and build networks of local people that engage with each other, having different opinions while still working together. These skills will be a base for when our state and federal political leaders start discussing major investments of our money. Other people's money that drives marketing campaigns for issues and candidates, lobbying, and other outside influence will be pushed aside and be replaced by informed, educated, and involved government consumers.

23.3. CDG is Economic

The goal is not to have some Kumbaya society where we all play nicely together, but to drive the economy. That energy is what provides jobs, and most of us spend the majority of our lives working. We all want to be paid well and to have job security. Money makes money and always will, so the rich will continue to get richer. But with all of our eyes open and fully vested in managing our government, the playing fields will be less tipped. Upward mobility should be more attainable, allowing our flywheel mass to be more evenly distributed along the flywheel radius and not overly skewed to a minuscule percentage of our population.

That economic energy is what enables us to stay on top of our maintenance and improvement investments that keep our economic flywheel spinning smoothly. Think of it as keeping the axle greased. If it gets covered with sand (crumbling infrastructure or inefficient systems), then the wheel doesn't spin as well, or the debt load requires more energy to fight through. Remember, not all debt is bad, but when the wheel is spinning slowly, too much debt can be crushing. When we have lots of momentum (size and speed), we may not even feel the debt burden. When that wheel is humming, it takes less external energy to keep it going, and additional investments can be made without increasing taxes.

With CDG, we start at the bottom and drive up for better value at less costs year over year. Fewer individual and business assets going towards taxes will shift more to us for leisure retirement or additional business investments. This is not the misleading concept of trickle-down economics that has lifted big boats and has let smaller boats sink, but a more balanced economic stimulus. Now, any other nation can do the same thing, and the smart ones will follow suit, but we have the opportunity to establish the first mover advantage and a lead we should not vacate.

Former chairman of the Federal Reserve Alan Greenspan used to talk about productivity growth, which is getting more out of the same investments. To grow economies, the economy needs to add value. Think of manufacturing or food production. You are creating something that has value. For net new value, you are rewarded for what you have created. Manufacturing is a smaller part of our economy, so we need to offset this shift with more food production, new businesses and technology, and the ability to get more out of the investments we make.

Our total government is the largest services business on the planet. CDG is the first step in driving productivity growth in our massive services company. We are starting with what we agree we must have; however, that is just a fraction of the government we have.

Chapter 24. Getting Started with CDG

First, we stop fighting over raising taxes or cutting government. We all have different opinions and that is fine. We start with what we can agree on. So, maybe just police, fire, and schools at the local level. This is CDG. It does not have to be the entirety of CDG, but it is something to get started with to build the tools, methods, and mindset for working together to manage this starting set of services.

We begin with putting our focus on this CDG and work together to make sure we are getting better services at a lower cost year over year. It may sound simple, but it will be more complex in the implementation. As a nation, we need to develop and excel at these skills. It starts with being extremely clear on what value each part of government should be providing (i.e., our expectations) and then quantifying how to measure it and establishing the bar (i.e., what is good or bad). With the baseline established, we need to hold each CDG entity responsible for making annual improvements and use the baseline to flag not doing so as failure. This may require additional investments, but many of us know from business that IT, systems, re-engineering, automation, and other investments are absolutely necessary to remain competitive. This also holds true for a service business, and our government is the world's biggest services corporation.

The process of getting our CDGs under control will convert us from pitiful consumers of government to fussy, high-demanding customers who settle for nothing less than excellent services and high value. Once we can get to this point, it is much easier to have discussions about the next layers of government. These can be aspects of our government that not everyone agrees are essential or should be done. However, as we have these discussions, the services in question will be evaluated on the basis of everyone being able to clearly understand the expected value, and how we will measure them and know that they will be working to become continuously cost-efficient and effective. In other words, we could begin to actually trust our government to be respectful of our money.

The CDG-focused process needs to happen at all levels: local, state, and federal. This creates opportunities for everyone. You can argue this is a choice. Our culture needs to change so that choosing to be responsible for managing our government is something we all want to do.

24.1. Taking Local Action: Steps Toward CDG

There are not many ways to measure your local economy, but this is where the impacts will be felt first on both flywheels. These local activities are the intersection of stopping the WTAT flywheel and helping to maximize economic flywheel energy. Start small, learn, and build. The key is to only bite off what you can chew. Communities need to start with elements of government that are small and locally controllable. Where can we find autonomy and local control? There will be more hands-on control in smaller communities and more of a challenge in larger cities. The complexities from a city being the smallest level of government could mean the first elements that show improvements are smaller sub-departments delivering government services. In some situations, there may not be controllable and delineated budgets or control mechanisms at precincts or local fire stations, so more budget assumptions may need to be made.

Some will be tempted to say all government services are needed. They may be right, or they may be wrong, but looking at all government services is not the first step. Start with just the top two or three and leave the rest for later. Ask what purpose or role this service provides. How it evolved is not why we have a service; the focus needs to be on what value it provides now. No one is going to say we don't need fire protection. A better question is, how much fire protection do we need? Do we know how many fires we have versus twenty years ago? Is it comparable, or is there a larger level of risk we are willing to accept based on new building materials, smoke detectors, sprinkler systems, and mutual aid? Are there other "services" the fire department provides beyond fire protection?

There are initial dimensions to these questions. The first is: what do we need? And the second is: what total services are we getting? To address the need, we should be asking hard questions. These are the strategy or planning questions. Based on the population and other trends, what is it we need now, and what do we need moving forward? We can then construct Venn diagrams of the available services in an area to figure out if we have too much, not enough, or just the right amount of service equipment for that area. For example, I built a table to show all of the fire equipment my community has in the adjacent small towns and the abutting city's Station 2 that borders three towns. From this table, it is clear how over-equipped the area is. There are just not enough people employed at the fire departments to use any sizable percentage of the equipment at one time. The reality is that if multiple things were happening, on-duty staff from other areas would arrive before we could get our extra local equipment onsite.

With a rapidly aging population, we need more ambulances and paramedics than big fire apparatus. Government tends to grow, but it is our job to ask the questions about rightsizing government. Many areas of the country are regionalized, so those regional services would not be the best places to start. These communities, like larger cities, may need to focus on other government services as they build the skills to ask questions and measure value delivered.

For your local police department or public works department, do you have the most cost-effective or the least cost-effective department? The evaluation must include not just employee/budget costs per people or area served, but also the services that group provides. You may be paying much more for a department than, say, a cousin in a different county, but if they are getting far less services, maybe you are getting more value for what you are spending.

Exact comparisons may be difficult, but we do not require the precision of a lunar landing. Ballpark comparisons should be sufficient for initial evaluations. Be wary of those who insist comparisons can't be made if everything is not exact apples to apples. Of course we would like comparisons to be as accurate as possible, but in many cases, close or approximate should be sufficient to identify if we are overpaying or underpaying, or if the services are not meeting our expectations.

A good starting place for comparisons is the budgeting code standards many states require for municipal budgets. If you are not involved with finance or accounting, you may not be familiar with charts of accounts, which are the structure of financial record-keeping. Businesses create a structure customized to their current business organization, but states require a level of consistency across municipalities. This standard coding for budgets and actual spending will help with comparing town versus town or city versus city. Note that it is not cut and dry, and some assumptions and manipulations will be made. For example, my town's police and fire department share a building, but building costs are in a standalone account, so these costs should be reallocated to each department.

There will be quantifiable metrics, such as what is spent, staffing, percentage of benefit costs, and number of people or area served. These numbers can then be analyzed by people in the community who have the analytical skills, as well as by others who can describe the story the numbers present. This story may include points such as a constant rate of growth, changes in ratios between equipment and employees, or trends in salaries or hourly and overtime costs. Nothing may leap out as significant, but no one is doing this analysis for us, so we need to do this work to better monitor and manage what we buy. Resist the temptation to have departments tell us what is going on. They may need to open their respective kimonos, but it's the consumer's job to determine value, not the stores or businesses providing the services.

Before we declare we are getting the best deal for our money, we must also tally what services are being provided. Some towns have trash pickup, others don't. What other community services do the police, fire, public works, recreation department, or library provide? To defend budgets by showing value, some departments may be tracking their own activities already. Our local library has posts about how they compare in statewide usage statistics. Similarly, our recreation department reports number of programs and people involved. Qualitative aspects are how easy or hard it is to work with the local government. Is department information online? Can you get service on Saturday morning? Are there extended hours one day a week? Businesses continuously use surveys to measure the qualitative aspects and make improvements.

24.2. Taking Local Action: Analyzing Budgets

At a budget committee meeting, I was lambasted when I asked that since we are paying much more for something, what more are we getting than last year? Afterwards, I started with what the town provided and I plugged the data into a spreadsheet. At first, I just grouped departments into single buckets so I could see trends. Eventually, another Rye Civic League member, Peter Crawford, took over the data and charting, while I focused on the story. For the past few years, we have provided residents an analysis of the town and school budgets (posted on www.ryecivicleague.org).

The challenge is that our attention is only on our town. Step two is to start looking at comparable communities with the same tools. We have done this a little bit, such as looking at how much government there is per person. When our police chief wanted to add an officer, I graphed the number of officers against population and could easily see overstaffed, understaffed, and others clustered around the data curve.

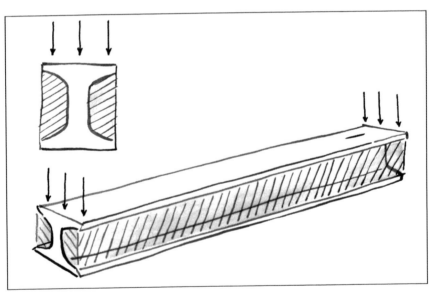

For the volume of money we spend on government, it is shocking how little we know about effectiveness. The government snowball keeps on rolling and we never get to look at the inner layers to see if we need them or not. Have you ever wondered why a steel I-beam is used instead of a solid rectangle? A majority of the load (stress and strain) is carried by the top, bottom, and material at the center. The value we get from all of the other material is negligible. That is why the other material is removed, leaving us the I-shaped beam. The removed steel was not doing much of the work. The beam strength is only reduced slightly, there are material cost savings, and the beam weighs much less. If you need to carry more of a load, you are better off with a larger I-beam than using a solid rectangular beam. Figuring out which government services are an I-beam section carrying the load and which are the sections that provide little incremental value is up to us to figure out.

24.3. Flywheel Idea: Purchasing and Investment Committee

We should change the name of every budget committee to the "purchasing and investment committee" to put more onus on what is happening with our money. Everything we fork over for local taxes is to either *purchase* government services or to make long-term *investments* in roads, equipment, buildings, recreation fields, etc. A budget is an organizational step, if the company revenue goal is X amount and Y is the funds departments will need to make this revenue goal. From the voter's perspective, the government budget tells us what we are purchasing for this year and what long-term investments will be made. Governments do not have revenue goals like a business; the goal needs to be maximizing services at lower costs and making sure our economic flywheel is constantly building energy.

24.4. Shareholders (Voters) Are Responsible for the Board of Directors (Who We Elect)

Today, when candidates run, they tell us about what they want to do and what their platform is, which is fine if we are trying to differentiate between candidates. However, the process is out of alignment with how an effective board of directors should operate. While the people the board hires can come to the table with ideas and suggestions, it must be the board of directors that, as the name says, directs. The voters are the ones who should be providing the direction and expectations for what we want to happen. The question is, which candidates are best suited to deliver results and meet the goals we establish?

Towns and cities have master plans that should be continuously reviewed and updated. The master plan is what sets the direction for zoning laws, what the planning boards should and should not be doing, and guidance for the activities of the rest of the government. Most corporations and businesses have annual and/or three-year strategic plans to guide executives and the actions of management. Whether it be master plans or different types of guiding documents, we are responsible for making sure these are in place and constantly maintained.

Wherever and whenever we are electing representatives, the voters need to clearly communicate what they are expecting their representatives to accomplish. At all levels, if we are hiring and paying people to get something done, it is not up to them to set the goals and objectives. We must set the expectations and how they will be measured. We need to establish how we will determine if the service is improving. While a community may agree to make investments in tools and other activities, these should be viewed as capital investments. The operational costs to deliver the service are what should be flat or decreasing with improved efficiencies. So, budgets may grow over time or with the need for capital expenditures or investments that enable future productivity gains.

For example, in the Northeast, the government owns and maintains the snowplows that keep roads cleared. This equipment is a capital expense that must be bought as capital budgets. However, what we spend on people and gas to keep the roads cleared are the operational costs. How much snow falls in a given year is an uncontrollable variable; the focus should be on finding ways of minimizing and reducing the operational costs of keeping the roads cleared. It could be anything from determining the hours when the plows are out working to maintenance. For example, when it comes to snow removal, there could be different guidelines for clearing roads on a weekday versus weekends or holidays, when the overtime expenses are greater and fewer people need to get to work or school.

24.5. Local Discussion and Debate

Governments and elected officials are not omnipotent. It is unrealistic to think that our governments or politicians can singlehandedly fix our largest challenges. A strong partnership and committed support from us—the consumers of government services—are required to reverse course on national challenges. Currently there are many groups across the country, working diligently and occasionally with well-coordinated national organizational structures, providing examples and lessons for driving bottom-up change.

Seldom will there be elegant solutions to complex problems. The foundation for broad-based changes is built on a strong base of trusted information, understanding, engagement, and local actions. This doesn't mean that everyone will agree on everything, but a majority of eligible voters can come to a consensus and compromise on clear expectations for our government and elected officials.

For a national dialog to be constructive and productive, discussions and information need to occur interactively at the local level. We all know that if you torture numbers long enough, you can get them to support any position. To combat spin city and marketing driving misinformation, local efforts must first define what the problems are and discuss solutions' pros and cons. The in-person discussions and dialog (not lofting attacks via blog posts) create the filters and exposure to alternate perspectives that filter out the misinformation. The local community responsibility is to facilitate the dialog and debate between people, assuring that voters comprehend the trade-offs, risks, and implications of different options.

For example, the community can't just be complaining about schools. What are our expectations for all of the education we are buying? How are we going to know our expectations are being met? How will we measure this? It can't be voting for a school board and telling them to give us a report at the end of the year. Are we setting parameters around cost increases we are willing to accept? Conversely, what kinds of efficiencies and productivity gains are realistic? How do we know if the schools are doing a bad job budgeting or a great job? Can we determine how much budget surplus is acceptable, or did they ran out of money? What defines good or bad budgeting—maybe budgeting accuracy is not the best approach to maximizing the return on our investments? Yes, it's not simple, but who doesn't like a good challenge?

Chapter 25. Managing Who We Hire

How would you like to never get performance reviews, or to know they have no impact on future pay increases? Would you be happy if people working for you were getting performance appraisals from their direct managers, but you were not allowed to see this information? Unfortunately, most of the people we are hiring (i.e., voting in) or funding the salary and benefits for are operating in some form of this model.

If we are going to manage elected officials, we need data points and analysis that help us understand the value we are getting, and an established baseline to measure improvements. Is my city council better than your city council? As a group, how do we know how Congress performed over the past term? Yes, how they vote is a data point, but does it matter if Congress got nothing done, made no improvements, and figured out no ways to make sure we are getting better service at less cost? We need to be looking at how people perform in individual roles (a mayor), as a member of a group (representative or board member), or in an executive department (hired by those who are managing for us).

25.1. Elected Bodies (People Who Are Part of a Group)

Elected bodies need to be measured on what they accomplish collectively. If the body fails to meet goals, all individuals failed. It is our responsibility to make sure every elected body is effective. We must insist that at the start of each term or session, each elected body agrees on and then communicates to us what they are going to accomplish that year. The elected government body must agree on how we can measure their degree of success. There are typically two sets of activities. One is the basic operation (budgets, filling roles, annual responsibilities) and the other is the tactical priority for that term. These could be making infrastructure investments, improving service delivery, addressing critical needs, and all other actions the body chooses to tackle.

For basic operations, there should be minimum expectations, such as completing the budget by a certain date and making sure information is available and digestible to the public in a set timeframe. The elected body should propose and set these measurable metrics and either report out or have the public monitor. Using the earlier example of school board budgets, the question is not whether the budget is up or down, but whether it was sufficient to meet expectations. Was there a shortfall or too big of a surplus? If there were not enough funds allocated, either the budgeting was not done well, or there were clear and well-known circumstances that caused the problem. Where I live, a year with many snowstorms can quickly drain a public works budget, even more so if the snow falls when employees get overtime pay. Most groups run surpluses, so they budget conservatively in order to not run out of money. When are surpluses extensive? What is an acceptable budget surplus? Some states allow school boards to retain no more than 4% (New Hampshire is 2.5%) of a budget surplus year to year.

The next set of operations is more difficult, especially if the elected body is divided across political parties. Each group needs to develop a way to agree yearly on what they will commit to accomplishing. Say the group has six goals that all agree to accomplish. How they determine which goals is up to them, but all members should have a say. So, if there is a political majority, the minority should at least have their top priority included. It should not be the majority's way or the highway, but a fair representation of the members. Once the list is set, everyone is personally responsible for achieving all the publicly committed goals, not just the ones their political side is driving.

If they can't agree on the list, then they should step aside, and not be returned to that job (i.e., reelected). The responsibility is to provide value, not to get paid for not getting things done. What would happen in your job if you only did the things you wanted and spent the rest of your time preventing other people your company employs from getting their work completed? It is easy to picture the US Congress—the ones we pay over $174,000 a year in salary and benefits, while also funding their supporting staffs. Now they clearly are not sitting on their hands; they do many things for their constituents while in office.

But they are group members, not in isolated positions. The collective job is to conduct the business we have assigned, not the goals of a political party. When was the last time all members of Congress came out at the beginning of the year and said, regardless of party, we are going to work together this year and here is what we are committing to complete by the end of the year?

25.2. Taking Local Action: Managing Groups

The work starts with us, not by telling the US Congress what to do, but by starting to demand that goal setting and measured progress are established locally. Local boards (select, planning, zoning, conservation, etc.) are not creating much change, but they can set operational milestones for improvements in the services delivered. For example, what can a land use board do to reduce cost and time for the individuals and businesses they interact with? For a select board, what will they accomplish this year, what could make working with them easier, and what would improve the value the public gets from their effort? While many of these may be volunteer boards and some communities may be currently strapped finding people to serve on boards, that will need to change as we all become more active in effectively managing our huge annual investments in government services.

The labor force for these activities will need to come from those of us who are motivated to not only meet the requirements of the board, but to move the needle in how the board provides value. Many years ago, before I started coaching our children's sports teams, I served on a local association board. Before I started, past boards just did what was needed to keep the lights on (i.e., to just keep the organization going). The board that preceded me had started the process of systematically addressing foundational problems that made running the association difficult. They started with the basics, like getting the financial books in order and recording what assets the organization owned. The next round of board members defined roles and responsibilities. We tried some things that worked, and other ideas that did not. The next group scrapped some of the things we did and made changes that were uncomfortable at first but, in the long run, were clearly better for the association.

The culture of this association changed to one where making incremental improvements was the norm, the mindset of continual improvement, and not constrained by "This is how it has always been done." That's what most impressed me. It wasn't just about getting the service delivered, but about asking how the service could be incrementally improved year after year.

Here is another example of that mindset in action. When I was completing the yearlong Leadership New Hampshire program, we got to spend a morning with the New Hampshire Supreme Court. One of the most interesting parts was learning that the court is also responsible for the operations of all other New Hampshire courts. These judges were well steeped in the challenges of massive process changes, even as they were pushing all the lower courts to strive to be as paperless as possible.

The goals each government body commits to must be put front and center. Not only must we see these goals, we must pay attention to what they are and put our officials' feet to the fire if they are not being met. If local newspapers are still thriving, they can be a primary vehicle for driving awareness of what our elected groups commit to accomplishing. This would be information tables in the papers or posted on local websites. We can even choose to fund a large flatscreen TV installed in a public spot that would continually display updates on these metrics (goals met, days late achieving actions, milestones completed on projects, etc.). The key is that we don't just check at the end of the term, but that we are focused on monitoring progress throughout the year.

While this approach can start with elected bodies, it does not have to stop there. Many executive (federal, state, city, and town) departments, everything from the EPA to your local department of public works, can have specific goals aligned to the value they are providing and improvements they are making. Over time, this will help eliminate the "do-nothing Congress" we pay for. If they are not getting things done and making our government more effective and efficient, then we are wasting our money.

25.3. Evaluating the Individual

If there is a board with five people, do they all do the same amount of work? Are they all equal in contributions and effectiveness? Most likely not. It is more likely there are stars, dead wood, and others somewhere in the middle of the spectrum. Whether or not this group meets the group's stated goals and metrics, we must also have an indication of how effective they are as part of a team of people.

If you are attending meetings, you can watch how the board members work with others, the questions they ask, whether they are prepared, and whether they volunteer for additional tasks. Do they know what they are doing or do they have an alternate agenda? If not, how do we know if they are the best or the worst? Voting records and attendance are just data points, as an up or down vote can be much more complex than a black or white answer. Their peers may not be critical of individuals, since they need to continue to work with each other and negative comments could be detrimental to working relationships.

25.4. Flywheel Idea: Monitoring Individuals

We are going to have to come up with methods and practices for getting us the information we need. Different communities or groups may select different methods or systems. The important thing is that we start taking the steps to provide more information than we have today. One approach is to have people an individual engages with complete an anonymous review of how they think the person is performing. It could be survey questions, using the many online tools that compile and analyze information, or it could be open-ended questions. Many businesses and hopefully public entities utilize a 360-degree model that collects feedback from superiors, subordinates, peers, and others people engage with. I personally like to get this type of data because some people can be better with one group than another. Not only will this data be helpful for us, but as constructive feedback it also assists the individual in improving.

The job performance information could also be compiled and reported by citizen volunteers who attend meetings or regularly engage with that person. Peers could also set the measurement areas, metrics, and evaluation method that would become available to the public. For anyone we elect, it is our responsibility to put systems in place. For employees of government who are hired and managed by people we put in place, we have less responsibility, but this information should not be completely hidden from the public domain. While there are laws that protect the "reputation" of individuals, either we're forced to have a high volume of trust in the people we hired, or more information should be available for our evaluation.

Should the public be sticking its noses into the business of every school department, police force, fire department, building inspector, library staff, and others? Most likely not, as this starts to become micromanagement, but there should be some aggregated level of feedback on the progress of employees. If they are not getting any increase in salary, besides some adjustments for inflation, there is not much for us to manage. However, if they are getting increases in pay beyond the cost of living, then we can expect them to be providing more or better services for that incremental cost we are incurring. If they are not providing better service or more value, why are we paying more if we are not getting any incremental benefit? If they are a rock star, we should know that and be willing to pay more.

In some cases, increased value or better service may be hard to quantify or to demonstrate, such as a person who does not serve the public directly and whose customers are all public employees. While experience can bring a measurable increase in efficiencies, there may be some valuable experience that is harder to quantify. Many public service roles have an element of intuition and accumulated knowledge that can enable people to read situations, understand ramifications, and possess other skills that help them be incrementally better and hence more valuable.

This will never be an exact science, nor does it need to be. What we need is directional (surveys, polling data, a few direct interviews) or comparable types of data points (ranking against peers or others with similar roles), which help us know if we are getting good value or if we are overpaying. For example, when we have good teachers or teachers that are continuously getting better, or if we have teachers that are not doing a great job, kids, parents, teachers, and administrators have likely noticed and can tell us. How else can we make sure those we hire to manage our schools are addressing problems? Once again, test scores are a metric, but they fall far short of providing enough granular information to effectively manage.

25.5. Hiring for Individual Roles

While much of what we discussed earlier can apply to someone we hire for a specific role, such as a mayor, a town clerk, or county positions, we can be much more granular about roles we know more about. If we hire an employment agency to find an ideal person, we need to provide guidance to say what the requirements are to succeed. Experience, certifications, and training are easy to qualify, but what are the intangibles that differentiate the stars from the "just okay" people for this job? If we get candidates running for a position, we tend to ask their views on one issue or the other, but we should first be focused on what it takes to succeed in this role. If they don't have the skills, disposition, and other attributes to excel in the job, their views or position are less important.

For the individual roles the voters directly hire, the same or similar performance metrics we develop to understand how effective they have been in office can also be used as the base of requirements when it comes to evaluating who we want to hire. As we develop these specific success attributes and put them in the public domain, this will greatly help us at election time. We need to be doing this work if we want a direct correlation between the ability to succeed and getting elected, versus the current system of who can raise the most money for manipulative marketing.

The idea is not to go metrics-crazy, but to look at what it takes to succeed, along with how someone performs in a role, much more critically. It's hard to create a metric that would say which mayoral candidate is better suited to lead in a crisis. We must rely on our people instincts from direct interaction rather than choreographed commercials, sound bites, or negative information from the opposition.

It may feel like a lot of work, but there are lots of people in this country, and once something is created it is much easier to adapt, modify, and enhance than to build from scratch. While you may not be able to change the way we elect the POTUS, you do have influence in what happens in your local community. So, start doing this where you live. As this becomes the norm or establishes the base for what is to be expected, we then can impact the process that involves people across our own municipal and then state borders.

25.6. Flywheel Idea: The Right Type of People to Hire "In the Aisle"

Jumping to state and federal governments, we use the term "crossing the aisle" when a member of one polarized political party offers to work with someone who has the same job, but whose campaign is funded by a different set of money. If we expect Congress to pass any bipartisan legislation, then we need to get some of our well-paid and amply benefited legislators to use this slogan: "In the aisle, where the real work gets done." We can start with any independents in Congress today, or perhaps the No Labels Problem Solvers (more information at https://www.nolabels.org/leaders/) are brave enough to start sitting in the aisles to make a point. They should sit in the aisles during discussions and engage with others in the aisles. . Soon people will acknowledge that it's in the aisles where all the work for the country gets done. So, we want people who are "in the aisle." We should not be reelecting anyone who spends most of their time "out of the aisle," i.e., only working with their own political party.

Chapter 26. Managing Government-Funded Projects

As a teenager, I was in the back seat going up north with my father driving and my father's friend (the late Mr. Bill Willis) riding shotgun. As we drove by highway construction projects with many construction workers standing together, clearly not working, Mr. Willis would roll down the window and scream for them to get back to work. One day, I summed up the courage to ask Mr. Willis why this bothered him so much. He went on to explain that he could never, ever afford to have that many workers standing around not working in his own construction business. The fact that our taxes were paying people to stand around and watch others work got under his skin.

From that point on, I have always taken notice to see how many people appear to be working and how many people appear to be watching. This level of observation also made me notice how frequently there is a sign saying "This project comes from …" and then lists the governor or some other elected official's name. How stupid do you think we are? No one else is going to be fixing the highway or installing massive infrastructure projects. The fact that we paid for people to discuss such a sign, order it, have it delivered, installed, and eventually removed and scrapped has always irked me.

Note: there is now an exception as we are seeing another type of infrastructure funding. These projects are referred to as P3 (public–private partnerships), which we are not immediately paying for; however, the following idea can also apply to them with information about the private component. I recently read David McCullough's *The Path Between the Seas* and learned that the Suez Canal was a private venture and that the Panama Canal started out as one.

26.1. Flywheel Idea: Project Dashboards

I would like to see a different set of signs around taxpayer-funded projects. We should be using LED signs to display project status.

Colors could be used from green down through yellow, orange, and red to show how costs to plan are running and the percentage completion compared to the original plan. Now if these numbers are on the green background, then fine, the project is on schedule and running at or below budget. Workers huddled around would not be a concern. On the other hand, if the sign is clearly communicating the project is running late and over budget, everyone should be working as hard as possible; even the management should be kicking in to get the project on track.

The signs letting everyone know the status of the projects would be a motivational factor, since the workers' friends, neighbors, and family and the general public would all know the project they are working on is costing them more than originally planned. If we are going to have signs telling us our tax dollars are hard at work, is it efficient work or inefficient work? It would be nice to know.

Once again, we don't need laws to make this happen, we just need to start on local projects. Whether it's upgrading Town Hall, making improvements to a school, or fixing an intersection, whenever your locally controlled government is making capital improvements or creating new capital assets, your community can start having these signs put in place and updated regularly. Local groups should feel free to sell advertising to help cover the costs, something the government should eschew. The more we begin to do this around the country, the more it will become the norm. After we start doing this for years, we may even get to track all the costs associated with the billions that go into our military assets. Wouldn't it be nice to keep running tabs on how much each aircraft carrier or other big investment is costing us versus plan?

26.2. Getting Public Support for Process Improvement or Re-engineering Service Delivery

Now this is not all about cutting, cutting, cutting government. If you are in business, you know that to get better, you need to make investments. This is not to say our government should not spend money; the bigger question is, when is it a good decision to spend more money? Obviously, it would be when the net benefits outweigh the cost of that investment.

For many people, the fear of incarceration or fines helps them make good choices. I will go out of my way to avoid having to participate in our legal system. Why? Sitting in a public court environment is torture enough for me. The only thing that comes close is staring at a wall of paper files or shuffling around a hospital with a growing stack of paper. It's the inefficiencies in these systems that are overripe for process improvements that torture the engineer in me. There is so much that could be done more effectively, but they don't. While I have no sympathy for corporations who are still using archaic technology, such as Budget's dot matrix printers or the DOS/AS400-style screens at airlines, it's our responsibility to make our government more cost- and value-efficient.

26.3. Flywheel Idea: Educating about the Value of Investing in Technology

Some of these process improvements use the latest buzzwords like "digital transformation." They are going to take a healthy investment to make this change. We can kill two birds with one stone if we create a reality TV show where the systems integrators (IBM Services, Accenture, Deloitte, etc.) compete to see who can best deliver cost and value improvements for government. For example, we could attack the welfare, criminal, or other system in, say, three states of comparable size and similar economics, such as Vermont, New Hampshire, and Maine. The first thing that would be exposed is how costly the implementation and delivery of these systems are. The second and more profound reaction will be: "Holy cow, how did it ever get this bad or go this long without improvements being made?" This will allow us to show everyone the gains that can be made if we are willing to invest.

For the competing firms, their out-of-pocket costs may not be more than what they spend on commercials and other advertisements. The firms would get tremendous exposure regarding their capabilities and how they can tackle complex problems. I will let Hollywood take it from here, but this is one way in which these firms and Hollywood could play a big part in educating us how our big government operates. Following seasons could bring in other vendors, states, and types of services ripe for improvement. When they run out of good state ideas and if they are brave enough, they could delve into parts of our federal government.

The outcome of this should be that future funding for improvements would be understood by voters and approved. It will cost money to fix things, and we need to be willing to make investments. The return will be better value from future dollars used to maintain government services that we all agree we do need to have.

Chapter 27. Called for Your Civic Duty (like Jury Duty)

I referred to this earlier when we talked about designating the Friday after Thanksgiving as National Civics Day. We can say transparency all day long, but it is too much for the average person to know what is going on at the local, state, and federal level. One approach is to have the information organized, digestible, understandable, and accessible to people. When I started to get involved with the Rye Civic League, I struggled to build an organizational chart of town government. This should have been a simple task, not the arduous endeavor it turned out to be.

A *Bloomberg Businessweek* editorial opinion in March 2015 cited a 2010 national civics test that found 73% of high school students were not proficient in civics.[71] So just about three quarters of the graduating seniors that year were launched into our democracy after being scored as deficient in civics. That same article advocated for high school students to pass the naturalization test as a graduating requirement (you only need to get 6 out of 10, so a D would be passing). It also pointed out in 2013, the Department of Education suspended national exams in history for high school seniors. We invest in public education because businesses can't function if the available workforce does not have the skills businesses require. Conversely, we also can't expect to have a healthy functioning democracy if our children are launched into adulthood without the basics of civic responsibility.[72]

We have two choices: we can agree to pay for more government to organize and present this information for us, or we can do it ourselves. While there are some things, such as getting the meeting minutes done, that are the responsibility of government, the overall responsibility of keeping everyone informed, educated, and engaged should fall on the collective society. The first task is to make sure we teach those of us who pay for our government to know how to drive for better services at lower costs. While everyone should be doing this, let's start with those of us who are vested and are paying for all this government. Eventually it could be expected that all who vote will contribute to this civic duty process.

27.1. Flywheel Idea: Civic Duty in Action

Civic duty will work like jury duty. When you are called up, you need to serve, and it can be enforced just like jury duty. For example, your civic duty job could be to research, prepare, and deliver a 10-minute (or less) presentation. The presentations would be loaded online and held at a large civics fair at the town, ward, or regional level. Of course, these will have food, marketing, music, and other draws to make this a can't-miss social activity for every community. People would circulate through the different booths to learn about the government service each person researched and is presenting. Subjects could be local, county, state, or federal, any government we buy. Yes, there will be some cost in the coordination of the event and getting people called to civic duty, but if we can't show we are managing our government, we need to do something different. I have no qualms about allowing corporate advertising and sponsorships to offset costs.

The process would start in high school to make sure those whose education we are paying for learn how to research and give these presentations before graduating. The presentation format would be a template for the financials, but the focus should be on a segment of government and its mission and goals, detailing how government is delivering on those, if we are paying more then what we are getting, and closing with how this segment of government impacts this community.

This baseline education should help foster discussion and debate with friends, neighbors, and colleagues. There could be awards such as best in class and other incentives to propagate the best ideas and analysis. Not everyone would attend, or would be forced to attend, but for those presenting, they would pull from their networks. Our society is in need of community events and activities that don't keep us isolated staring at electronic screens.

As communities begin to deploy a Civics Day, how they organize, present, record, promote, share, etc., can be structured into blueprints other communities can copy and adopt. There is no need to constantly reinvent the wheel, so it can instead be a continual process of learning from each other to improve the information to better manage our government.

Chapter 28. Who Coordinates the Ants

Even if by some miracle, people get off the couch and decide they are going to carve out free time to manage our government, we need to help them get started and coordinated. Each community, town, and state, and eventually the federal government, needs a way of directing people to find tasks that they can embrace with their unique interest and skill set.

One of my earliest ideas in this area was to create a website that would be a clearinghouse for people to discover who is doing what for campaign finance reform, tracking government, and other initiatives, then to see how they could contribute. A good friend was working in campaign finance reform and told me that even in this key area, there were a multitude of disjointed groups. That is because many are advocating different paths to achieve a similar goal. It's easy to say, "Why don't they work together?" But then the challenge falls to which one? We don't know which approach has the best chance of success; it may be a combination of several actions that gets us campaign finance reform. This cause should have an army of volunteer supporters, but they need a way of connecting and allocating assignments to all who want to help.

How do we efficiently coordinate the skills with the needs? Here is where technology steps in. We have the base technologies in place, such as dating platforms, LinkedIn, and artificial intelligence. What is needed is a clearinghouse of tasks so that individuals can step up. Over a decade ago, I started a WordPress site called New Hampshire Managing Our Government (NHMOG). When people reviewed my first version, they said I needed to include more examples, and that led me to the Rye Civic League.

We have many architects, programmers, and database people who can build, manage, and improve this system through open-source tools. We should build information services that help us manage our government. While we can have openness and transparency, information is not helpful unless some of us go the extra mile and produce the analysis that tells the story.

Think about how that software can be adapted to help people find tasks to work on and to help groups who want to get something completed but need the individuals to do the work. Groups focused on managing specific aspects of the government we are buying would put in the types of skills they need, time, effort, and other attributes, and the software would narrow down matches by a variable set of attributes. The software then presents matches; in this case, it will be matching opportunities to help to what people are capable or willing to do. Individuals could also search (and set up alerts) for when tasks appear that match their skill set or interests. This can be one massive (cloud-based, obviously) application that allows you to limit the view or focus area, geography, or other variables.

Focusing on the money in politics, there already are some great tools, such as OpenSecrets.org, and state websites are now providing better information on where the money is coming from. But it still takes effort to get at the information and to figure out what the analysis is telling us. Each Congressional, Senate, or state (for the governor) area only needs a few people to be using this site to produce the analysis. The information needs to be put in a context and format that is digestible.

The below analysis is from Committee for Economic Development of The Conference Board, but it is at the highest level, so the next set of activities is to look at each candidate and get the details around the missions of these groups.[73] When I dug into this, I found that some group names (PACs) were intentionally obscure to make it harder for the average person to see what is happening.

Table 1: **Overview of Federal Election Financing, 2013–2014** *(total by type of spender)*

		Adjusted amount ($ millions)	Percent of total
Limited Sources	Candidates[a]	$1,229.1	27.0%
	Parties[b]	1,143.9	25.1
	PACs[c]	1,351.8	29.6
	Subtotal	**$3,724.8**	**81.7%**
Unlimited Sources	Super Pacs Receipts[d]	$666.1	14.6%
	Social Welfare Org. Expenditures[e]	118.8	2.6
	Trade Association Expenditures[e]	41.3	0.9
	Union Expenditures[e]	3.1	0.1
	Other[f]	5.5	0.1
	Subtotal	**$834.8**	**18.3%**
	Total	**$4,559.6**	**100%**

Table 2: **Overview of Federal Election Financing, 2015–2016** *(total by type of spender)*

		Adjusted amount ($ millions)	Percent of total
Limited Sources	Candidates[a]	$2,733.6	36.2%
	Parties[b]	1,543.9	20.5
	PACs[c]	1,456.0	19.3
	Subtotal	**$5,733.5**	**76.0%**
Unlimited Sources	Super Pacs Receipts[d]	$1,602.7	21.2%
	Social Welfare Org. Expenditures[e]	147.3	2.0
	Trade Association Expenditures[e]	33.9	0.4
	Union Expenditures[e]	21.6	0.3
	Other[f]	5.9	0.1
	Subtotal	**$1,811.4**	**24.0%**
	Total	**$7,544.9**	**100%**

Source: Based on data reported by the Federal Election Commission and Center for Responsive Politics

[a] Adjusted Candidate receipt totals do not include contributions from PACs, party committees or other candidate campaign committees to avoid double counting.
[b] Adjusted Party receipt totals do not include candidate to party transfers or contributions to avoid double counting.
[c] PAC receipts include amounts raised by traditional PACs subject to contribution limits.
[d] Adjusted total does not include Super PAC to Super PAC contributions to avoid double counting.
[e] 501(c) social welfare organizations, trade associations, and unions do not report total receipts to the FEC but are required to report federal election spending on any independent expenditures, electioneering communications, or labor union communication costs.
[f] This category includes independent expenditures or electioneering communications by individuals, corporations, or miscellaneous types of organizations.

Source: https://www.ced.org/reports/the-landscape-of-campaign-contributions

This is just one example, but there are countless other ways a few individuals in each community can do the heavy lifting that enables all of us to better understand what is happening with the government we buy.

Along with civic duty service, this type of clearinghouse is going to be absolutely essential for us to be coordinating our activities. Think about how complex a big corporation is; there should be even more of us engaged in managing our government.

28.1. Flywheel Idea: Recognition for Those Who Have Contributed

People wear their "I voted" stickers with pride. The same needs to happen for those who have done their part.

We should give people more credit and visibility to hopefully move away from having the same small set of people do all of the work locally. Communities could take inventory of who has volunteered and taken action for managing local government. This could be posted and tracked. Maybe they get special car stickers for preferred parking spaces, etc. Maybe it is just a sticker that changes colors every five years, so you serve in year one and that sticker stays on for five years. After that time, we move to a new sticker. The idea is to assign social recognition and pressure for the people who do serve. Maybe it's something that goes on a mailbox or a house, or social sites like Facebook or LinkedIn can apply the sticker to your online image.

To get this done, towns could utilize middle school or high school students to take surveys and report who has volunteered, voted, and attended meetings. This is not to spy but to continually get data that helps motivate and encourage a high level of responsibility and participation, which must be one of our goals.

Chapter 29. The Rye Civic League, a New Hampshire Example

What the Rye Civic League is currently doing can and should be duplicated in every town, city ward, and county regions across the United States. Alex Herlihy resurrected the Rye Civic League. I asked Alex to provide the original Rye Civic League background, which follows:

Roots of the Rye Civic League by Alex Herlihy

In 1968, Frances Holway, Joan La France, and Marjorie Miller established the Rye Civic League (RCL) for the purpose of educating townspeople about Rye town government and publishing a monthly *Town News*, which reported on town board meetings and other town news. The free publication was placed around town in red bags and members received copies in the mail. The RCL quickly became a catalyst for active citizens, and the three founders made a lasting contribution to town civic life. Frances was a go-getter and provided the basement and mimeograph machine, Marjorie was one of the main editors of the *Town News* and kept it going for the last few years, and Joan was knowledgeable about legal affairs and the state Revised Statutes Annotated (RSA) and was often the most intelligent person in the room during select board and planning board meetings. In 1992, the RCL disbanded due to low membership.

Inspired by the original Rye Civic League's history, a few people revived the organization in 2009. By 2011, a core of dedicated and skilled residents were editing and publishing a monthly online "Civic News" sent to over 1100 residents. With people so busy and so many town meetings to pay attention to, the Rye Civic News delivers key points in a digestible format that enables residents to stay informed and become more active in civic life. Links provide more detailed information that is posted on www.ryecivicleague.org and the town website. Almost half of the people open the Civic News every month and average over two clicks per person.

The RCL is a 501(c)(3) incorporated, nonprofit membership

organization, independent of town government, with a board of directors. It produces the *Rye Citizens' Handbook*, presents the annual PowerPoint of the "story" behind the town and school budgets, and sponsors the annual town candidates' night as well as the statewide candidates' debate every other year. RCL members attend or watch recorded videos of most public town board meetings and are able to go beyond the official minutes published by the town.

29.1. The Rye Civic League in 2019

The Rye Civic League's core delivery is the free monthly e-mail newsletter we call the "Civic News." While we list upcoming meetings, the bulk of the newsletter is short summaries of the key meeting points, including the top five or six topics and links to the official meeting minutes and recorded video.

We learn what people are interested in based on what they click in the newsletter. For example, we found that many want to see what properties are requesting variances from the zoning board. Eventfully the town started putting up signs at those locations. For major developments, the RCL has created a place for people to get more detailed information. For busy people, it is extremely hard to stay informed because the local paper no longer covers town news like it used to. While the town has a website, it is far from easy to use.

The more meetings I went to, the more I learned about what is not getting into the town meeting minutes. For example, if you are building in a protected wetlands area, do you start with the conservation commission; get the variances first from the zoning board; or start with the planning board? It is not clear. When the RCL brought this up at a meeting, the uncertainty seemed to be coveted by developers as it gave them some wiggle room. The lack of information also makes it incredibly hard if you are an abutter to a development. Unless you have been through the process, it is hard to figure out when and where you can interject. The budget process is also like this. Public input is welcome, but it is coming so late in the process, after all of the work has been done, that board members do not appear to be motivated to incorporate changes.

29.2. Rye Citizens' Handbook

When you move into a community, how do you know how the local government works? If you grew up in a city and moved to a rural community, the way the local government operates can be significantly different. I don't think anyone's ever taught a class about how all our different forms of local government work. I was shocked how long it took me to understand all of the relationships between the different boards and departments. In hindsight, it seems relatively simple, but moving into a new form of government is not straightforward.

I mentioned earlier how I tried to map out town government. At the time, there was nothing published that clearly communicated this information to a newcomer. My little sketch became a complicated multisheet diagram with too much information. It could never clearly communicate all that people needed to understand.

Fortunately for us, one of the RCL's members, Mae Bradshaw, decided that the details needed to be captured and singlehandedly took on the task of building the first *Rye Citizens' Handbook*. If all she had to do was go to each group and get their process documents, job and role descriptions, and operating guidelines, it would not be much of a story. But it turned out little information existed, was centralized, or was current or accessible. Coaxing the details from each group and getting them to review and contribute was no easy task.

The annual book provides basic information such as who is in what role, contact information, history of Rye, and annual events; the bulk of the book explains the different entities in town. It documents the three districts, describes the master plan, our form of government, the process we follow, and finally the many boards, committees, and commissions. This book, produced by residents for residents, is the only document in town that concisely explains the function of our local government. Producing the handbooks would crush the meager finances of the RCL, so after a few initial sponsors, the local assisted-living facility Webster at Rye has provided the funds enabling us to print handbooks each year.

If other towns follow suit, these descriptions along with the budget details will help us to compare the different segments of services we buy with similar communities.

What boards, committee, or commissions do and don't do must be included in any comparisons, not just the budget dollars or the budget increases. The bigger question is what services and value they deliver; if this information is not captured, how will we know what we are getting? The question for your community is: who will step up and get your town, ward, or city handbook created if it does not exist already?

29.3. Rye Civic League Annual Presentations

There is a big difference between meeting requirements and effectively communicating. In New Hampshire, the rules from the state are referred to as the Revised Statutes Annotated (RSA). These are the "rules" local governments must follow. Some are antiquated, such as saying public notice must be posted at Town Hall and the library or included in the local newspaper. Now, how many people do you know that wander up to Town Hall to read notices, or if they go to the library, make the time to read the notice board? Even if local papers exist, many residents are not subscribers, or they depend on the online version. So, the intent of the RSA is that municipalities communicate, but the letter of the law says that doing these old-fashioned actions are sufficient.

Our local government may be meeting the letter of the law, but they are falling far short on the intent. You can see the same type of "communication" when it comes to engaging with residents about budgets. Our town provides a one-page document that shows top-level budget account values and the variances (changes from last year). Scanning, you can only ask about the biggest items and the biggest changes percentage wise. There is no story or analysis presented or discussed about the town purchasing and investment choices.

Telling the story of our investments is something only the Rye Civic League is doing for Rye residents.

Before we dive into the discussion of school and town budgets, we need to step back and review a point I brought up earlier. In the corporate world, companies start with forecasting the possible revenue they can create, then ask what investments are needed to achieve the forecasted revenue. So, based on those sales and margin targets, what (people, investments, marketing) must be in place to accomplish those goals? A company first sets a goal, then works to ensure it has the means of achieving those goals. The budgets are the allocation of investments to hopefully enable the company to achieve its fiscal goals.

At times, it can feel like the goal of government is to drive revenue through taxes. But the goal of government is not revenue, but to provide and deliver the services that the people say they need. The allocation of money is not about creating revenue, but deciding on and prioritizing the services we purchase or investments. That is, how funds are allocated in a budget is a community statement about what is valued or important. Many people have said that for a government, a budget is a moral document, since it documents the choices that society has made about priorities.

A corporation has a strategic plan to produce revenues and budget is allocated to achieve those revenue goals. What is the plan that drives the budget decisions for a government? Unfortunately, much too often it is, "What did we spend last year and can we justify the budget increase?" I had hoped when I first went to budget committee meetings that the focus would be on value, not spend. Oh, how wrong I was. Many of the members couldn't even grasp the concept. I tried to rephrase my questions to ask, "If we are paying this much more, what additional value are we getting?"

So, what is the job of the budget committee? In my town, it's about keeping taxes to a minimum. There is no strategic planning. Yes, there is a master plan, but it does not get the funding and community attention this crucial document requires.

The RCL now produces an annual town and school budget analysis that tells the story. If you buy into the concept that a governmental budget is a moral document, it is important to understand the trends. Case in point, after the analysis, we saw that our junior high school budget had remained flat for almost ten years, but we knew that salaries and health costs had gone up. While some savings could be contributed to declining enrollment, the analysis also showed a shift to more spend for special education, so that begged the question, where had the cuts been coming from to keep a flat budget? The answer was the total available staff. That is an example of how budget decisions (intentional or not) impact the community.

The first thing the analysis did was help quantify what the drivers were of the budget. For the town, there were the big five town operations: police, fire, public works, and debt payments. A bar chart clearly showed the comparison between these segments and year-to-year shifts. The same type of bar chart for schools is what made the flat spending at the junior high school so obvious. Based only on what the school was providing, no one would have seen that long-term trend.

For the town, the multiyear bar chart also pointed out that while taxes were remaining relatively flat, the consistent drop in debt payments was masking steady budget increases. The year-to-year information the town was providing did not tell that story, nor were town officials discussing it. The more we looked at the numbers and produced different types of charts, the more stories began to emerge. To see or know the complete picture, someone needs to be doing the analysis. This is one of the chores we need to do ourselves, or agree that we are going to outsource it and add more tasks to government.

Once the quantitative budget analysis work is completed, communities can then layer on the qualitative piece, that is, the services delivered. Community comparisons can then show who is overpaying and who is getting good value. The qualitative is important since departments (police, fire, recreation, public works) don't provide identical services. For example, our police department runs a bike rodeo along with the recreation department.

When your house is on fire, or when you need an ambulance, you want to know you have a good fireman or a good paramedic. How do we know if we are paying the rates for great services, but only getting OK services, if we are not measuring and benchmarking? We need to be more responsible for the government we buy, but it's not easy to understand what we are getting for what we pay. This is our responsibility to fix. Some communities may decide that a mediocre fire department is acceptable, but they want great public works, or vice versa. Let the communities decide, but at least make sure they understand what they are getting and the costs.

29.4. Warrant Articles

At our town meeting, we vote for elected positions, and all other matters are called warrant articles. To provide the background, the Rye Civic League produces a presentation that provides the background and supporting information for anyone who chooses to be better educated. The format provides the basic information, such as why you would be for the article (pro position) or why you would be against the article (con position). For some articles, it takes me a fair bit of effort to fully understand the implications and drivers. If I need to invest that much time, it is a good bet that most voters are not making the same investment and may not fully grasp the different perspectives on an article.

Some years there can be twenty-five or more warrant articles, and many voters start to reach their saturation point. We can work to have fewer topics on the ballot or develop ways so that more voters have the patience and drive to understand all they are voting on. Regardless of how busy or not someone is, everyone can benefit from a concise and direct guide to the warrant articles. To help here, the RCL has been producing a warrant article list that provides short descriptions along with what a "yes" or "no" vote would be saying. This allows people to have some semblance of understanding to guide their choices.

The warrant article table has links back to the longer warrant article presentation the RCL produces. I have seen other towns produce information sheets to help voters. Some do their best to take a neutral position, and others clearly are advocating a specific view. As an author of many of these tools, it is extremely hard to be neutral, so the Rye Civic League is far from perfect, but we try hard.

29.5. Rye Candidates' Night

Every year prior to the town election, we give all candidates the opportunity to make a statement about why they are running, and when there are competitive races, we allow residents to pose questions.

Attendance is respectable, and we see that a fair number of people are watching the recorded video. I have been pleasantly surprised over the years by the positive responses we received from people who watched the videos. It turns out that there are many people who are interested but just could not get to the venue that evening.

We also host a similar candidates' night every other year, when we elect our state house representatives, state senator, and executive councilor.

29.6. Taking Local Action: Making Candidates' Night Happen

Hosting a candidates' night only requires a little bit of planning and organization. Pick the date well in advance and get candidate confirmation on the saved date before you publicize. We use a moderator and a timer to keep things fair. Questions should be for all candidates, not just one, in order to eschew attack questions. We prepare a few questions in advance in case the audience is silent. To promote the event, we create a trifold brochure that has a short statement about the candidates and any links to online sites, both neutral and candidate-supported.

In getting the background for the following Portsmouth Listens section, I learned of an alternate approach where residents sit at small tables in a large room. The candidates for the different positions get to move around and meet and listen to residents' concerns. This is a great process that could also work well between the elections, maybe around a potluck dinner or neighborhood event. If you have ever seen speed dating, it is like that, but the candidates are moving to tables with multiple people.

29.7. Taking Local Action: What Does It Take to Serve?

Some communities feel fortunate to have people to fill open positions in town. Elections would be more interesting if there were fewer uncontested races. The most effective way to get your feet wet is to be an alternate, since this allows you to sit at the table, ask questions, and if members are absent, to be a voting member. You can thus ease into how the board works.

In an effort to help more people get involved, to have competitive races, and to get the vacant alternate spots filled, the RCL has hosted two information nights about opportunities to serve. We invited a member from each board, committee, and commission to the library, where they talked about what it is like to serve. The town has never offered educational nights, so it is really up to us to motivate more people with the skills, experience, and commitment to serve.

When we posted a list of members and the end dates for terms, we were surprised to see consistent and healthy interest in this concise and comprehensive list. New positions and open positions had previously only become known after the town report publishes.

29.8. Flywheel Idea: Tavern Nights

Let's pretend there is no internet, TV, Netflix, or other activities that keep us isolated in our homes. We could have neighborhood groups gather at a home or establishment for a potluck or other type of dinner and call it "Tavern Night." The seating should be small tables or areas where groups could gather together. At each table would be information on the upcoming election. It could be the information on warrant articles, budgets, or candidates. This information would be discussion prompters for people who could discuss this topic or could rotate to other tables or areas for other discussions.

If you remember from earlier sections, discussion and debate is one of the core components for democracy that has withered over time. The goal of tavern nights is to get people to have conversations. Rather than regurgitating sound bites or the latest tweets, people could have cohesive thoughts and ideas of their own.

While my little town has the RCL, our neighboring city, Portsmouth, has been leveraging listening circles.

Chapter 30. Portsmouth Listens

In Portsmouth, New Hampshire, there is often a win-win between the public and those responsible for managing city government. Now, not everything is perfect in Portsmouth and no one said that success must be a utopia. However, some city groups don't talk at the public; instead, they work with them to mine the collective wisdom and achieve a level of community support before they move forward.

When I participated in Sustainable Portsmouth (a Portsmouth Listens initiative focused on reducing Portsmouth's ecological impact) effort, I was fortunate enough to meet the co-founders and co-chairs of Portsmouth Listens, John Tabor and Jim Noucas. Noucas provided me with additional reading before we met to make sure I had all of the background and history.

Portsmouth Listens has tackled a number of problems in the community, including middle school bullying, building or renovating the middle school, and working on the city budget, the master plan, and sustainability. They were working on affordable city housing when I met with them.

This is how I recall Sustainable Portsmouth proceeded. Several hundred people met in the high school cafeteria for a day. We were split into small groups and talked. We got to know our group and discussed why we were there and what we hoped to achieve. We then wrote down our achievement goals. We were then mixed up again and we discussed in different small groups and brainstormed all the things we thought Sustainable Portsmouth should do. So, say we had two hundred people and that first part took four hours. That is eight hundred hours of deliberation, ideas, and contributions.

The facilitators then hung sheets of paper across the cafeteria and each group went through their ideas. We created groupings or categories on the big sheets; the number of sticky notes (i.e., ideas) would be clustered around sub-themes. When all was said and done, there may have been eight different categories packed with ideas. We were then asked to go pick a category we wanted to work on and assembled at the category. I ended up on a "communication" team, which had suggestions for how to get groups working together, getting the word out to the community, coordination, etc.

The next session was a team meeting. As a team, we were given our marching orders to develop a plan and a documented sub-report and presentation. Our group built an inventory of all the different types of sustainability activities that were already in place and what we wanted to achieve, and we discussed the other ideas that ended up with us.

We had meetings, brainstormed, did research, had conference calls, divided up the work, and completed our report. All groups then presented at the final meeting, where we took turns presenting our recommended actions.

Yes, believe it or not, my ideas and what I wanted to achieve were not the panacea I believed them to be, nor were they the most important thing to get done. My original ideas barely made it into my group's final report. While it was humbling that everyone did not rally around my great idea, in the end I could not argue. The group chose to focus on more appropriate actions for Sustainable Portsmouth. The Portsmouth Listens co-founders let me know that going in with an agenda and leaving being part of an output that didn't mirror my original expectations was common. Many people came into discussions with a certain set of beliefs, opinions, or mindset, and walked out with a newfound respect for other perspectives and a realization that the world does not look the same to everyone.

Sustainable Portsmouth marches on and the results are visible. There are recycling bins all around the city. Most counter-based restaurants have recycling systems; food is composted; home food composting is available for residents; bicycles are available for transportation; municipal buildings and residential homes are now consuming less energy; solar energy is pervasive; and many others. While Sustainable Portsmouth was not the only driver for these actions, this non-government, no-cost organization contributed through direct efforts. A sustainability fair and other actions played a key role in making Portsmouth a more sustainable community.

30.1. Key Points from Portsmouth Listens

One of the strongest points from the Portsmouth Listens process is that its actions come from deliberation. A body of people put forth ideas, suggestions, and recommendations, add information, and hear different perspectives, then discuss, adjust, and build toward a consensus. This is far different from an elected body sitting up high, bringing in "experts," and then deciding what is best for the people. Much of your government is managed the latter way. Lobbyists and other experts write legislation for your representatives to submit. There are many complexities to be managed and subject matter experts provide value. However, what they propose, the impacts, and the trade-offs all need to be deliberated and vetted, not just rubberstamped.

In my younger years, I remember watching President Reagan at a State of the Union address pulling up a stack of legislation and saying how many pages it was and how much it weighed. His point was that he couldn't be reading all of this and then signing off that he understood it all. If he wasn't going to read it all, how were the citizens going to understand what was being proposed? Everything was much too complex, and he was urging Congress to keep it simple, to reduce the complexities and hence reduce costs. A good example is our federal tax code. Completing my federal taxes requires documenting some energy investments using forms called Schedule K-1. The complexities (loopholes and incentives) that have evolved around taxes for energy firms are mind-boggling.

Having someone else (experts and lobbyists) do all the work is easy, but citizens in a healthy democracy can't be taking the easy road, we need to do the work. Americans mock the state planning approach (e.g., the politburo in the Soviet Union and China) that assumes a small number of people know better than everyone else (i.e., the elite dictating to the masses). However, when Americans don't deliberate, when the representative bodies don't deliberate, when one side dictates their views and approaches to the only competing side, how much different are we in the United States than the communist state planning style of decision making?

A key tenet of our judicial process is the right to a jury of our peers. Does this jury have experts come in and tell them what to do? Do they make decisions based on political party agendas? No, they deliberate. They are required to discuss, raise points, and convince each other and agree on what the conclusion should be. Sometimes the jury can't move one way or the other. This is not a failure of the process but a confirmation that a particular case is not clearly one way or the other; both perspectives have about equal merit.

In a dialog and discussion, one sound bite or tweet can't rule the day or drive the discussion. During discussion and debate, all points get questioned, and they must be defended and understood to be accepted. The process of listening, formulating your own ideas, and engaging is what can lead people to change their minds or to develop a healthy respect for a differing viewpoint. The dialog process acts as a filter or sponge that lets the water through but pulls out the dirt. In a world of sound bites or tweets, ideas are not nourished, contributions are not made, and communities are not formed. Humans are social beings; interaction and relationships with the community are core parts of who we are. To deliberate and engage, we need to step away from being a receptacle for the deluge of one-way information flow and find ways to leverage the power of many people sharing and contributing.

During my discussion with the Portsmouth Listens founders, they told a story about how a city committee was formed and came back to the city council with a set of absolutely unrealistic recommendations. Yes, the committee could have deliberated, but handpicked or orchestrated committees with many likeminded people are perfectly happy skipping down a trail they all agree to. They were picked to produce a predictable output. This is not to say that all ideas from listening circles are great, but the majority of the recommendations have passed through layers of dialog to filter ideas and suggestions. Elected officials or appointees just don't have the bandwidth or diversity of views to create a broad marketplace of ideas or the time to allow better solutions or suggestions to percolate upwards. When the leaders that voters put in place pick a group of people who are similar to them, see things the way they do, and have the same set of beliefs and expectations, the conclusions and recommendations are going to be predictable.

There is no magic that makes a process like Portsmouth Listens deliver huge value for the community and the municipality. The positive results come from a whole set of enabling activities. One is the lack of budgets or need to continually focus on finances. This frees up the volunteer leaders to be doing what they volunteered for, not spending time raising money. Through the partnership with the city, facilities and some other costs don't exist and donations and contributions fill in the gaps. Locally, having the area newspaper as a co-founder and co-chair provides a stamp of credibility and the communication channel is a huge advantage. However, if there is any magic, it's having a neutral third party or facilitator to enable stakeholders with differing views, perspectives, and agendas to help people lay down their weapons and work together.

Part 7

We now have a shared view of how our democracy evolved as boundary conditions dissolved, a shared mission of changing the direction of the WTAT flywheel, the economic flywheel vernacular to assist with discussion and debate and a multitude of ideas to rally around. How each of us embrace our civic responsibilities will differ, but the essential element is that we all need to be doing our part, no matter how small or large.

Chapter 31. Closing Thoughts

31.1. Primary Mission

Briefly recapping, we started out discussing how the boundary conditions needed for the democratic equation to work have eroded from the days of our Founding Fathers. These conditions are:

- discussion and debate
- the press as information and journalism
- disseminating new ideas and information
- civic responsibility of the voters

Our responsibility is to understand and restore the function performed by the boundary conditions. Businesses respond to markets, so we leave the press and journalism out of the discussion, letting the power of commerce shape how the function of independent journalism evolves. Ramping up our investment of skills, effort, and time toward civic responsibility will lead to civil discussion and debate along with more ways for new ideas and information to spread.

Yes, the Way Things Are Today (WTAT) flywheel is large and has a massive amount of energy. Stopping that flywheel and getting it spinning the other direction is a daunting task. If we do nothing, it will keep on gaining energy, making it harder to stop every additional day we do nothing. To slow that flywheel down and get it moving in another direction requires citizens to take action.

At first, these efforts will be imperceptible as they push back at the WTAT flywheel. However, as we begin to do more and more, the impact from those efforts will get noticeable. The WTAT flywheel will begin to lose speed and energy, and the slower it goes, the easier it becomes to slow down. Through thousands of communities and millions of people doing small things, we can bring that flywheel to a stop. Then as many, many people continue managing the government services we buy, the flywheel will start to move in the other direction. All those efforts will add energy and momentum as a new culture takes over that demands better value at less money year over year from our government.

The new norm will be much more civil discussion and debate. We will have the skills to look at many sides of a question and have the flywheel vernacular framing the discussion in relation to our economic flywheel. We are not going to agree on everything, but we will ask questions, we will listen, we will be heard, and then we will move forward. Stagnation and partisan pendulum swings will eventually become a thing of the past.

It is not going to be easy, and most would prefer to be doing anything else but managing our government. The higher road is less traveled because it takes effort, and it means other activities need to be sacrificed. The higher, less-traveled road is harder, but if our nation wants to be getting better value for the government we are buying, we have to commit to the climb.

The work starts at the local level. What we have been doing with the Rye Civic League is an example of the little things. Residents have more information and there has been more voter engagement. The RCL is just one of the changes. For example, the town capital improvement plans (possible large departmental expenditures for the next five years) went from being updated every five or so years to an annual process. People are different; we have different interests, skills, experience, and abilities. The trick is to align skills, interests, and tasks. Some may crunch the numbers, others may craft the analysis or the story, creating infographics and making presentations, flyers, social media, information booths, and other ways of communicating.

The services are just as varied as the people. These span planning, libraries, community services, events, utilities, IT support and technology, recreation, public works, cemeteries, schools, and more. Find something that you are interested in that aligns with your passions, interests, or hobbies. You may ease into an activity, just observing until you choose to do more. The key to slowing the WTAT flywheel down is the choices citizens need to make. We need to choose to make the time. Some years, life may not leave much time; those are your sabbatical years. It could be when you have infants, are caring for parents, or multitasking between school and work or multiple jobs. That is OK, as long as your sabbatical comes to an end at some point.

The activities at the intersection of our economic flywheel and our responsibilities as consumers of government services require larger time investments. These tasks will be pulling back on the economic flywheel brakes; scaling back the weights our economic flywheel must fight through on every revolution; and removing the sand and constantly greasing the axle so our economic flywheel builds energy. Citizens need to start locally figuring out how to approach challenges. Our youth and those with technical skills are going to play a critical role leveraging technologies that drive efficiencies. Technology is a force multiplier we need to be fully leveraging. When one group discovers or creates an approach or a solution that works, that progress can't be left in isolation.

Going back to the Rye Civic League deliverables, these can be repeated at communities across the country. The RCL website is far from optimal, but imagine what countless web developers could do with multiple types created, tailored towards small towns, small cities, and larger cities with wards. How the RCL analyzes town and school budgets could be standardized to help in comparing similar towns or cities. The RCL has a vision, but we lack the technical expertise and people to implement it. Ideally after each meeting, the key meeting points would go out on tweets and be posted to Facebook or similar platforms. The recorded videos would have tags allowing citizens to jump to that specific topic segment. The work to compile the monthly "Civic News" would diminish as the newsletter would build itself from these continuous posts.

Expectations must also be realistic; just because an individual feels or thinks they are doing the right thing does not guarantee it will work or be successful. The RCL approach may not be right for every local community. For example, Durham, New Hampshire, doesn't need its own "Civic News" because the town administrator's "Friday Updates" serve a similar function. Every community has the responsibility of deploying a solution and approach that works best for them.

Some individual contributions may just be communicating out

what is happening locally, how it is working, what makes it succeed, and what has failed. Others may be creating tools that make the sharing of ideas, process, measurement, and communicating easier for communities. If private ventures jump in to monetize, that is fine too. Maybe tech companies will take my New Hampshire Managing Our Government idea and build community-focused clearinghouses that match skills with needs and share best-in-class practices.

There is no one single path for us to be walking down, nor do we need to think of it as lining up to push on the same spot on the WTAT flywheel; that would not be efficient. We need to be pushing against everywhere we can. It is not the strength or impact of a single person, but the accumulated impact from many of us doing a little bit each year that will make a difference. From an individual vantage point, progress may be hard to see, but it will be clearer to journalists, pundits, academics, and thinktanks monitoring from the outside.

Citizens can't wait for someone to come and tell them what to do. As I tell my children, they are responsible for the decisions they make and what they choose to do or not to do. All citizens are individually responsible to make those choices. It can start with a self-assessment of what kinds of tasks they would be interested in, what they are good at, and what skills they possess. The next step would be for them to look for local activities and get involved. If there isn't a group, it's time to start one. In the early days, citizens should stay focused on the CDG, services we agree we need to have, where the discussion is about maximizing value and reducing costs.

Once a community has developed skills to view a topic from multiple perspectives, engage in face-to-face discussion and debates, and work together separating fact from fiction, then the activities can expand to political party differences. Our national goal of working towards government services that continually increase in value and minimizing total costs should cut across party boundaries. The same holds true when it comes to improving the effectiveness of our public education, battling the cost of girth, reducing the massive costs of crime, and tackling other flywheel brakes and weights.

In this time and this place, it falls on us and the next generations to walk the harder and higher road. To keep us working together, the flywheel analogy and vernacular will enable efficient and effective discussions. We can ask if something is a brake or a weight on our economic flywheel. Is something sand on the axle, or will an investment or a new way of monitoring and managing our government services be grease for the axle?

Together, our most important national mission must be to have the most cost-effective and efficient government in the world. This is across all aspects of government from federal and state to local. The goal is not to cut government, but to look at every single aspect of our government and make sure we are continually getting better service and value at lower costs year over year. Yes, some government may be eliminated, but we may find the need to invest in systems and process improvements that will provide significant advantages in the long term.

Remember, it's all about the economy, and if the economy is not humming, everything else is a secondary concern. Efficient government will help us make more investments in our infrastructure and keep more personal income in the private domain (savings and investments). In 2017 I estimate that total federal and all US state government spending was about $5.6 trillion a year. (I used one 2017 state spending data point.[74]) The year is not important; anything around $5 trillion is a very, very big number. Apple had 2017 revenues of just over $229 billion, so we had government services and investments twenty-four times greater than Apple's global revenue. If our federal and total state government were the GDP of a nation, our federal and state budgets add up to be the third-largest GDP in the world. It's a *huge* amount of money that does not even include all of the local governments (city, town, and county).

We own the biggest corporation in the world (our federal, state, and local governments), and I am willing to say it is the worst-run and most inefficient mega-corporation. We are the board of directors, who are doing a lousy job, and as the stockholders, Americans are losing their shirts.

We need to collectively commit to continuously drive all levels of our government to provide better service and value at lower costs year over year. Obviously, we should be able to make huge leaps in the beginning, but the process of improving and getting higher value and service can never end. This does not happen by voting; you spend about ten minutes a year doing that, and no politician or political party is a panacea for all of our problems. Getting our money's worth will only come from every one of us committing to allocate a larger percentage of our time to managing our government.

31.2. What Will You Choose to Do?

The ultimate question is: what are you going to do? Reading this book was a good first step, but if you do not choose to allocate time and effort, we are not going to stop the WTAT flywheel and get in sync to maximize our economic flywheel energy. Remember, it took a lot of years for our nation to get into this predicament, and there is no magic that will make the path easy or automatic. While a few galvanizing people may rise up and be catalysts for change, the real power must come from a commitment by the masses to take individual actions. On some topics, like campaign finance reform, many people have been working on different aspects and solutions for years, but citizens need to get on the same page and start working together.

Taking campaign finance reform as an example, I did a lot already; I worked with another resident and got a town warrant passed forcing the selectmen to notify our state representatives that our town is in favor of campaign finance reform. I participated in the NH Rebellion for a number of years and donated to other groups. However, not much seems to be changing.

These campaign finance reform actions are not working together. One could be hitting the WTAT flywheel on the broad side, another on the left or right, coming into the flywheel at angles that will not have much impact, pushing in the direction of rotation and not against it. The actions do not all need to be the same, but there needs to be some coordination so they push back on the flywheel spin and help slow it down a little. Lots of little actions can have as much of an impact as a large event, especially if the smaller efforts are coordinated.

I don't have all of the answers, but I can sense the potential dormant energy lying untapped in our country. Despite our never-ending differences of opinions, we need to stop those details from preventing progress on change that a majority wants to happen. It's up to Americans to choose to be American and embrace the challenge of being responsible for managing our government. Wearing hats and voting for people who say they want America to be great does not fix our problems. Only Americans choosing to do many great American things will help make and keep America great.

I have provided many suggestions for activities people can begin to pursue at the local level. Each of us is only a single individual, but the accumulation of our activities will get the flywheel weights reduced, force the brakes to let up, get the sand cleaned out of the axles, and institute a continuous maintenance program to keep the axle greased.

It's been nine or more years for me working on the Rye Civic League. While there has been lots of progress, we have much more work to do before the RCL reaches its full potential. I am hoping more people step in, contribute, and evolve the RCL to let me move aside and onto other things. For any of the actions I have discussed, it will take lots of people, patience, failures, learnings, and improvements. But if we are relentless and don't give up, we will maximize our economic flywheel energy.

It's a lot easier to watch TV, play a video game, follow social media, watch a movie, read a book, go fishing, or do other things when you are not working. The tasks that lie in front of us are a lot less fun and exciting, but the choice is yours. Can you choose to make the time and do great American things for the future of our nation? It is no one's choice but your own for how much, when, and how you will contribute.

I know I will continue to try. Even if nothing changes after this book, my children, my wife, and maybe future grandchildren will know I tried to make a difference. If our big problems continue from the failure of the governed to manage our government, and future generations bemoan the state of our nation and democratic health, I will have a clear conscience because I chose to put in the effort. It has been my choice—now what are you going to choose to do?

Appendix: Applying Your Engineer's Brain to Government

Why do we need the engineer? Silly question: everything is always better when an engineer is involved! (Just kidding.) Creating mathematical models to describe how things work is something engineers do—and it's something you can do, too. It just takes a little training. If you want to design a flywheel or make sure you understand how it works, the engineer has been trained to develop the mathematical equations describing everything that impacts the flywheel. Moving forward, when we engage in respectful discussion and debate, we can use flywheel mechanics to discuss what is happening.

This section is for those who want a little more grounding in the flywheel metaphor and the engineer's approach to problem-solving before jumping into the meat of *Consuming Government*.

Appendix Chapter 1. Economics & Engineering Project

In *Consuming Government,* we focus on the energy of our economic flywheel. The following brief sections on energy, kinetic energy, inertia, mass, shape, and angular velocity are only introduced to develop a feel for flywheel mechanics.

A1.1. Energy

The energy in the flywheel, known as kinetic energy, is the strength of the economy. If the flywheel is at a dead stop, it takes a lot of energy to get it moving, but once it is moving it takes a lot less to keep it going or to make it spin faster. If it is barely moving, something minor is able to bring it to a complete stop. On the other hand, if the velocity (angular velocity) and mass are high, minor blips or interference will not impact the flywheel much. So mass, speed, and the shape of the flywheel combine to create kinetic energy, or in our case, economic energy. Everyone's goal and our focus should always be about what this will do to help increase the economic energy of our flywheel. Avoiding or minimizing negative impacts that suck out economic energy enables us to build energy as our population increases.

A1.2. Using the Energy

Picture an old mill powered by a stream. The water turned the water wheel and that energy was converted to power for grinding and other tasks. If we view our economic flywheel as connected to a shaft (with gears, pulleys, etc.) connected to all our economic activity, the flywheel energy is a measure of our economic strength, such as gross domestic product (GDP). The more energy, the more economic activity is happening. That energy is what creates job growth, wage increases, and the revenue for governmental services. Assuming there is some natural (minor) rate of inflation, the increases in flywheel energy helps absorb those cost increases. If there are things holding back our flywheel from spinning, diminishing those negative impacts will also help increase our flywheel energy.

A1.3. Inertia

A leaf does not have much inertia. A massive rolling boulder has lots of inertia. A square boulder can have the same mass (remember, weight is the force of gravity pulling on the mass off an object) as a round boulder, but the round one will take a lot less energy to keep moving. Open a door and poke a few inches away from the hinge; does it close? Now give the same poke near the doorknob and watch the door close. That is the effect of the lever arm from your high school science classes. So mass, the radius, and shape all impact inertia. Shape is the tricky one. In the inertia equation, a constant (K) is assigned for shape. It can be complex, but inertia is a key component of the energy driving our economy, and we can relate those components to what is happening in our economy: all of those business transactions, jobs, and consumer spending.

A1.4. Mass

The sheer size of the economy helps make an economy more robust. The bigger the economy, the more mass and inertia that economy has. Economies with less mass are more fragile or susceptible to losing energy when external forces are applied. As an economy grows (i.e., volume of economic activity), even if it does slow down, it still has a large amount of economic energy. If it slows down too much, an economy with less mass will require less energy than a more massive flywheel to get spinning again, so the bigger the economy, the more important it is to keep it moving effectively.

A1.5. Shape

The inertia equation uses a constant (K) in many books to account for the shape of an object. Academics can have a field day figuring out how to assign the constant to what is happening in an economy. Energy can be physically measured. If we can agree on some way to measure what the other economic energy components are (mass, radius, and angular velocity), then we can solve for K. The fun comes in when we look at what makes the shape of an economy different. This could be the structure of government, how well it is managed by the stakeholders, or other factors. We have been picturing a nice round, solid flywheel. If a country did not have high-speed internet connections or if it had laws that prevented it from maximizing all potential human capital, those factors could force the wheel to be more oval or to have holes (picture a solid wheel compared to a wheel with spokes).

A1.6. Radius

If the economic flywheel starts out small and more mass is added to it, that mass will have a greater impact if it makes the wheel larger rather than denser. In the inertia equation, the radius is squared so it has a large impact on the inertia. So yes, the bigger economy has a physical advantage compared to a smaller economy. When we think of trade and the impact of other flywheels on ours, the larger radius creates opportunities for more interconnections.

A1.7. Angular Velocity

We want our economic flywheel to spin and to spin fast. The faster the flywheel spins, the more energy it has. Picture a big flywheel moving slowly; even if it is huge, it may not be that hard to stop if it is moving slowly. Our speed can mask our problems, but removing the flywheel brakes, weights, and sand can give a flywheel more energy without adding mass or additional stimulus. Measuring it and tracking it can provide helpful information on what and how things may be impacting our flywheel. We can also be looking at acceleration and deacceleration, as this is the rate of change in the velocity.

Appendix Chapter 2. Flywheel Mechanics

In a true mechanical system, the flywheel would need to be attached to an axle and something would need to hold that axle. We are using a model, so our flywheel is just going to spin on an axle.

What happens if the flywheel is not solid at the axle or not completely symmetrical, or has gaps or chunks missing? The wheel could have wobble or be jerky from soft or missing material, which would lead to a loss of energy and unpredictable impacts from external actions. Think corruption, redundancies, poor cooperation, bad management structure, and other factors that make delivering governmental services not as efficient as possible. How our government operates drives these factors. While we can't control it, we need to monitor, look for the effects of problems, and not let our government operate in a black box.

If you are familiar with ball bearings, those hard, round balls are well lubricated to allow something to spin efficiently. Sometimes it can be a well-lubricated shaft sitting inside another shaft. Either way, for the flywheel to spin, it needs be well lubricated. The degree to how effective this connection is lubricated could be related to the productivity of our elected officials. There are things we can do that help our flywheel spin effectively, or we can let it be and suffer the economic consequences of inefficiencies.

Picture our US Congress. The polarization from the primary process has created a situation where a victory is making the other party look bad by not accomplishing activities. However, there are some basic responsibilities of the US Congress that need to move forward regardless of party views. This is the appointment of positions, passing of budgets, and helping executive branches succeed with their missions. A "do-nothing" Congress (i.e., one that neglects basic Congressional responsibilities) can be viewed as putting sand on our axle. Our flywheel will spin, but it must now grind its way through every revolution.

There can also be too much lubricant or the wrong type of

lubricant. Which works better: grease or honey? A thick, viscous fluid could clog things up. Trying to do too much can also cause problems. In New Hampshire, the four hundred state representatives and twenty-four state senators put forward so much legislation, no one can keep up with it. Too much activities or a process that enables too much to get on the axle can also be detrimental to our economic flywheel motion.

A2.1. Stimulus

When you want to add energy to the flywheel, where you push and how you push can make a big difference. If you want to make something spin faster, can you engage with the object at the same speed? If you want it to move faster, your hand (i.e., a stimulus) has to be moving faster than the object to get it moving faster. So, a stimulus that worked when the economy was spinning slower will not work as well when the economy is moving faster.

Where you insert that stimulus can also matter. The outside edge of the wheel covers a greater distance on each rotation, so it is moving at a faster speed than a point closer to the axis. The closer point to the axle does not need to travel as far to complete a revolution, so it is moving at a slower speed. As the economy expands, what you did before won't work the same way again. You need to increase the speed or move the stimulus closer to the center of the axis, which is not as easy as pushing from the outside edge. The bottom line is what worked last time needs to change to get the same level of benefit.

A2.2. Flywheel Connections

Clans, villages, city-states, and modern countries all have trade in common. One economy has an impact on another economy. How economies are connected explains how one economic flywheel impacts another. Picture a loose, long string between flywheels; the impact is not great. Now, what happens if there is a metal or rigid connection between flywheels? There is going to be immediate impact on every revolution. What if the connection is a rubber band? There will be a delay before the band gets taut, and the force will be strong and brief.

If the connection is a string, the interaction may be minimal.

How has trade or the impact of one economy on another changed over time with technology? Compare the effort of crossing a river to trade a seashell versus moving billions of dollars to the other side of the planet with an electronic transfer.

These changes in technology have made those connections much more rigid. So, a stimulus to our flywheel, or even the self-perpetuating energy we create, does not stay in our flywheel. The stimulus energy is dissipated to other flywheels much more efficiently than it was in the past. We also have more connections and they, too, are more rigid than ever. The opposite is also true, where other economies have a greater impact on our flywheel.

A flywheel with more inertia (kinetic energy) helps protect our flywheel from being impacted by other flywheels, but also makes our impact on other economies even greater.[75]

Endnotes

1 https://colonialamericantaverns.weebly.com/entertainment.html. Entertainment in Colonial Taverns. Also: https://cupola.gettysburg.edu/cgi/viewcontent.cgi?article=1026&context=ghj. *The Gettysburg Historical Journal*, Volume 1 Article 7 2002 "The Tavern in Colonial America," Steven Struzinski

2 https://www.michiganradio.org/post/founding-fathers-never-intended-permanent-political-class-controlled-wealthy, Michigan Public Radio "The Founding Fathers never intended a permanent political class controlled by the wealthy." Jack Lessenberry April 18, 2016 Accessed May 14, 2018

3 "Policy Basics: Where Do Our Federal Tax Dollars go?" Center on Budget and Policy Priorities, updated January 29, 2019, accessed March 17, 2019, http://www.cbpp.org/research/federal-budget/policy-basics-where-do-our-federal-tax-dollars-go.

4 US Debt Clock, March 2019, accessed March 2019, http://www.usdebtclock.org.

5 "Current health expenditure (% of GDP)," World Bank, accessed March 17, 2019, https://data.worldbank.org/indicator/SH.XPD.CHEX.GD.ZS?view=chart.

6 https://money.cnn.com/2017/08/05/news/economy/high-deductibles-insured-health-care/index.html CNN Business "When high deductibles cause even insured patients to postpone care" Pauline Bartolone, Kaiser Health News August 5, 2017 Accessed May 14, 2019

7 https://www.hcup-us.ahrq.gov/reports/statbriefs/sb216-Mental-Substance-Use-Disorder-ED-Visit-Trends.jsp?utm_source=AHRQ&utm_medium=EN-1&utm_term=&utm_content=1&utm_campaign=AHRQ_EN1_10_2017 Healthcare Cost and Utilization Project. "Trends in Emergency Department Visits Involving Mental and Substance Use Disorders, 2013-2016 December 2016 Audrey J. Weiss, PH.D., Margureite L. Barrett, M.S., Kevin C. Hestlin, Ph.D., and Carol Stocks, Ph.D., R.N. Accessed May 14, 2019

8 https://www.reuters.com/article/us-new-prescriptions-study/many-patients-may-never-fill-new-prescriptions-idUSTRE61G3QX20100217

Reuters Health News Feb, 27, 2010 "Many patients may never fill new prescriptions" Amy Norton Accessed: May 14, 2019

9 Scared Straight! 1978 Documentary Directed by Arnold Shapiro, Golden West Television. Keep America Beautiful 1971 "Crying Indian" Ad campaign

10 Governor's Task Force on the Seacoast Cancer Cluster, "Governor's Task Force on the Seacoast Cancer Cluster: Final Report," New Hampshire Department of Health and Human Services, October 13, 2017, accessed March 18, 2019, https://www.dhhs.nh.gov/dphs/gtfscc/documents/gtfscc-final-report.pdf.

11 "Geographic Variation in Pediatric Cancer Incidence – United States 2003-2014," Center for Disease Control (CDC), June 29, 2018, accessed March 18, 2019, https://www.cdc.gov/mmwr/volumes/67/wr/mm6725a2.htm.

12 Michael Goodman, Joshua Naiman, Dina Goodman, and Judy LaKind, "Cancer Clusters in the USA: What do the last twenty years of state and federal investigation tell us?" *National Library of Medicine, National Institutes of Health; Critical Reviews in Toxicology,* April 21, 2012, accessed April 6, 2019, https://www.ncbi.nlm.nih.gov/pmc/articles/PMC3408895.

13 Thomas Frieden, "CDC Weight of the Nation Press Briefing [transcript]," Center for Disease Control (CDC), July 27, 2009, accessed March 17, 2019, https://www.cdc.gov/media/transcripts/2009/t090727.htm.

14 Doyle Rice, "More than 2 billion are overweight or obese globally, new study says," *USA Today,* June 12, 2017, accessed March 18, 2017, https://www.usatoday.com/story/news/health/2017/06/12/wide-world-more-than-2b-overweight-obese-globally-study-says/102776692/.

15 American Diabetes Association (ADA), "Economic Costs of Diabetes in the US in 2017," *Diabetes Care,* March 2018, accessed March 18, 2019, http://care.diabetesjournals.org/content/early/2018/03/20/dci18-0007.

16 "Suicide Statistics," American Foundation for Suicide Prevention, accessed March 19, 2019, https://afsp.org/about-suicide/suicide-statistics/.

17 "Suicide Rate by Country 2019," World Population Review, accessed March 19, 2019, http://worldpopulationreview.com/countries/suicide-rate-by-country/.

18 TIME Staff, "The Opioid Diaries," *TIME,* March 6, 2018, accessed March 19, 2019, http://time.com/magazine/us/5170229/march-5th-2018-vol-191-no-9-u-s/.

19 WatchBlog, "How Much Does Crime Cost?" US Government Accountability Office, November 29, 2017, accessed March 18, 2019, https://blog.gao.gov/2017/11/29/how-much-does-crime-cost/.

20 "U.S. Military Spending vs. the World," National Priorities Project, accessed March 18, 2019, https://www.nationalpriorities.org/campaigns/us-military-spending-vs-world/.

21 "DoD Releases Fiscal Year 2018 Budget Proposal," Under Secretary of Defense (Comptroller), accessed March 18, 2019, https://comptroller.defense.gov/Portals/45/Documents/defbudget/fy2018/fy2018_Press_Release.pdf.

22 Chris Mai and Ram Subramanian, "The Price of Prisons – Examining State Spending Trends, 2010-2015," Vera Institute of Justice, May 2017, accessed March 18, 2019, https://www.vera.org/publications/price-of-prisons-2015-state-spending-trends.

23 The Council of Economic Advisers, "Returns on Investments in Recidivism-reducing Programs," May 2018, accessed March 18, 2019, https://www.whitehouse.gov/wp-content/uploads/2018/05/Returns-on-Investments-in-Recidivism-Reducing-Programs.pdf.

24 Daniel Terrill, "NRA Releases Financial Statement Showing Revenue, Expenses for 2016," Guns.com, May 5, 2017, accessed March 18, 2019, https://www.guns.com/2017/05/05/nra-revenue-expenses-in-2016.

25 Trevor Nace, "Humanity Has Officially Consumed More Than Earth Can Produce This Year," Forbes, August 3, 2017, accessed March 18, 2019, https://www.forbes.com/sites/trevornace/2017/08/03/humanity-officially-consumed-more-earth-produce-year/#5d88831759a4.

26 Dan Boyce, "IE Questions: How Much Do Energy 'Vampires' Cost Us?" Inside Energy, May 8, 2015, accessed March 18, 2019, http://insideenergy.org/2015/05/08/ie-questions-how-much-do-energy-vampires-cost-us/.

27 "Standby Power," Berkeley Lab, accessed March 18, 2019, https://standby.lbl.gov/.

28 Erin Baldassari, "'Worst-case scenario:' High-speed rail costs jump $2.8 billion to $10.6 billion," The Mercury News, Bay Area News Group, January 17, 2018, accessed March 18, 2019, https://www.mercurynews.

com/2018/01/17/worst-case-scenario-high-speed-rail-costs-jump-2-8-billion-to-10-6-billion/.

29 "List of equations in quantum mechanics," Wikipedia, accessed March 18, 2019, https://en.wikipedia.org/wiki/List_of_equations_in_quantum_mechanics.

30 Sjoerd Nienhuys, "Seismic Building Codes: Global and Regional Overview," Evidence on Demand, November 2015, accessed March 18, 2019, https://assets.publishing.service.gov.uk/media/57a0897c40f0b652dd000242/EoD_HDYr3_59_November2015_Seismic_Building_Codes.pdf.

31 Editorial Board, "Leaky Pipes Are a Fixable Climate Threat: Natural gas seeping through lawns and sidewalks traps heat with dangerous efficiency," *Bloomberg Businessweek*, May 8-14, 2017, 8.

32 J.T. O'Donnell, "The Rise of 'Employer Shaming' (and Why Your Company Should Worry)," LinkedIn Talent Blog, March 7, 2016, accessed March 18, 2019, https://business.linkedin.com/talent-solutions/blog/employer-brand/2016/the-rise-of-employer-shaming-and-why-your-company-should-worry.

33 "Interest Expense on the Debt Outstanding," TreasuryDirect, accessed March 18, 2019, https://www.treasurydirect.gov/govt/reports/ir/ir_expense.htm.

34 Christopher Chantrill, USGovernmentSpending.com, accessed March 19, 2019, https://www.usgovernmentspending.com/us_fed_spending_pie_chart.

35 Jennifer King Rice, "The Impact of Teacher Experience: Examining the Evidence and Policy Implications," National Center for Analysis of Longitudinal Data in Education Research, Brief 11, August 2010, accessed March 19, 2019, https://www.urban.org/sites/default/files/publication/33321/1001455-The-Impact-of-Teacher-Experience.PDF.

36 Abigail Hess, "The 5 states that spend the most on students," CNBC Make It, April 17, 2018, accessed March 19, 2019, https://www.cnbc.com/2018/04/16/the-5-states-that-spend-the-most-on-students.html.

37 Jay Fitzgerald, "Disruptive Students Affect Long-term Prospects of their Classmates," *National Bureau of Economic Research (NBER) Digest*, May 2016, accessed March 19, 2019, https://www.nber.org/digest/may16/w22042.html.

38 Stephen Exley, "Ofsted: Bad behaviour costs pupils more than a month of teaching a year," *Tes*, September 25, 2014, accessed March 19, 2019,

https://www.tes.com/news/ofsted-bad-behaviour-costs-pupils-more-month-teaching-year.

39 "Head Start Facts and Impacts," National Head Start Association, accessed March 19, 2019, https://www.nhsa.org/facts-and-impacts.

40 David Leonhardt, "The Case for $320,000 Kindergarten Teachers," *New York Times*, July 27, 2010, accessed March 19, 2019, https://www.nytimes.com/2010/07/28/business/economy/28leonhardt.html.

41 "Teen Brain: Behavior, Problem Solving, and Decision Making," American Academy of Child & Adolescent Psychiatry, No. 95, September 2016, accessed April 2, 2019, www.aacap.org/aacap/families_and_youth/facts_for_families/fff-guide/the-teen-brain-behavior-problem-solving-and-decision-making-095.aspx.

42 "Lawsuit Abuse Impact," US Chamber Institute for Legal Reform, accessed March 19, 2019, https://www.instituteforlegalreform.com/issues/lawsuit-abuse-impact.

43 Thomas Sullivan, "Defensive Medicine Adds $45 Billion to the Cost of Healthcare," *Policy & Medicine*, May 5, 2018, accessed March 19, 2019, https://www.policymed.com/2010/09/defensive-medicine-adds-45-billion-to-the-cost-of-healthcare.html.

44 James Hirby, "What Percentage of Lawsuits Settle Before Trial? What Are Some Statistics on Personal Injury Settlements?" The Law Dictionary, accessed March 19, 2019, https://thelawdictionary.org/article/what-percentage-of-lawsuits-settle-before-trial-what-are-some-statistics-on-personal-injury-settlements/.

45 "Lawsuits Cost Small Businesses $105 Billion, Study Shows," US Chamber of Commerce, July 7, 2010, accessed March 19, 2019, https://www.uschamber.com/press-release/lawsuits-cost-small-businesses-105-billion-study-shows.

46 Julie Kurtz and Farm Aid, "Farm Bill 101," May 22, 2018, accessed March 19, 2019, https://www.farmaid.org/blog/farm-bill-101/.

47 AP, "Farm Population Lowest Since 1850s," *New York Times*, July 20, 1988, accessed March 19, 2019, https://www.nytimes.com/1988/07/20/us/farm-population-lowest-since-1850-s.html.

48 "Farms and Farmland: Numbers, Acreage, Ownership, and Use," *USDA.Gov Census of Agriculture*, ACH12-13, September 2014, accessed March 19, 2019, https://www.nass.usda.gov/Publications/Highlights/2014/Highlights_Farms_and_Farmland.pdf.

49 John, Sophie, and Jesse Javna, *50 Simple Things You Can Do to Save the Earth* (New York: Hyperion, 1990), https://www.amazon.com/Simple-Things-You-Save-Earth/dp/1401322999.

50 Stacey Selleck, "Fundraising a Top Priority Mandate to D.C. Politicians," US Term Limits, April 26, 2016, accessed March 19, 2019, https://www.termlimits.com/congress-fundraising-priority/.

51 Nancy Scola, "Exposing ALEC: How Conservative-Backed State Laws Are All Connected," *The Atlantic*, April 14, 2012, accessed March 19, 2019, https://www.theatlantic.com/politics/archive/2012/04/exposing-alec-how-conservative-backed-state-laws-are-all-connected/255869/.

52 Jessica Leber, "When Lobbyists Write Legislation, This Data Mining Tool Traces the Paper Trail," *Fast Company*, October 26, 2015, accessed March 19, 2019, https://www.fastcompany.com/3051823/when-lobbyists-write-legislation-this-data-mining-tool-traces-the-paper-trail.

53 "Organizations," National Institute on Money in Politics, accessed March 19, 2019, https://www.followthemoney.org/resources/organizations.

54 "Options for Reforming Money in Politics," League of Women Voters, accessed March 19, 2019, https://www.lwv.org/league-management/voting-rights-tools/options-reforming-money-politics.

55 "Contribution Limits," Federal Election Commission, accessed March 19, 2019, https://www.fec.gov/help-candidates-and-committees/candidate-taking-receipts/contribution-limits/.

56 Joe Miller, "No WMDs in Iraq," FactCheck.org, February 19, 2008, accessed April 8, 2019, https://www.factcheck.org/2008/02/no-wmds-in-iraq/.

57 "The FEC and the Federal Campaign Finance Law," Federal Election Commission, updated February 2019, accessed March 19, 2019, https://transition.fec.gov/pages/brochures/fecfeca.shtml.

58 Norah O'Donnell, "Are members of Congress becoming telemarketers?" *60 Minutes*, April 24, 2016, accessed March 19, 2019, https://www.cbsnews.com/news/60-minutes-are-members-of-congress-becoming-telemarketers/.

59 Ryan Grim and Sabrina Siddiqui, "Call Time for Congress Shows How Fundraising Dominates Bleak Work Life," *HuffPost*, updated December 6, 2017, accessed March 20, 2019, https://www.huffingtonpost.com/2013/01/08/call-time-congressional-fundraising_n_2427291.html.

60 Nicholas Confessore, Sarah Cohen, and Karen Yourish, "2016 Presidential Election Super-PAC Donors," *New York Times*, October 15, 2015, accessed March 20, 2019,   https://www.nytimes.com/interactive/2015/10/11/us/politics/2016-presidential-election-super-pac-donors.html?mtrref=undefined.

61 *Granny D Goes to Washington*, October 23, 2006, https://www.imdb.com/title/tt0893336/.

62 Eric Vega, "The Most Gerrymandered Districts in America," Ranker.com, accessed March 19, 2019, https://www.ranker.com/list/most-gerrymandered-districts-in-america/eric-vega.

63 Anne Stych, "Many Americans can't pass U.S. citizenship test," Bizjournals.com, October 16, 2018, accessed March 19, 2019, https://www.bizjournals.com/bizwomen/news/latest-news/2018/10/many-americans-cant-pass-u-s-citizenship-test.html.

64 Drew DeSilver, "U.S. trails most developed countries in voter turnout," Pew Research Center, May 21, 2018, accessed March 19, 2019, http://www.pewresearch.org/fact-tank/2018/05/21/u-s-voter-turnout-trails-most-developed-countries/.

65 Sandra E. Garcia, "An 'I Voted' Sticker Can Get You Free Stuff. (But Is It Legal? Well…)," *New York Times*, November 6, 2018, accessed March 19, 2019, https://www.nytimes.com/2018/11/06/us/voting-free-stuff.html.

66 Mike Maciag, "Voter Turnout Plummeting in Local Elections," Governing.com, October 2014, accessed March 19, 2019, http://www.governing.com/topics/politics/gov-voter-turnout-municipal-elections.html.

67 "New Hampshire Election Laws," Chapter 655, New Hampshire Secretary of State, accessed March 20, 2019, http://sos.nh.gov/ElecLaws.aspx.

68 Annabel Acton, "Why Every Brand Must Think and Act Like an Entertainment Brand," *Forbes*, August 22, 2017, accessed March 20, 2019, https://www.forbes.com/sites/annabelacton/2017/08/22/want-to-win-in-the-digital-age-act-like-an-entertainment-brand/#21d335a25070.

69 Scott Keeter, Nick Hatley, Courtney Kennedy, and Arnold Lau, "What Low Response Rates Mean for Telephone Surveys," Pew Research Center, May 15, 2017, accessed March 20, 2019, http://

www.pewresearch.org/2017/05/15/what-low-response-rates-mean-for-telephone-surveys/.

70 Todd Selig, "Friday Updates," Durham, New Hampshire, accessed March 20, 2019, https://www.ci.durham.nh.us/fridayupdates.

71 Editorial Board, "Citizenship Tests Are Good for Citizens, Too," *Bloomberg Businessweek*, March 13, 2015, accessed March 20, 2019, https://www.bloomberg.com/opinion/articles/2015-03-13/give-high-school-students-a-citizenship-test.

72 "U.S. History 2010: National Assessment of Educational Progress at Grades 4, 8, and 12," The Nation's Report Card, National Center for Education Statistics, 2010, accessed March 20, 2019, https://nces.ed.gov/nationsreportcard/pdf/main2010/2011468.pdf.

73 Committee for Economic Development of The Conference Board, "The Landscape of Campaign Contributions: Campaign Finance after *Citizens United*," Committee for Economic Development, July 10, 2017, accessed March 20, 2019, https://www.ced.org/reports/the-landscape-of-campaign-contributions1.

74 "Total state government expenditures: Fiscal Year 2017," Ballotpedia, accessed March 20, 2019, https://ballotpedia.org/Total_state_government_expenditures.

75 If you want to better understand flywheel mechanics, I found this site to be helpful: "Flywheel Kinetic Energy," The Engineering ToolBox, accessed March 17, 2019, https://www.engineeringtoolbox.com/flywheel-energy-d_945.html.

Acknowledgments

It's been a long road from my first letters to the editor to the release of this book. I need to start with Deidre Randall from Peter E. Randall Publisher and editor Zak Johnson, as they recognized I had something worth spending time on. Zak was kind enough to tell me the book lacked structure and a theme, so I had to create an outline. From there, he suggested I share it with some friendlies. So, courageously, Alex Herlihy, Dr. Everett Lamm, Jeff McLean, Frank Hyer, and Rich Luff plowed through the first version. They provided edits and let me know it was not the most readable book and that specific content needed to go. While their feedback was constructive and honest, there was no greater motivation than the support of people I admire, especially when they donate their precious time and exhibit genuine enthusiasm for my efforts.

From there, Jeff Deck stepped in and suggested I use the flywheel as the central theme of the book. Jeff cut up what I had and took the first pass at reassembling the book into the flywheel segments. Jeff made corrections and pushed me to get more resources and support for my claims so it just wasn't me saying something. Most of the numbers and supporting information come from his prodding. That process took another seven or more months, before I went back to Zak Johnson, who helped improve the structure, chapters, footnotes, and many "book" things I had no idea about.

While John Klossner is credited up front as the illustrator, I am fortunate that he was willing to work with me to envision and create these illustrations. As a novice author, I was lucky enough to be introduced to Ken Lizotte of emerson consulting group, inc., who led the crucial marketing for this, my first book.

If not for the support from my wife, Amy, there would be no book. I would like to say our two boys were instrumental in the research and creation of this book, but watching me type was never too riveting. Rumor has it they will read the book when it publishes.

About the Author

Steven Borne received his B.S. in mechanical engineering, with minors in ocean engineering and business from the University of New Hampshire. While working full-time, he graduated Beta Gamma Sigma from Northeastern University with an MBA. He has spent the past thirty years as a controls engineer, project engineer, program manager, and marketing and sales manager for small businesses and multinational corporations.

2019 will be his twenty-eighth year riding the Pan-Mass Challenge, which raises funds for the Dana-Farber Cancer Institute (www.pmc.org, rider number SB0011). He has coached his sons through thirteen seasons of youth sports, and graduated with the Leadership NH class of 2017.

Borne's first foray into the 1999 NH primary process exposed him to the inefficiencies of the presidential campaign process and gave him experience writing letters to the editor. His letters tended to not complain but to offer solutions to problems. An aggregation of all these ideas led to a fledgling independent party incorporating many of his ideas. Failing to get this party on the New Hampshire ballot, he realized that the New Hampshire election laws needed to change. His Republican and Democratic state representatives championed his initiative until the subcommittee decided to make it even more difficult to establish a New Hampshire independent party.

As he engaged in a few more New Hampshire presidential primaries volunteering with No Labels, the NH Rebellion, the Coffee Party, and other groups promoting moderates and independents, he realized that the way to revitalize our democracy was not through political parties but to get us citizens to change our behavior. In an attempt to catalog the myriad groups attempting to address campaign finance reform, Borne realized there should be a centralized place to match individuals and activities. As he began to build the website New Hampshire Managing Our Government, he discovered best-in-class examples were needed just as the Rye Civic League was restarting. Ten years in, the Rye Civic League has made tremendous progress (Borne has been president the past five years).

Through two decades of civic engagement, the siren song calls to the engineer in Borne to help our nation self-correct how we might best manage all the government services we buy, and develop practical action steps for doing so.

S.borne @
concqot.net

603-770 1743

Consuming Government